THE ANGUISH OF SURRENDER

For Trustie and Lily, good friends and fond memories covering several countries and continents, with affection.

Rick Straus

THE ANGUISH OF SURRENDER

JAPANESE POWs OF WORLD WAR II

ULRICH STRAUS

An ADST-DACOR Diplomats and Diplomacy Book

University of Washington Press
Seattle and London

This publication was supported in part by the Donald R. Ellegood International Publications Endowment.

University of Washington Press
PO Box 50096, Seattle, WA 98415
www.washington.edu/uwpress

Library of Congress Cataloging-in-Publication Data

Straus, Ulrich.
    The anguish of surrender: Japanese POW's of World War II /
    Ulrich Straus.
        p. cm.
    "An ADST-DACOR diplomats and diplomacy book."
    Includes bibliographical references and index.
    ISBN 0-295-98336-1 (cloth : alk. paper)
    1. World War, 1939–1945–Prisoners and prisons, American.
    2. Prisoners of war–Japan.   3. Prisoners of war–Asia, Southeastern.
    4. World War, 1939–1945–Concentration camps–Asia, Southeastern.
    5. Asia, Southeastern–History.   I. Title.
DS805U5 S77   2004
940.54'7273'092252–dc22   2003053379

CONTENTS

ILLUSTRATIONS

Photograph insert follows page 76.

FOREWORD

For more than 225 years extraordinary men and women have represented the United States abroad under diverse circumstances. Their dedication and achievements remain little known to their compatriots. In 1996 the Association for Diplomatic Studies and Training (ADST) and Diplomatic and Consular Officers, Retired (DACOR) created a book series to increase public knowledge and appreciation of the involvement of American diplomats in world history. The author of the newest volume in the series, former Foreign Service Japan expert Ulrich A. Straus, exemplifies—with this exhaustively researched and deeply moving account of Japanese POWs of World War II—the professionalism and humanity that characterize the best career diplomats.

Of the many books in English on the twentieth century's greatest conflict, none focus on the Japanese prisoners of war it produced. Now, in *The Anguish of Surrender,* Rick Straus recounts the painful dilemma individual Japanese soldiers and sailors faced when, despite intense indoctrination to the contrary, they were forced to confront the reality of becoming captives. Straus examines in depth how Japanese POWs dealt with this dilemma, which put them truly in extremis—between life and death—and compelled them to drop their illusions. He shows how trained Allied linguists, including many Japanese Americans, extracted useful intelligence from their psychologically unprepared captives by affording them humane treatment. In the course of his research, Straus interviewed and corresponded with former POWs in Japan and delved deeply into POW interrogation records at the National Archives, the sparse material later written by their U.S. Army and Navy interrogators, interviews of America's Japanese language officers and enlisted men, and Japanese source material, including publicly and privately published books and articles by former Japanese POWs.

Rick Straus lived in Japan a total of twenty-one years, beginning in the period 1933–40, when he was a child. He returned there as a U.S. Army Japanese language officer in early 1946, serving in the Occupation, at the Tokyo major war crimes trial, and in the Intelligence Division (G-2) of GHQ, to which he returned during the Korean War. While in Japan conducting doctoral research under a Fulbright grant in 1955, he took the Foreign Service examination and, in 1957, joined the State Department. Fully half his thirty-year Foreign Service career dealt directly with Japan—ten years in Japan, in the political section of Embassy Tokyo and as consul general in Okinawa, and five at the State Department working on U.S.-Japan relations. Among other assignments, he served in West Berlin, as political counselor in Bern, as State Department director of Philippine affairs, and as adjunct professor at the National War College in Washington, D.C. Since retiring from the Senior Foreign Service in 1986, he has taught and lectured on Japan and U.S.-Japan relations at George Washington, Georgetown, Johns Hopkins, Michigan, Michigan State, Indiana, and Grand Valley universities, the College of William and Mary, and Hope College, and he appears as a local PBS foreign affairs commentator in Interlochen, Michigan.

In *The Anguish of Surrender,* Rick Straus combines scholarship, expertise, and empathy to convey, for the first time in English, the truly dramatic and deeply human stories of Japanese POWs, from their prewar indoctrination through unexpected prison camp experiences to postwar reintegration. In the process he advances our understanding of the paradoxical wartime roots of postwar Japanese-American friendship.

KENNETH L. BROWN, President
Association for Diplomatic Studies and Training

ROBERT L. FUNSETH, President
Diplomatic and Consular Officers, Retired

PREFACE

In my experience, Americans have generally been astounded to learn that we had taken any Japanese prisoners at all during the Second World War. This is hardly surprising. Wartime reports only stressed kamikaze attacks from the air and banzai charges on the ground, reinforcing the image of a fanatic enemy who would never allow himself to be taken captive. By the war's end, only about 35,000 Japanese had fallen into Allied (including Nationalist and Communist Chinese) hands, a tiny fraction of the 945,100 German and 490,600 Italian POWs in camps in the United States and elsewhere when the war ended in Europe. Just over 5,000 Japanese POWs were in captivity in the continental United States, with the rest in Hawaii, Australia, New Zealand, India, Burma, the Philippines, Okinawa, and scattered additional locations. Relatively few Americans ever saw, let alone came into contact with, Japanese prisoners of war in the United States.

When I tried to explain the subject of my research to friends and acquaintances, most found the topic interesting. However, their follow-up questions indicated that half believed I was talking about Americans taken prisoner by the Japanese, while the other half thought I was referring to the incarceration of the West Coast Japanese Americans during the war. Japanese POWs in Allied hands were simply not a part of their frame of reference.

A recent flood of books in the United States on the biggest conflict of the twentieth century includes none on the Japanese prisoners of war it produced. From a Western perspective, wartime Japan's moral revulsion concerning POWs was an extreme position, one that tended to dehumanize the enemy. Japanese POWs faced a dilemma when, despite all their assumptions and expectations, they were forced to confront the reality of becoming prisoners. How they dealt with this dilemma merits examination.

A study of Japanese POWs of the Second World War at this time provides us with a far more nuanced picture than was possible during the war, or even in the decades that followed. We can now read books and articles written by the former POWs about their wartime experiences and, while there is still time, interview at least a representative sampling of them before they pass from the scene. It is clear that the experience of falling into Western captivity was for them a defining moment in their lives. By contrast, for the Japanese-speaking Caucasian-American officers who dealt with Japanese POWs, this was a passing phase that was largely forgotten once the war was over and they could look forward to resuming their "normal lives." For Japanese-American army intelligence personnel, who were forced to prove their loyalty and had family incarcerated in relocation centers, memories about wartime contacts with POWs tended to remain more acute. With the passage of a half century since the war, the former prisoners not only reflected more on what took place but also, to some extent, dwelt less on aspects of events they believed should never have happened. Through their eyes we also have a much better sense of how well they were able to reintegrate into the society of which they believed that they would never again be a part.

When the war ended on August 15, 1945, I was in the final days of an eight-week basic training course at Fort McClellan, Alabama, designed to transform bookish Japanese language students into reasonable facsimiles of soldiers. I had already had a year of intensive study of written and spoken Japanese at the University of Michigan and could look forward to another half year of intensive study at Fort Snelling, Minnesota, concentrating on the oral and written language used by the Japanese military. If the war had gone on for another six months, I could well have been one of those interrogating prisoners or translating documents in the planned second invasion of Japan near Tokyo in early 1946.

I had been accepted into the army's intensive Japanese language program by virtue of having lived for over seven years in prewar Tokyo. At the time my family was still German, but as Jews our situation was becoming precarious owing to the ever-closer relationship between Germany and Japan. We were most fortunate to be able to emigrate to the United States in late 1940 when tensions were rising in East Asia. It was in 1943 that Capt. (later Lt. Col.) Paul Rush visited my family in New York. He was on the trail of former students of the American School in Japan (ASIJ) to recruit them for the army's Military Intelligence Service Language School (MISLS) at the University of Michigan. Informed that my former classmates at ASIJ would be getting into the army program, I jumped at the opportunity to head for Ann Arbor after graduation from high school in June 1944.

A few obstacles remained to be overcome. My status at the time of graduation in June 1944 was that of an enemy alien because I had yet to complete the five years needed to obtain American citizenship. Under the peculiar regulations of the time, enemy aliens were subject to the draft but could not volunteer. The draft, however, would not catch up with me for another nine months. Hoping for the best, I presented myself to the University of Michigan with a view to enrolling in the regular Japanese language course offered in the catalogue, as well as other courses appropriate for a freshman. I was told that the Japanese course had been canceled because the army required the service of all Japanese language instructors, but perhaps another way could be found for me to learn Japanese. In a matter of days it was arranged for me to join the ongoing MISLS class. My parents had known Col. Kai Rasmussen, the director of the MISLS program, when he was the assistant military attaché in Tokyo, and that no doubt helped my cause.

I cannot recall whether it occurred to me then how utterly absurd it was for a civilian "enemy alien" to be enrolled in an intelligence language program while almost all of our Japanese-American teachers had been denied their rights as American citizens. Most had spent time in the so-called "relocation camps" where their relatives were still detained. Later it bothered me that I had embodied an unwitting example of the racial discrimination so prevalent in the United States during that period.

The army's sixteen months of Japanese language training gave me the basis for my lifelong interest in Japan and American-Japanese relations. I served at General MacArthur's headquarters (GHQ) during the Occupation, including six months at the Tokyo war crimes trial of Japan's top war criminals. My knowledge of both Japanese and German came in handy for supervising the translation of official German documents used at the trial. Later I served in the G-2 (intelligence) section at headquarters. Recalled to active duty during the Korean War, I was again assigned to G-2, GHQ in Tokyo. I was on a Fulbright grant in Tokyo to collect material for a doctoral thesis when I passed the Foreign Service examination and joined the State Department in 1957. In the ensuing thirty years, I spent another ten years in Japan, in both Tokyo and Okinawa, plus five more years at the State Department working on U.S.-Japan relations.

Upon retirement in 1987, my interest in the country and people of Japan remained undiminished. I turned to teaching about Japan and U.S.-Japanese relations at various universities in the Washington, D.C., area and exploited numerous opportunities to return to Japan to renew friendships and soak up new impressions. My original interest in Japan's political developments turned gradually toward seeking a better understanding of Japan's underlying values and its people's psychological makeup.

Through the years I kept running into colleagues and friends who had served as Japanese language officers and enlisted men during the war. For a time these encounters assuaged my abiding curiosity about the Japanese prisoners of war. Eventually, though, I determined that the time was ripe for me to take another look at our unexpected "guests" in the midst of what Professor John Dower aptly characterized, in the title of his book, the "war without mercy."

Since that war, two generations have grown up whose passions have receded with the passage of time. In Japan, the shame at having been taken prisoner has faded and, in most cases, disappeared. Reluctant to write or even talk about their wartime experiences at first, former Japanese POWs have become much more eager to leave behind a record of what they went through in the hell of war and the conflicting emotions resulting from their being taken prisoner. A surprising number of autobiographies by Japanese veterans have been published, especially in the past two decades. Several noted Japanese scholars have also begun to show an interest in Japanese POWs.

This study deals only with those Japanese who became prisoners of the Western Allies (the United States, United Kingdom, Australia, and New Zealand) during the war. Millions more were added to their small numbers at war's end when the emperor broadcast his surrender message and the rest of Japan's military gave up peacefully. They were scattered from Burma in the west to pockets of Japanese forces in the Philippines and Guam in the east, including those in Indonesia, Malaysia, Thailand, Indochina, and many islands that had been bypassed in the South Pacific. Some of them ended up in the camps that housed POWs taken during the war, usually creating little or no tensions.

In addition, more than 1.6 million more Japanese surrendered to Chinese and Russian forces at war's end. This study does not cover their surrender and subsequent treatment as POWs. Both deserve separate treatment because their experiences in captivity were entirely different from those accorded Japanese prisoners of the Western powers.

In China, Japanese forces were engaged in war against both Nationalist and Communist forces from 1937 to 1945. During that period, Japan's military presence was by far the most powerful one in China. Up to the end of the war, Japanese forces were generally on the offensive, suffered relatively few casualties, and gave up few prisoners of war. Once the United States became involved in the war, combat in China diminished in intensity as both the Nationalists and Communists husbanded their resources in anticipation of the civil war that was to follow. For the Japanese troops, the conflict in China was far less intense than combat in the Pacific and Southeast Asia, and their postwar treatment at the hands of the Chinese Nationalists was, as Japanese veterans recall, "magnanimous." Although the Japanese expected revenge, there was no mass retribution from the Chinese, who had suffered grievous military and civilian losses at the hands of the Japanese. Both the Nationalists and Communists held war crimes trials for those suspected of specific crimes. The Japanese surrendered largely to the Nationalists, partly because the United States arranged it that way, but also because it coincided with their own preference. The Nationalists' primary interests were (1) that they seize all weapons from the Japanese forces, which had not been defeated in China; (2) that the Japanese departure not result in a security vacuum exploitable by the Communists; and (3) that Japanese troops not be used against them by the Communists. With the tacit concurrence of the American forces just coming on the scene in modest numbers, these interests ensured that the Nationalists treated their 1.2 million Japanese POWs with kid gloves, on occasion even with considerable deference.

Japanese forces in Manchuria opposite the Soviet Union endured yet another fate. For several years they had kept the Soviets from shifting the bulk of their Far Eastern forces to the defense of the homeland from a German threat and subsequent invasion. When the tide of war turned against Japan, substantial Japanese forces from Manchuria, including some of their elite and best-equipped units, were sent to the active fronts in the Pacific. The Soviet Union attacked the weakened Japanese forces in Manchuria on August 8, 1945, in compliance with its pledge at the Yalta Conference and in response to President Truman's request at the Potsdam Conference. It swiftly occupied all of Manchuria and northern Korea down to the thirty-eighth parallel, Sakhalin Island, and the Kuriles, and captured 600,000 Japanese soldiers in the following weeks. Like the German prisoners taken by the Soviets, these Japanese endured years of captivity, hard labor under primitive conditions, malnutrition and disease, and over 60,000 of them died. The others were eventually repatriated, some after having been brainwashed or recruited to furnish intelligence to the Soviets. Many of these survivors have written accounts of their ordeal under the Soviets, experiences totally different from what prisoners of the Western allies, or the Chinese, underwent.

This study of Japanese POWs captured by the Western Allies is based on a variety of sources. On the American side this includes the POW interrogation records at the National Archives, the sparse written material subsequently penned by American army and navy personnel who conducted the interrogations, and interviews of America's Japanese language officers and enlisted men. It also relies extensively on Japanese source material. This included publicly and privately published books and articles written by former Japanese POWs.

As a result of a letter sent to the editor of the *Asahi* newspaper, in which I asked former POWs to contact me, I developed an extensive correspondence with a large number of former POWs. In the spring of 2000, I followed up with thirty-five personal interviews in

Japan with ex-POWs, selected largely on the basis of our previous correspondence. These interviews were conducted in coffee shops, restaurants, hotels, and private homes. Lasting two or more hours, each covered a wide range of issues and helped to clarify for me the experiences, thoughts, and feelings of former POWs during those exceedingly stressful times. Our meetings were often quite emotional.

On one occasion, sitting in the crowded confines of a coffee shop filled with tobacco smoke, I noticed that a man sitting at the next table was greatly interested in our conversation. He strained to hear every spoken word and even tried to read some written material that passed at our table. Finally, he could contain himself no longer and in a thoroughly un-Japanese way, joined quite spontaneously in our discourse. He, too, had been a prisoner after the Second World War. I have a strong sense of gratitude toward all the former POWs for sharing their intimate, painful thoughts with me, a stranger from another country.

I am aware of the possibility that the former Japanese POWs who responded to my appeal through the *Asahi* might be a self-selected group with special reasons (perhaps of gratitude for the treatment received at the hands of Americans) for wishing to communicate with me. What I learned from them, however, generally agreed with the writings on wartime experiences by other Japanese veterans, who would have had no reason to believe that their accounts would ever be read by an American.

I was also aware of the evident fact that I was dealing with the recollections of events and attitudes of fifty-five and more years ago, and that some episodes of that stressful era may well have been repressed in the recesses of the mind. For example, a number of Japanese claimed to have been unconscious when captured; it seems more likely that they were exhausted, weak, ill, and perhaps confused by stress, and unconsciously wanted to bury realities that were too painful to bear.

My sources served in many different combat zones. They were captured at various times in the war, and their experiences of becoming prisoners of war varied greatly. Nevertheless, there were enough common, recurrent themes to give me confidence that they represent a reasonably broad spectrum of the limited number of Japanese captured during the war. The relatively small number of diehards were a notable exception. They sought to make life as difficult as possible for their captors throughout the period of their incarceration. Although my sources and Japanese historians have written and spoken of this element in the POW camp population, apparently none has published his wartime memoirs, and none ever responded to my appeals for contact.

Nobody is more aware than the former POWs themselves that the generation that fought, bled, died, and became prisoners during and after the Second World War is now rapidly passing from the scene. The survivors of that war, on both sides of the Pacific, cannot and should not forget their comrades who died on its battlefields. Fortunately, such bloody wartime memories have not prevented Japanese and American veterans of such brutal conflicts as the battle of Iwo Jima from joining in organized unit reunions, as well as in one-on-one get-togethers. Such reunions have been taking place for decades, in fact, with little or no publicity, and have contributed to a new era of better understanding between the people of our two countries.

Since beginning this study, I have received several eager requests from American veterans of the Pacific War asking me to help find a Japanese whom they captured in a battlefield cave and with whom they now eagerly wanted to get back into contact. The difficulty of finding someone about whom they knew next to nothing made my task impossible, but the strongly expressed desire testifies to the meaningfulness of the brief encounters over a half century ago, probably for both men.

Before the outbreak of the Second World War, Japanese and Americans hardly knew one another. Only a tiny percentage of Japanese had ever met and talked with an American, and very few Americans had ever spent time with any Japanese. We knew each other largely through caricatures that were further embellished during the war. The prison camps became the place where large numbers of Japanese encountered Americans in any number for the first time. Elements on both sides apparently felt a desire to communicate across the linguistic and cultural barriers, despite the mutual hate and disdain brought on by the war. These tentative encounters established a new pattern of discourse and understanding. A significant number of Japanese actually came out of the war genuinely appreciating aspects of the American way of life. Meetings under those exceptionally difficult circumstances were a prelude to the far broader and more meaningful encounters during the Occupation of Japan, and, eventually, to the mutually productive relationship of today.

If the ability of wartime Japanese POWs eventually to reintegrate fully into their postwar society was a test of the fundamental societal changes that have occurred in postwar Japan, we can be well satisfied that the Japanese have accomplished that task far better than anyone might have thought possible in 1945. Since that time our two countries have built a solid partnership based on mutual interest and mutual understanding, unprecedented for the United States in the sense that it was created with a non-Western nation. For the Japanese, too, the partnership with America represents their first really meaningful national collaboration with another country in history. I like to think that the first broadly based encounters of Americans, Australians, New Zealanders, and Britons with Japanese germinated in the unlikely locus of Allied prison camps. Wars can have unintended consequences.

A NOTE ON JAPANESE NAMES

Throughout the text, I have followed the traditional Japanese convention in which the family name precedes the given name, except in the case of Japanese Americans, for whom I followed the usual Western order of given name first, family name last.

ACKNOWLEDGMENTS

First and foremost, I wish to acknowledge the contributions made to this book by the more than eighty former Japanese prisoners of war who responded to the appeal for contact that I placed in 1999 in a letter to the editor of the *Asahi Shimbun,* a major Japanese newspaper. One of these respondents even wrote a follow-up letter to the editor that referred to my request for contacts and urged former POWs to write me. The ex-POWs who contributed to this book included veterans whom I subsequently interviewed during a trip to Japan in 2000, individuals who suggested others whom I might want to contact, and those who provided me with privately and commercially published autobiographies and related publications. I am especially grateful to these men because my subject covered a period of great inner turmoil and pain in their lives.

I am indebted to two outstanding Japanese historians, Fukiura Tadamasa and Hata Ikuhiko, who have pioneered academic writings on Japan's wartime POWs. Professor Fukiura allowed me to draw on both his own work and his extensive personal library for my research. I also relied upon Professor Hata's well-known, groundbreaking two-volume study on the historical background and wartime experiences of Japanese POWs.

I owe a great deal of thanks to the tireless staff at the U.S. National Archives & Records Administration in Washington, D.C. They patiently responded to my many requests for relevant material amid many blind alleys. Most especially I am grateful for the friendship and advice of archivist John Taylor, the grand old man of the archives, who steered me in the right direction on numerous occasions in the course of my research.

Ms. Akiba Yoko, Area Specialist in the Japan Section of the Library of Congress, was instrumental in bringing to my attention the existence of autobiographies written by wartime Japanese prisoners of war. The six such autobiographies she found were the first of many more I eventually read.

I am indebted to the countless graduates of our army and navy Japanese language schools who told or wrote me about their participation in interrogations of Japanese prisoners. Their anecdotes significantly assisted me in describing the atmosphere in which such contacts took place. I am especially grateful for the help given me by Otis Cary, a navy language officer who published all his writings on wartime experiences in Japanese.

Two stalwarts at our small public library in Northport, Michigan, librarian Deborah Stannard and assistant Barbara Waddell, handled my endless requests with their usual aplomb, even when they involved Japanese language books from the Library of Congress. I could not have completed my research without their assistance.

Stanley Falk, an old friend, fellow student at the army's Japanese language school, colleague, and U.S. Army historian, made many helpful suggestions after looking over an early draft of this book. The University of Michigan's Center for Japanese Studies provided funding to launch my initial research in the United States.

Pamela Grath was most helpful in looking over my manuscript and proposing linguistic changes that resulted in a smoother text. Dennis Alleva helped me in dealing with an occasionally incomprehensible computer. Dick Pflederer kindly created exactly the right maps to enhance my text.

I am grateful for the unfailing encouragement given my research by Kato Mikio, Executive Director of the International House of Japan in Tokyo.

Margery Thompson, Publishing Director of the Association for Diplomatic Studies and Training, was a steadfast friend, prodder, and adviser during the process of getting the manuscript ready for publication. I owe her a lot.

I dedicate this book to Sarah, my wife and helpmate, and to the memory of our children, Kuri-chan and Andy, who are buried in the Foreigners Cemetery in Yokohama.

THE ANGUISH
OF SURRENDER

Japanese POW camps in East Asia, 1942–46

Map 1. Japanese POW camps in East Asia, 1942-46. In addition to the five camps shown on the map, Camp Bikaner near Quetta in western India (now Pakistan) housed Japanese prisoners.

INTRODUCTION

For the Allied armed forces, the war against Japan was the most bitter, pitiless combat of the Second World War. The Japanese enemy was relentless in advancing and tenacious in defending every piece of ground it had taken. The mercilessness of the fighting was ensured when the Japanese government branded being taken prisoner the most heinous moral dereliction imaginable for any imperial soldier or sailor. There were to be no exceptions to this harsh edict; whatever the circumstances under which a member of the military might become a prisoner, exoneration would never be possible. The government further reinforced the ban on surrender by making it known informally that any returning Japanese POW would be put to death. It went without saying that the disgrace of surrender would also attach to the family of any soldier or sailor who dared to transgress this harsh code.

The official position of wartime Japan toward its own military inevitably affected Japanese attitudes toward prisoners captured by the Japanese. Such prisoners, believed by the Japanese to have disgraced themselves, were seen as legitimate objects of their captors' scorn, contempt, and much worse.

When war came, the American government was prepared to abide by the international agreements governing the humane treatment of prisoners of war, and for the most part American and other Allied forces lived up to these commitments. In the first two years of the war, however, it proved difficult to translate government policy into behavior on the battlefronts. Americans were consumed by hatred of an unfathomable and alien foe that had adopted a very different set of rules on the battlefield. American attitudes were also dictated by a desire to revenge the "sneaky" and humiliating attack on Pearl Harbor and the brutal treatment of American prisoners taken not only on Bataan but also on Guadalcanal, where Japanese atrocities included torture, murder, and mutilation that left the marines with an undying hatred. Prewar racial antipathy toward the Japanese, as exemplified by discriminatory legislation and, once war broke out, the shameful incarceration of Japanese-American citizens, also played a role. All of these factors not only stiffened the Americans' resolve not to be captured; they also diminished any inclination they might have had to take Japanese prisoners.

In combat areas the conflict between contrasting modes of acceptable behavior on the battlefield predictably led, at first, to the adoption of the much lower Japanese standards as the common denominator. It was only after the Western Allies slowly went on the offensive and senior officers became convinced of the potential intelligence value of Japanese POWs that Americans and their allies placed increasing emphasis on the taking of prisoners.

In the European theater of operations, Americans faced an equally cunning and determined foe, with the difference that the Germans, in combat against the Western Allies, generally lived up to their obligations under international agreements covering the treatment of POWs. (That was not the case in Germany's war against the Soviet Union; even so, the eastern front produced millions of both German and Soviet prisoners.) As brutal and merciless as combat often was in Europe, it never reached the depths seen in the Pacific. The Japanese willingness, seemingly even eagerness, to die rather than give ground or surrender was the additional crucial difference.

American public opinion about its two major enemies also made a sharp distinction between the two. The public consistently hated the Japanese and German governments more than their people. In polls taken in July 1945, 52 percent of the public believed that the Japanese people are incurably "warlike and want to make themselves as powerful as possible," while only 39 percent of the public believed the same of the Germans. Questioned as to which people were "more cruel at heart," 51 percent picked the Japanese, 13 percent the Germans. The rest believed they were equally cruel. As late as October 1946, 47 percent of Americans felt that Japan "could never become a good nation." Americans expressed the view that the Japanese were the greater threat to the United States and favored harsher postwar treatment of the Japanese people.[1]

When Japanese soldiers and sailors reached the limits of human endurance, they faced the difficulty of wanting to adopt the right and appropriate course of action dictated by their government and societal norms. At the same time, not a few retained the all too human desire to remain alive. Seldom have such large numbers of people been left to their own individual devices to come to terms with the fundamental issues of life or death. Especially when they found themselves alone or with just another buddy or two, they discovered how strong the will to live could be. Those who chose life or had it chosen for them by circumstances beyond their control ended up in Allied prison camps. Many more, for a variety of reasons, chose to die rather than be captured.

Rooted in a group-oriented society, the individual Japanese POW faced a totally unprecedented situation. Since unit surrenders hardly ever took place until close to the war's end, the one, two, or three who became prisoners at the same time found themselves having to establish entirely new relationships with unfamiliar compatriots. To add to the complication of establishing solidarity in prison, Japanese prisoners often sought to hide their true identity not only from their captors but also from fellow prisoners. Most Japanese in Allied prison camps, therefore, suffered enormous mental anguish, despite their physical well-being.

Following Pearl Harbor, the U.S. Army and Navy launched an unprecedented effort to teach Japanese language skills to thousands of Americans in order to gain combat and strategic intelligence about an inadequately understood enemy. With some exceptions, virtually all the teachers were Nisei, second-generation Japanese Americans, who were mostly recruited out of the so-called relocation camps. The army eventually took thousands of Nisei into its intelligence programs, where they made major contributions to hastening victory in the Pacific.

Having achieved a significant capability in Japanese language skills, intelligence officers in the Pacific launched a major effort to convince senior officers, and through them the frontline troops, that Japanese POWs could well provide vital intelligence to the Allied war effort. It was a hard sell, given the implacable determination of the Japanese to avoid being taken prisoner. Not unreasonably, many Americans believed that any fanatical Japanese unlucky enough to be captured would keep their mouths firmly shut during interrogations. In reality, many Japanese, finding themselves in a situation they never expected to be in and for which they had received not the slightest instructions, reacted in myriad, quite unexpected ways. Some hard-liners never did change and sought to carry on their war against the Allies throughout their imprisonment. Others behaved in completely counterintuitive ways by cooperating with their captors. A majority adopted positions somewhere between these two poles.

Once captor and POW met face-to-face, racial stereotypes tended to disappear and both Japanese and Americans began to see each other as human beings. The widespread use of the Nisei in the interrogations played a vital role in bringing this about.

As Ruth Benedict pointed out in her groundbreaking 1946 study, *The Chrysanthemum and the Sword,* Japanese POWs in many instances utterly surprised the Allies by providing them with significant information of intelligence value. Some assisted the Allies in a number of other ways, such as helping to write surrender leaflets and even returning to the caves they had fled in order to urge others to surrender.

The story of the POWs begins with the education of young Japanese in an increasingly militaristic society in the 1930s. It continues with their indoctrination during an unimaginably tough basic training and their testing on battlefields where the tides of war were turning sharply against them. Some wrestled with a strong instinct to live, against the ironclad strictures forbidding surrender. A remarkably small percentage of Japan's armed forces simply came to the end of their rope and resigned themselves to a fate they imagined might be worse than death itself. In the prison camps they faced interrogations that many succeeded in erasing from memory. Many saw Americans or Europeans for the first time in their lives and became aware of the immense disparity in behavioral patterns and living standards between Japanese and Westerners.

Most Japanese POWs could not possibly imagine a situation that would allow them to return to Japan and remain alive. Then the emperor surrendered, and it happened. How would their families receive them, having been convinced that their sons and husbands had died glorious deaths in the defense of the fatherland? Many POWs feared the uncertainties inherent in their return home as "ghosts."

On coming back to a devastated homeland, they had to deal with rejoining families that had presumed them dead, who had participated in memorial services for them, and received death benefits from the government.

In modern times no other POWs have ever returned to their fatherland and their loved ones with so many unanswered questions in their hearts. In most cases, the anticipated problems did not arise. Former POWs were able to reintegrate into postwar Japanese society relatively smoothly. Their concern soon became that of all other Japanese—how to survive another day and, eventually, how to contribute to the reconstruction of their homeland.

With few exceptions, the men who once served the emperor now believe that Japan has been so completely transformed that their grandchildren fail to comprehend what life once was like for them, and the moral code that dominated behavior in wartime Japan will not, nor ever should, be resurrected.

1

PRISONER NUMBER ONE

It was the night of December 6, 1941, and Ensign Sakamaki Kazuo of the Imperial Japanese Navy was frantic as he saw all the meaning of his entire young life unravel. A graduate of the naval academy, he had been carefully selected as one of five skippers of the Imperial Japanese Navy's two-man midget submarines whose suicide mission was to breach the Pearl Harbor defenses. Their operational targets were sufficiently important to have merited a meeting in October with Admiral Yamamoto Isoroku, commander-in-chief of the Combined Fleet, on his flagship. The admiral had emphasized at that time how much the navy counted on the midget submarine crews. They were about to engage in an operation offering far greater glory than much more senior officers in the surface navy could hope to win.

Sakamaki was a superb example of the type of officer produced by Japan's naval academy at Etajima. Life at Etajima was mentally and physically rigorous. It left no room for individual thinking, emphasizing instead the need for absolute obedience to military superiors. Sakamaki had been taught that no middle ground existed between victory and defeat, and he had come to believe that it was "critical for us to die manfully on the battlefield." Armed with this romanticized notion of war, Sakamaki and a friend had bought perfume "to be fit for a sudden and glorious death" when they learned that war with the United States was imminent.

Crews for the suicide subs had not been volunteers. They had been picked for the select honor by reason of their mental and physical resilience, unmarried status, and fighting spirit. At twenty-one years of age Sakamaki fully met the criteria. His mission was to sink the battleship *Pennsylvania* with his two torpedoes, but from the very start of the mission he was dogged by bad luck. Even before his forty-six-ton submarine was launched from its mother ship, the supersized submarine I-24, his gyrocompass had malfunctioned, and without it he had no chance of finding the entrance to Pearl Harbor, let alone striking his target.

Remarkably, Lt. Comdr. Hanabusa Hiroshi, the commander of the five midget submarines, asked Sakamaki whether he wanted to proceed with his mission with malfunctioning vital equipment. Caught up in the excitement of the moment and unwilling to be left behind when his comrades were risking almost certain death, Sakamaki opted without further thought to carry on with the launch as planned. It is quite certain that he knew there was only one proper response, but even if the command had wanted him to abort the mission, Sakamaki would have fought desperately to proceed with it out of a sense of solidarity with his fellow midget submarine officers. Sakamaki's superiors saw no reason to change their plan. The virtual certainty that he would not be able to locate and hit his target without a functioning gyro was subordinated to the "spirit" of the moment. The possibility of fixing the gyro and using the midget submarine in a subsequent military operation was apparently not considered. The certainty that by sending a crippled warship into combat the Japanese navy would lose two trained men did not enter into the decision process. Sakamaki realized that the Japanese navy's inferiority to the American and British navies necessitated unusual combat techniques, including midget submarines. Sakamaki felt "the weight of duty and heavy responsibility filling my mind."[1]

As Sakamaki was blindly careening around off Oahu, his chief concern was to avoid surfacing and thereby giving away the impending attack. He was grimly determined to accomplish his mission unaware that the *Pennsylvania,* his target, was still in dry dock. He sighted several destroyers guarding the entrance to Pearl Harbor but did not want to "waste" his torpedoes on "mere destroyers." He barely avoided getting hit by the destroyer *Helm* and managed to submerge, later hitting several reefs and damaging both his torpedoes and launch tubes. With "tears of chagrin" he decided that his only option was to try to ram the *Pennsylvania*. He soon realized that even this was not possible since there was no way he could find, let alone breach, the entrance to Pearl Harbor without surfacing. Later he admitted that he was "not thinking clearly." With no clear idea where he was and a return to the mother ship impossible, he headed for what he presumed was the midget submarine assembly point, off the island of Lanai. But with pressure within the submarine rising to dangerous heights, causing a sharp buildup of temperature and electrical malfunctioning, Sakamaki later contended that he lost consciousness and all control of his ship. His submarine eventually hit a reef near Kaneohe on Oahu. The impact split open the ship and threw him into the water. Sakamaki was able to swim five hundred yards to the nearest shore, but his shipmate perished.

Sakamaki came to land some fifty miles from Pearl Harbor. He was picked up on the beach before dawn on December 8 and taken into custody by a military patrol led by Sergeant David Akui, a Japanese-American member of the Hawaii Territorial Guard. A fellow member of the guard, Roy Terada, had witnessed the attack on Pearl Harbor while on maneuvers the previous day. Both Akui and Terada were as surprised to find an enemy sailor on Oahu as Sakamaki was to be made Prisoner No. 1 of the war in the Pacific. Two days later, the damaged submarine was spotted, brought to land, and thoroughly inspected for whatever secrets it might yield on the capabilities of a new Japanese weapons system. Some documents were also found on the submarine. The ship was then put to use as an attraction for war bond drives in the United States. Several years later, while Sakamaki was a POW at Camp McCoy in Wisconsin, he was asked whether he wanted to see his submarine again at a nearby town. Sakamaki politely declined.

Only one or two midget submarines actually managed to penetrate the antisubmarine barrier defending the Pearl Harbor anchorage. None returned from their missions. They apparently caused no damage, and the Japanese high command lost all confidence in this particular secret weapon. Still, the midget submarine crews who were missing and presumed dead had one more mission to fulfill. They were memorialized by the government-controlled Japanese press as the "nine heroic warriors" and the "nine gods of war." When the nine were given a mass funeral in downtown Tokyo, some in the audience could deduce that one man of five two-man crews was not included, and therefore could be presumed to be a prisoner of war. In due course, in accordance with the Geneva Convention governing treatment of POWs, the United States notified the Japanese government through the International Committee of the Red Cross that Sakamaki had been taken captive. This placed the Japanese navy in a quandary. No death notice was ever made public, and Sakamaki's family was never notified about his fate. In the Japanese navy's officers list of March 1942, next to Sakamaki's name it was noted that he was "attached to the Yokosuka Navy Yard (Top Secret)." In August 1944 this was changed to "reserve status," but his real fate became more or less an open secret among naval officers. Cropping Sakamaki's visage from a photograph depicting the ten midget-submarine crewmen, then circulating as part of the government's propaganda effort, did not help to hide the embarrassing truth.

Meanwhile, the only thing clear to Sakamaki was that his life was a total failure. He had not accomplished his mission by dying a glorious death. Worse, he had let his submarine fall into enemy hands and had suffered the ultimate shame of becoming a prisoner of war. His entire psychological support system was shot as he found himself in a completely unexpected situation for which he had received not the slightest instruction. He was utterly on his own. To his way of thinking, it was unlikely that there would be any other Japanese prisoners of war. Nobody could help him in this predicament. Not surprisingly, Sakamaki fell into a deep depression, a zombie-like existence in which he had what he described years later as "thoughts about committing suicide and surreal emotions." He was guilt ridden when he thought about his fellow midget-submarine commanders, all of whom, as it turned out, had similarly failed in their mission. He was overcome with shame as he thought about having besmirched not only his own honor but, even more important, that of his family.

During his first eight weeks of captivity in Hawaii, Sakamaki was repeatedly interrogated by Nisei lieutenant Gero Iwai and by Douglas Wada, the only Nisei employed by naval intelligence. In his autobiography he noted that initially the interrogators used a soft approach but hinted that when he refused to provide detailed answers to many of the questions, the interrogations became rougher. Like many other Japanese prisoners, he implored his captors to kill him, but his interrogators told him they could do no such thing. Some of the lower-ranked Americans, however, were inclined to take Sakamaki's plea seriously and wanted to take out their anger against all Japanese by "honoring" his request. He had more than a few anxious moments when he believed his captors might carry out their threats.[2]

For Sakamaki, life as a prisoner was much harder to bear than the death he had anticipated. He reports having been intensely frustrated with the Americans for denying him the means to commit suicide, but like many other Japanese prisoners, he made no serious attempt to seek death. Sakamaki wrote that he felt so guilty about having "luxurious" prison accommodations while his comrades-in-arms faced great hardships that he refused to take hot showers in winter even after he was relocated to Wisconsin. He also declined to sleep on his bed and took care not to come near his stove. His only activity was to read newspapers and books. He made every effort to avoid having his picture taken, to the extent of burning tobacco his guard had given him and using the embers to disfigure his face. Sakamaki was determined that his actions, already so shameful, should not further disgrace his family.

Even Sakamaki himself later conceded that he had been "half mad" during that period of his life. The widely admired POW facility commander at Camp McCoy in Wisconsin, Lt. Col. Horace Rogers, became so concerned about Sakamaki's mental state that he ordered a psychiatrist to see him. Following the passage of many months, however, Sakamaki slowly recovered his mental equilibrium. Eventually, he was judged no longer suicidal and even found meaning in life again, especially after he was joined by other Japanese prisoners and could assure himself that he was no longer unique. As his surreal emptiness receded, he became increasingly aware of the "humaneness of the Americans," something totally at variance with everything he had previously known and believed.

The interrogations ceased once Sakamaki arrived in the continental United States, but because the United States took no additional Japanese prisoners for some time, he remained alone in his confinement. The few additional prisoners seized on Attu in the Aleutians were confined at a different POW camp. It was only in November 1942 that Sakamaki first experienced some pleasure in being together with other Japanese prisoners, crew members from the carrier *Hiryu* who had been rescued at sea after the Battle of Midway, but even this meeting initially did not go well. The group included naval officers who were senior to Sakamaki, so that with their arrival he was no longer his own boss. He did not open up to the *Hiryu* group, and they refrained from confiding in him until much later. Sakamaki's bitterness over his fate persisted.

Only in early 1944, when he had already been imprisoned for over two years, did Sakamaki have a change of heart. He determined then to become a model prisoner by making the best he could of his circumstances. As leader of about a thousand Japanese prisoners, he even took some pride in being able to avert an outbreak of violence at Camp McCoy sparked by the camp's hard-liners. Among the prisoners, no one was better at identifying and analyzing the various factions in the camp and in retaining at least a semblance of surface harmony among them. Sakamaki was given high marks for his intelligence, and it helped that he managed to learn excellent English.

Nonetheless, Americans called him a "hard egg to crack" and were annoyed by his "petty and unending complaints" to the authorities, including his dislike for having American women work in the camp laundry. He also conveyed charges of this nature to Spanish diplomats acting as the protecting power, as provided for in the Geneva Convention.[3] The Americans did not at first appreciate Sakamaki's skills in managing to keep the lid on potential violence in the camp. Eventually, however, they learned to respect him for his toughness, leadership qualities, and powers of persuasion. Sakamaki repaid the confidence placed in him by telling newcomers to the camp that they were about to "begin life as civilized, organized and cultivated persons, fit to receive the benefits of international law." He urged his fellow prisoners to thank the American authorities "for saving our precious lives so that we can once again serve Japan." To those who talked about killing themselves or instigating violence he said: "If you are going to die, do it for a big cause; you are a fool if you lose your life over a small matter."[4]

Following Japan's surrender, Sakamaki was returned to his war-devastated homeland along with all the other prisoners of war. At the port of debarkation, he was debriefed on his wartime exploits by a senior former naval officer who was compiling a history of the war. A Japanese repatriation official told him not to feel ashamed or worried about his former POW status. But, when the Japanese media picked up his story, Sakamaki received more than one nasty letter from people who complained that he should have committed suicide. One man even offered to come to his home to show him how to commit hara-kiri. He was relieved to discover, however, that most Japanese received him back into their ranks with a simple "well done."

While the media soon lost interest in other POWs, its focus remained on Sakamaki. Called on as a witness for the prosecution at the International Military Tribunal for the Far East (informally called the Tokyo trial), Sakamaki testified that the Allies' treatment of Japanese POWs had been good. Many years later in interviews he amended this to say that he had been hit a few times, even by officers. Despite this, the overall impression he left behind in his books and interviews was that he had been treated fairly by the Americans and that he appreciated their humane approach toward prisoners of war.

Sakamaki married, wrote about his experiences, and briefly remained a celebrity. He found employment with the Toyota Motor Corporation and had a successful career. Sakamaki drove himself very hard, as if to restore his honor. He was also propelled by a strong sense of mission to make Japan into a first-class economic power. His career culminated in ten years as manager of Toyota's extensive operations in Brazil.

Following his retirement from Toyota, Sakamaki attended a symposium on POWs in Austin, Texas. There he finally saw again at a war museum the submarine he had commanded in the Pearl Harbor attack. When his old midget submarine was being broken up for scrap in Hawaii, he gave yet another interview, speaking freely about his experiences, but on returning home to Japan for the last time, he refused to talk further to the press. When an American journalist sought to interview him on the occasion of the fiftieth anniversary of the attack on Pearl Harbor, he declined. Near the end of his life, when asked to comment on how Japan had developed in the post-war era, Sakamaki stated that Japan was still somewhat feudal and needed to grow and adjust to the globalized world.[5]

When Sakamaki died on November 29, 1999, his death was not initially made public pursuant to the family's request. The array of top Toyota officials at his funeral testified to the high regard in which he was held by the company. His death was later noted with a brief obituary in the press, to whom he was still Prisoner No. 1.

Sakamaki's experiences as a prisoner of war were similar to those of others who followed him into captivity, although every prisoner went through his own travails. Initial interrogations were followed by more detailed ones, in some cases repeatedly. For largely administrative reasons, many Japanese POWs were moved from camp to camp within the continental United States. Camp life gradually settled into a routine, with a good deal of boredom interspersed with a variety of recreational activities and, in the case of enlisted personnel, work details.

For the great majority of prisoners, the prospect of an end to the war could not bring relief to their anxieties, no matter how the war might come out. They could not face the thought of returning to Japan if the Allies won the war. Yet if, as many still hoped to the very end, Japan were to win, their futures looked at least as bleak, if not even more hopeless.

The contrast between the experiences, hopes, and fears of American and other Allied prisoners of war in Japanese hands and those of the Japanese prisoners in Allied POW camps could not have been greater. The Allied prisoners encountered torture, beatings, death, starvation, poor medical care, and extreme working conditions, often at the hands of cruel prison guards who despised them for their "weakness" in having surrendered. The Japanese made no pretense of living up to the requirements of international law, although Japan's foreign minister had indicated at the outset of war that they might do so. Allied prisoners of war were sustained during their long period of incarceration by their common hatred of the enemy and the hope and faith that they would eventually be liberated, returned to their country with honor, and reunited with their families and loved ones.

The Japanese POWs in the hands of the Western powers, meanwhile, endured a very different kind of hell. This resulted from their ingrained belief that their lives were essentially over, that they had committed the most heinous lapse imaginable by allowing themselves to be captured, and that they would never be able to return to the home they had known, except to be executed. Shamed beyond redemption by becoming prisoners of war, they believed they had lost both their country and their families. Initially, even the excellent treatment they received at the hands of the Americans—the good and ample food, the freedom from strict discipline and beatings, and excellent medical care—could not overcome their personal malaise. Over time, most came to terms with their predicament, at least to some extent. Once the emperor surrendered, all but a small contingent of POWs became convinced that the unthinkable had happened. After the shock wore off, their thoughts turned to how they would fare in a defeated, devastated Japan and how they would be received by their families.

Beginning in late 1945, the POWs joined the millions of Japanese soldiers and sailors being repatriated from all over East Asia. Their transition to a war-ravaged land was by no means easy initially, but over the years the shame of having surrendered became attenuated because the emperor's surrender had made prisoners of all Japanese. Time did the rest.

2

JAPAN'S POLICY
ON PRISONERS OF WAR

During the Second World War, the Japanese government maintained a policy that in effect forbade its soldiers and sailors to be taken as prisoners of war for any reason whatever. This policy had ample precedent in Japanese history. Until the advent of modernity with the Meiji Restoration in 1868, Japanese history recorded only two examples of foreign military conflict–the aborted invasion by the Mongols during the thirteenth century and the Japanese invasion of Korea in 1592. Both were extremely bloody wars, with captives routinely slaughtered on both sides.

During the incessant clan wars in the twelfth and thirteenth centuries and for some time thereafter, prisoners of war in Japan's internal wars were treated with utmost harshness. As George Samson pointed out: "The killing of prisoners was subject to certain rules in Europe, whereas in Japan it seems to have been the custom. There was no practice of ransom in Japan, but it was the usual practice to reward a warrior who had captured an enemy of high rank or great prowess. This practice helps to explain the decapitation of prisoners, since it was easy to produce a severed head as evidence when claiming a reward."[1] Although there were instances of mercy toward the vanquished foe, history has primarily recorded cases where the prisoner's expressed wish to die was granted.

With the establishment of the Tokugawa Shogunate in the early seventeenth century, the requirements of Bushido, or "the way of the warrior," came to form the moral ideals of the samurai (warrior) class. Prisoners, including the sick and wounded, were routinely killed. A

Japanese samurai took immense pride in his loyalty, his stoicism, and above all, his physical bravery, choosing death over the dishonor of capture. Suicide by ritual disembowelment (seppuku or hara-kiri) was also the means of avoiding almost certain torture at the hands of the victorious party. After the climactic Battle of Sekigahara in 1600, Shogun Ieyasu attempted to assure his defeated foe, General Mitsunari, that it was by no means rare for soldiers to be taken prisoner and that it was not shameful to meet such a misfortune. Mitsunari, however, insisted on being beheaded, and Ieyasu complied a few days later.[2]

Mercy was not expected for either self or foe in Japan. In contrast to the European practice in medieval and later times, prisoners of war were regarded as having forfeited their right to live. Samurai fought to the last ounce of their strength rather than surrender. Nevertheless, there were exceptional cases where captives were "turned" to fight against their former lord, as well as occasions when a feudal leader would deal harshly with conspirators in his own ranks but treat others, including prisoners, more leniently.

In medieval Japan, warfare was still largely restricted to the feudal samurai class that ruled over other classes of society. The Bushido code of behavior applied only to this ruling class. In the Meiji period (1868–1912), samurai morality was gradually extended to all classes through the process of conscription, along with some Western influences, but the first "modern" effort to express the morality of a Western-style military still retained most of its Japanese traditions. This can be seen in the "Imperial Precepts to Soldiers and Sailors" issued in 1882. Above all, this document stressed prudence, self-control, and especially loyalty: "Our relations with you will be most intimate when We rely upon you as Our limbs and you look to Us as your head. When We are able to guard the Empire, and so prove Ourselves worthy of Heaven's blessings and repay the benevolence of Our Ancestors. . . . The soldier and sailor should consider loyalty their essential duty. . . . Never fall into disgrace and bring dishonor by failing in moral principles. . . . The soldier and sailor should esteem valor. . . . To be incited by mere impetuosity to violent action cannot be called true valor. . . . The soldier and sailor should stress faithfulness and righteousness . . . (and) make simplicity their aim."

Stressing "Loyalty to the Throne" as the "essential duty," the precepts urged military men to bear in mind that "duty is weightier than a mountain, while death is lighter than a feather."[3]

Confucian in tone, the precepts said nothing about the necessity for soldiers to die for the emperor, but it was clearly implied. The precepts also intimated that the self-identification of the soldier and sailor with the emperor conferred a "purity" that was motivated not by expectations of gain or advantage but by one striving for a higher good. The imperial precepts were always read during the high school courses on ethics and spiritual training. By the 1930s such ceremonial words may have had little effect on students destined for university training. For the great majority of the more naive peasants' and workers' children, however, the impact remained profound.

Through the decade of the 1920s, Japan still tended to downplay its indigenous moral code as it sought Western acceptance by embracing most aspects of continental Europe's legal system. It was also at this juncture that the West, dealing for the first time with more "democratized" fighting forces in the First World War, attempted to legislate new international norms for the treatment of prisoners of war.

Japanese government policy toward its own soldiers who fell into enemy hands evolved gradually in the modern era. Seeking acceptance in the comity of so-called civilized nations in the Meiji period, Japan became a party to a number of early international treaties dealing with the conduct of war, including the Brussels Declaration of 1874 and the Hague Conventions of 1899 and 1907. In the 1920s, in the aftermath of the horrors of the First World War, international efforts were redoubled to humanize the conduct of war and provide better treatment for prisoners of war. The improvements were codified in the Geneva Convention of 1929, which the Japanese government signed but ultimately failed to ratify, believing that it lacked true reciprocity. This was the most sweeping convention negotiated on POWs, and it was the last one prior to the outbreak of the Second World War.

During the Sino-Japanese War of 1894–95, Japan stated that it would abide by the Brussels Declaration on prisoners of war, the first such international effort to regularize and humanize the reciprocal treatment of POWs. In that conflict, the Japanese captured 1,790 prisoners, while only one Japanese soldier was taken prisoner by the Chinese. Japan treated its prisoners humanely.

The Hague Convention of 1899 on the treatment of POWs was operative during the Russo-Japanese War of 1904–05 and was generally observed by both sides. At the end of the war the Japanese held 71,802 prisoners, while the Russians had captured 1,626 Japanese soldiers and sailors, including 26 officers. The Japanese government of that time, unlike the one during World War II, acknowledged the existence of Japanese prisoners in enemy hands, including a regimental commander. Japan even sent a request through the U.S. government, which represented Japan's interests in Russia during the war, asking that conditions be improved for Japanese POWs in Russian prison camps. It also facilitated the sending of letters and packages to Japanese POWs through international Red Cross channels. In line with this willingness to acknowledge the status of its captured military personnel, a regulation of Japan's POW Information Office at that time stipulated that the name, rank, and other information of each POW would be published when received. (This regulation was voided on December 27, 1941.) Japan and Russia also agreed to several exchanges of prisoners while fighting was still going on.

Upon their return to Japan, all prisoners from Russia were subjected to interrogations on the circumstances of their capture and on their conduct during imprisonment. The interrogations of enlisted personnel were fairly perfunctory, but officers were questioned more closely, and seven officers were required to forfeit their rank and decorations. The most senior Japanese officer captured by the Russians received only light administrative punishment, a few additional officers were disciplined, but other returnees eventually received decorations for their combat service. A common view in Japan during World War II, one fostered by the government, held that returning Japanese POWs had been treated harshly after the Russo-Japanese conflict. It seems beyond doubt, however, that by and large the Japanese government of the day exercised leniency toward its POWs. Despite this record, it was helpful to Japan's ideological objectives in the years leading up to war with the West to have ordinary Japanese believe that an uncompromising policy of rejecting even the possibility of becoming POWs had always been the special pride of Japan.

On the Allied side during the First World War (1914–18), Japanese forces took only a few weeks to capture the entire 5,000-man German garrison at its colony in Tsingtao, China. By all accounts the Germans were well treated, in accordance with existing international law, for most of their four years of imprisonment in Japan. Some of them thought well enough of their treatment at Japanese hands that, following a brief stay in Germany, they returned to Japan to resume their business interests. The Germans took no Japanese captives during the war.

Despite liberalizing political trends in Japan between 1915 and 1930, an atmosphere that branded the status of POWs as shameful for Japanese servicemen began to grow. Japan eventually decided not to ratify the 1929 Geneva Convention it had initially signed because "according to the Imperial Soldier's belief, it was contrary to all expectations that he might become a prisoner." The Japanese government officials charged with deciding whether to ratify the convention clearly recognized that Japan's position on this issue was unique.

These officials came up with four reasons why the convention was inappropriate for Japan. The most important of their arguments was that, while the international treaty that Japan had signed was technically reciprocal, in practice only Japan would have to assume obligations under the treaty, given Japan's view of the matter. Japan would have to feed and house POWs, while other countries would be spared the onus of caring for Japanese prisoners because there would be none. This made the treaty unilateral.

Japanese officials also anticipated that ratifying the convention might encourage the kind of enemy operation that actually did occur in the Doolittle raid on Tokyo in 1942. It reasoned that Japan's putative enemy (that is, the United States) might contemplate long-range carrier-based air attacks on Japan. Such attacks would incorporate a willingness to accept a likelihood of running out of fuel, in turn implying a willingness to run the decided risk that enemy airmen would become prisoners of the Japanese. Japan's decision not to ratify the

Geneva Convention on POWs, the government reasoned, might thus serve to deter certain specific enemy war plans.

Moreover, at a time when government hysteria about foreign espionage was rising, the convention's provision of access to POWs by neutral parties without an official Japanese presence provoked fear of undesirable leakage of military information to the enemy. Finally, the Japanese government believed, accurately enough, that acceptance of the convention would require the Japanese to treat POWs better than it treated its own military personnel. Since that would entail unthinkable revisions of existing Japanese army and navy laws and regulations, the provisions of the convention were unacceptable to the Japanese.

Japan's policy makers, including military leaders, had fully convinced themselves that it was feasible to wage modern war with solidly indoctrinated military personnel who would never, under any circumstances, allow themselves to be captured. The moral disdain for prisoners of war, which included an element of almost physical revulsion for prisoners of war, led to remarkably few Japanese becoming POWs during World War II. Since the Japanese military man considered himself the bearer of a higher spiritual code of behavior, it became inevitable that Allied prisoners would be treated with contempt for their "weakness" in allowing themselves to be captured.

Government indoctrination of the younger generation was thorough in Japan. The spirit of the modern Japanese warrior, with all his idealistic feelings of superiority, was well represented in the statement of one Japanese prisoner of war: "Now what is the Japanese Spirit? When I was on the [battleship] *Mutsu,* the commanding officer said to me: 'The Japanese Spirit is the strength of the mind to carry on with added determination when difficulties arise.' Therefore, surrender is absolutely unrecognized. To give in when beaten is the spirit of the Americans and British, and not that of Japanese, who will fight all the harder when defeat stares them in the face."[4]

In the beginning of the 1930s Japan began a more active pursuit of imperialist policies. The Kwangtung Army, stationed on the Asian mainland, instigated the seizure of Manchuria in 1931 without the prior sanction of the Japanese government and then carried it out with the government's reluctant consent.

Scattered clashes between Japanese troops and Chinese Nationalists took place on Chinese soil over the next few years, culminating in a full-scale Japanese attack in 1937. This war became known in Japan as the "China Incident," even though it was to last eight years. Japan's reluctance to call its conflict with China a war continued to the end and was based on domestic and international political considerations. Since in Japanese eyes the conflict was not legally a war, it followed that China was not in a position to take Japanese prisoners of war, and the status of Chinese captives of the Japanese was similarly clouded. Such interpretations led to convoluted explanations when the Chinese did, in fact, take Japanese prisoners.

The Japanese generally treated the Chinese as inferiors who ought to be grateful for Japan's willingness to lead the struggle against Western colonialism and to establish a new order in East Asia under its leadership. Although the Chinese at times offered stiff resistance, more often they fell back before better-trained and better-equipped Japanese forces, and not a few surrendered. As combat in China became unexpectedly prolonged, the Japanese ultimately could no longer avoid having to deal with the issue of their soldiers falling into Chinese hands. Since the Imperial Army was on the offensive, it would obviously collect large numbers of Chinese POWs as well. As demonstrated by the record at the International Military Tribunal for the Far East, the Japanese cruelly mistreated their Chinese prisoners, using them for bayonet practice, for slave labor, and in laboratory tests for chemical and bacteriological weapons. Operating on the pretense that Japan was involved in an "incident" rather than a war, the government generally left the handling of POWs in the hands of subordinate unit commanders, seeing no need to elucidate an all-embracing government policy. Some Chinese POWs were "allowed" to join the army of the Japanese-controlled puppet regime led by Wang Ching-wei. Others were released to perform hard labor, and many perished. Few records of the fate of Chinese POWs were maintained, and inspections of POW camps by the International Committee of the Red Cross were not permitted.

The Japanese mind-set concerning POWs that developed during the Sino-Japanese conflict was carried over into the internationalized war that began on December 7, 1941. Although the Sino-Japanese conflict was often ignored by the American media, major elements of the Japanese army remained bogged down in China, advancing further into the interior but failing to deliver a knockout blow. As the war expanded along the entire length of China, some Japanese soldiers became prisoners. Pilots were also captured when shot down or forced to crash-land behind Chinese lines.

The precise number of prisoners taken by the Chinese Nationalist and Communist forces during the entire period of the conflict (1937–1945) is unclear. The best estimate is that on August 15, 1945, a combined total of around 8,300 Japanese prisoners were in the hands of Chinese Nationalist and Communist forces.

By and large, the wartime treatment of Japanese prisoners by Nationalist and Communist forces was not based on international agreements. Japanese authorities were not at all dismayed by reports of poor Chinese treatment of POWs since information of this nature would discourage Japanese soldiers from even considering the possibility of capture. By terming its aggression an "incident," Japan would have been unable to seek protection for its POWs under international law in any event.

Of much greater concern to the Japanese authorities were rumors of humane treatment of Japanese POWs, especially by the Chinese Communists. In May 1941 the Communist Eighth Route Army established the Japanese Workers and Peasants School under the leadership of Nozaka Sanzo, who became one of the top leaders of the Japan Communist Party in the postwar era. Three hundred Japanese POWs were enrolled in the school, and the Communists successfully used a significant number of its graduates in anti-Japanese, antiwar propaganda activities such as the production of leaflets and loudspeaker appeals to defect. Some prisoners were even returned to their old units to spread Communist propaganda. These efforts were effective enough to cause considerable Japanese government concern.

Already before the Red Army's school for Japanese POWs went into high gear, however, the Japanese top command in China had produced a pamphlet, stamped Top Secret, entitled "Lessons Concerning Prisoners of War." Issued in March 1941, this analysis determined that some Japanese soldiers became prone to surrender (1) when they were separated from comrades or wounded and became depressed; (2) when they were attacked while engaged in road construction or supply operations and failed to react fast enough; and (3) when they failed to heed army regulations and standard operating procedures. The paper went on to describe Chinese interrogation techniques and how the POWs reacted to them, based on the recollections of POWs who had returned to Japanese control. The document concluded that Japanese POWs "tended to be easy marks, reveal information on our troops and even praise the enemy." Such behavior had led some Japanese to join the ranks of the antiwar elements and participate in the enemy's propaganda broadcasts. The study's conclusion was that "our men generally resist stubbornly until they fall into enemy hands, but once taken prisoner, their spirits are broken . . . and many are softened up." This state of affairs was clearly intolerable. Something needed to be done to deal with what the Japanese army termed an increasing incidence of "lax discipline" among the expeditionary forces in China. Japanese soldiers were taking the no-surrender policy all too lightly. Before the army high command resolved its dilemma, another relevant armed conflict intervened.

Japan's last military conflict prior to Pearl Harbor took place between Soviet/Outer Mongolian troops and Japanese/Manchurian forces. It was geographically confined to the area around Nomonhan, then in the remote Manchukuo/Siberian border region, now the northwest corner of China's Heilongjiang Province. The origin of the August 1939 clash remains in dispute, but what began as a minor skirmish between Japanese and Mongolian forces soon turned into a major battle. Whether or not the Japanese instigated the conflict, it ended with the Soviets besting the Japanese in the largest tank battle the world had seen prior to World War II. The localized battle exposed extensive deficiencies in the quality of Japanese tanks and artillery, as well as in Japanese tactics and leadership.

These factors were to affect the course of world history. In the fall of 1941, when German troops were within sight of the Kremlin, Nazi Germany urged its Japanese ally to attack the Soviet Union on its weakened Siberian flank. The Japanese army in particular had long regarded the Soviet Union as its prime military and ideological enemy and had geared its war planning to that end. With the lesson of its failures at Nomonhan in mind, however, and for a number of other cogent reasons, the Japanese government chose instead to attack the largely unprotected colonies of the Western powers in the southwest Pacific and America's principal Pacific base at Pearl Harbor.

Nomonhan also proved to be another step in the increasingly severe policy of the Japanese government toward prisoners of war. Either because of Soviet-Mongolian military superiority or because the Japanese were more inclined to kill their prisoners, for the first time in history there were more Japanese in the hands of the foe than vice versa. In any event, Japanese and Soviet representatives negotiated two prisoner exchanges during the mini-war. The Soviets may have precipitated negotiations by releasing the names of their prisoners in propaganda broadcasts. Perhaps Japanese prisoners, to hide their shame, had by then already falsified their identity during Soviet interrogations. The record is unclear. Whatever the details, these exchanges required Japan's army ministry to establish a new policy governing the returning POWs. By this time, extreme detestation of the thought of Japanese soldiers being taken prisoner had thoroughly taken hold in the army but had not been codified in military law. While the death penalty or indefinite imprisonment was provided for desertion, it was recognized that such punishments would not necessarily apply in the case of a soldier inadvertently taken prisoner.

The army minister (war minister in American parlance of the era) ordered investigations of all soldiers returning from Soviet captivity. Where crimes had been committed, charges were to be brought. Even when the investigation did not lead to formal charges or an individual was judged not guilty, the returning prisoner would nevertheless be subject to "severe disciplinary measures." After an unspecified disciplinary period, any former POW still requiring redemption would be forced to perform organized public welfare work. Finally, after the entire process had run its course, the government would assist the individual in seeking his livelihood "outside" of Japan. This generally meant Manchukuo or Korea, then under tight Japanese control.

In effect, then, POW policy was changed by this order to treat all returnees harshly, irrespective of the circumstances of their capture. For Japanese soldiers who might have felt that "honor" was an insufficient inducement to offer their lives blindly to the emperor, this policy ensured that the alternative was made as unappealing as possible.

Pursuant to the new policy, all Japanese officers returning from Soviet captivity were given the opportunity to commit suicide. Evidence suggests they did so willingly, but clearly the system also required their suicides. Enlisted soldiers, on the other hand, were treated with what the government believed was considerable leniency. They were advised, however, upon completing their compulsory public service, to avoid "telling their families that they had been prisoners, forming any associations of ex-prisoners, and meeting members of their former military units." In return, the military would help them find new jobs, usually joining the Japanese-controlled Manchukuoan military, working as civilians on military construction projects, or similar government-connected work. None were permitted to resume their careers in the Japanese army. This made clear that their stained honor could never be completely cleansed. Ironically, those who joined the Manchukuoan police or military forces to expiate their transgressions subsequently faced double jeopardy when, in 1945, the invading Soviets led them into prolonged captivity again.

There remained the embarrassing question of how to deal with Nomonhan returnees from Soviet camps whose families had been notified of their deaths in battle. In a "top secret" process, those ex-POWs not charged with crimes had their honor restored, and their families were informed accordingly. Nevertheless, the Japanese public resisted the effort to remove the stain of dishonor, and the aversion to imperial prisoners of war only grew.

Not until the late 1980s could some former Japanese prisoners taken at Nomonhan bring themselves to attend reunions of their former comrades-in-arms, and finally unburden themselves by speaking of the fate they had endured for having been captured.

In light of the intense sentiment within the army against POWs that existed already at the time of Nomonhan, it is not surprising that some Japanese POWs decided to take their chances with the Soviets instead of returning home. While exact numbers are not available, it appears that as many as five hundred to one thousand did just that. The Soviets apparently never forced Japanese POWs to remain behind permanently, but were prepared, possibly even eager, to have them settle in the Soviet Union. For its part, the Japanese government undertook no special measures to urge them to return home. Japanese soldiers captured by the Soviets in August 1945, on returning to Japan two to four years later, reported that they had encountered Japanese veterans not only of Nomonhan but even of the Russo-Japanese War, living reasonably secure lives in their Siberian surroundings, usually with Russian spouses.

Some months after the war started in the Pacific, a message from the Japanese commander on the Burma front stated that he had learned from captured documents that the Allies had obtained especially valuable intelligence on the "size of our forces based on POW interrogations." The commander ordered strict guidance to be provided to all soldiers "concerning the fidelity of the imperial forces." This elliptical language on a delicate subject was probably interpreted as a need to reinforce the doctrine that Japanese forces should always choose suicide over surrender; the order made no mention of international agreements governing the humane treatment of prisoners of war. The guidance also failed to address what soldiers were to be told about their comportment if captured, since the Japanese military remained unprepared to deal with any such possibility.

Despite evidence it had that Japanese POWs in Allied hands were talking, the Japanese government saw no reason to change its policy. Blindly, it plunged on, simply reiterating that harsh punishment would be meted out to any Japanese unfortunate enough to become a POW. A Japanese army circular of August 1942 entitled "Notes on the Treatment of Returned Prisoners of War" captured in June 1944 in Burma laid out government policy that followed the outlines established after the Nomonhan debacle. It stipulated that returned POWs, "if found not guilty" of any wrong conduct beyond becoming POWs would still be required to undergo "severe corrective punishment." Those requiring further punishment were to be sent to a training unit. Returned POWs would be allowed to live in countries other than Japan "to safeguard them," presumably from the scorn and anger of an aroused Japanese population.[5]

Reacting to the shock of Japanese becoming prisoners of the Chinese and the Russians despite the strict government policy, the then army minister, Tojo Hideki, ordered, a year before Pearl Harbor, the setting forth of army doctrine on POWs in clear and unmistakable words. The result was a powerful, unambiguous instrument, which hundreds of thousands of soldiers and sailors took with them to their deaths, although it proved insufficient to deny the elemental urge to live among at least some Japanese. This became increasingly apparent to the Japanese high command when combat with the Western powers proved infinitely more stressful to the combat arms than the conflict with the two Chinese camps.

A few days after Japan's opening of hostilities on December 7, 1941, the American and British governments inquired of the Japanese government through Swiss intermediaries whether Japan intended to conduct itself in compliance with the 1929 Geneva Convention governing the treatment of prisoners of war. Foreign Minister Togo Shigenori responded through the same channel that while Japan had not ratified the convention, it would abide by it. There is no evidence that the Japanese government, especially the armed services, ever seriously intended to implement this decision. In the event, Japan failed to abide by the Geneva Convention in all respects.

The United States and its allies lived up to the conventions they had ratified by notifying the Japanese government, through their respective protecting powers, of the names and other identifying information on all prisoners. The transmittals were translated but closely held within the Japanese government to retain the illusion that Japanese POWs did not exist. Families of POWs were not notified that sons or husbands were alive, even after the war ended. During the war the Japanese government was convinced that the families would not welcome news that their kin had been taken prisoner. In most cases, families did not realize their son or husband had survived until he appeared at the front door.

3

INDOCTRINATION INTO THE *SENJINKUN*

Japan's uncompromising stand concerning Japanese prisoners of war must be understood in the context of the prevailing Japanese political scene and the wider geopolitical events playing out in 1940–41. Japan's brief experiment with an increasingly broad electoral enfranchisement and parliamentary-style party politics had run its course. The electorate widely regarded the party-led governments of the 1930s as hopelessly corrupt and incapable of dealing with Japan's economic problems during the Great Depression era. As demonstrated by the increasingly frequent ascension of generals and admirals to the prime ministership, the military, with de facto veto power over cabinet formation, had become Japan's dominant political force. Right-wing political elements and their allies in the military gradually shunted aside elements urging a cautious foreign policy, including those in the political parties, the foreign ministry, and even in the navy, which held a healthy respect for the American and British navies. In the atmosphere of ultranationalism that overtook Japan, a country that prized unity and consensus, more and more courage was required to speak out against the war psychosis promoted by the rightists. Ultranationalists in the army and other organizations instilled fear in their more moderate opponents by several successful assassinations of prominent politicians and business leaders.

By the summer of 1941 the Japanese leadership felt that it had arrived at a decisive stage in history. Japanese forces were plunging ever deeper into China, without any indication that victory was in the offing. Unwilling to recognize the strong nationalistic and anti-

Japanese feelings of the Chinese people and their rejection of the Japanese-installed puppet regime, the Japanese government persuaded itself that Nationalist China's continued resistance was due to British and American military assistance. In reality, Western assistance at the time was more symbolic than tangible and hardly affected the course of the war. But allegations of a vast Western supply corridor to Chungking served to sustain Japanese beliefs that the Chinese government was inherently weak, susceptible to Japanese leadership, and would soon fall if Western aid could only be cut off.

The Japanese army in particular was deeply embarrassed by its failure to finish off the Chinese Nationalists. The idea of withdrawal from China was unthinkably humiliating, but that was the price the Western powers were demanding. While the European colonial powers were engaged in a death struggle with Nazi Germany, the conquest of Southeast Asia became increasingly appealing as a means of redeeming Japan's honor and cutting off Allied supplies to China. For its part, the Japanese navy, squeezed by the Western oil embargo, saw major advantages in securing the natural resources of the Dutch East Indies and Malaysia.

The army had long regarded the Soviet Union as its primary adversary, and its right-wing political allies considered Communism their principal ideological enemy. However, the army's humiliating defeat at the Battle of Nomonhan in 1939 had cooled its ardor for a conflict with the Soviets. Moreover, by the fall of 1941 the Soviet Union was occupied in a death struggle with Germany. This removed Japan's fear of a potential threat to its rear in the event Japan opened hostilities against the Western powers.

In fact, with the Germans sitting astride virtually all of Europe and striking deep into the Soviet Union, many military observers in Japan and even in the West thought that its days were numbered. In these circumstances, German advice to its Axis partner had considerable credibility: A "new world order" was arising from the ruins of the old; if Japan struck now it could seize the decisive moment to defeat the remnants of Western power in East Asia; Japan would partake in the spoils that were sure to fall into its lap. This litany fell on fertile soil among the expansionist nationalists. German interests were confined to knocking out the United Kingdom. Germany had absolutely no interest in taking on the Americans at that point, but the Pearl Harbor attack made the issue moot.

It would be wrong to think that the Japanese decision to attack the Anglo-American powers was motivated solely by expectations of material gain and glory. On the contrary, the military propelled itself to political leadership by appearing to be the only idealistic and truly patriotic element in society. Japan was undergoing a nativist reaction to the heavy doses of Western influence in the first three decades of the twentieth century. Domestically, the military portrayed itself as untarnished by the profit motive. In foreign policy, the concept of a Greater East Asia Co-Prosperity Sphere under benign Japanese leadership caught the popular imagination.

Unable to pull back and resolve the problems it had created for itself in China, the Japanese government proceeded to lunge forward rather blindly in a different direction without a sober weighing of the risks and advantages of a strike against the United States and Great Britain. It lacked any real strategy on how to achieve its war aims and the costs those objectives might entail. Japan's military power was considerably inferior to and less modernized than Germany's, even though it had developed some exceptional new weapons. Japan recognized that at least potentially the United States was militarily far superior. Nevertheless, the Japanese government felt that crucial decisions about its future course had to be made, believing that it did have some tangible military advantages. Japan had developed the Zero, regarded during the early stages of the war as possibly the best fighter plane in the Pacific. Japan had a number of secret weapons in place or being built, including both midget and extra-large submarines, and the world's largest battleships. Japan had also created a large fleet of aircraft carriers, recognizing their key role in the naval battles to come. It was the first to perfect the concept of multicarrier strikes over long distances, an idea carried out on December 7, 1941.

In the first year of the war, Japan was actually militarily superior in both manpower and equipment to the United States and its allies in the Pacific, who were forced to carry on a two-front war. The Japanese military leaders were not so blind, however, as to believe that Japan could maintain equality, let alone superiority, in the sinews of war once America placed its industrial power on a war footing.

Any appraisal of the odds forced them to fall back onto the "spiritual superiority" of the Japanese soldier and sailor. This plainly meant the Japanese warrior's readiness to endure any hardship and to fight to the death. This "spiritual quality," the military leaders were certain, would ultimately wear down the Americans and the other Westerners and sap their will to fight a prolonged conflict.

The fanciful notion that the emperor of Japan was planning to ride his white horse down Constitution Avenue in Washington as a symbol of Japan's total victory was never more than the product of the fevered imagination of American propagandists. Japan's leaders thought that ultimately the United States would weary of waging a war that might last decades, even "a hundred years" as some propagandists projected. Exhausted by the ever-ready Japanese willingness to die, the United States eventually would be prepared to cut a deal leaving control of East Asia in Japanese hands. This miscalculation of the extent of America's determination once aroused by what it regarded as an unprovoked attack, plus faith in a German victory in Europe, provided a basis for Japan's hopes for an improvement in its strategic position and a way out of its embarrassing dilemma in China.

The official Japanese view of Americans and British saw them as "ogres" and "devils," but ultimately flabby, disunited, and weak. Still somewhat confident as a result of a string of easy victories in China, the Japanese predicted that Western forces would bend and break before their determined bayonet charges and boundless determination to prevail at all costs. They viewed the U.S. Army's doctrine as a "simplistic belief in weaponry and matériel superiority." Japan did not need to be materially stronger because it was spiritually more powerful than America.

The official glorification of death in pursuit of national goals had thus become an integral, essential element of Japan's military strategy. Indoctrination began in the schools. The Imperial Rescript on Education of 1890, drafted by the Meiji government, designated the emperor as the father of all Japanese children. Every school had a Shinto shrine at which the emperor's picture was prominently displayed. The rescript was ceremoniously read by the principal on all appropriate national holidays. Many of the children, especially younger ones, listened uncomprehendingly to language that was arcane even then, but the occasions were solemn and the children were rewarded with gifts of *mochi* (pounded rice usually served at festive times such as New Year's).

The text of the rescript began with an explanation of Japan's polity and its establishment in prehistoric times under the aegis of the Sun Goddess, going on to stress the importance of filial piety in terms of obedience to parents and loyalty to the emperor and his laws. It noted the need to risk one's own life in defense of country and the emperor. To lend emphasis, the rescript stressed that this had been handed down to the children and their parents by their ancestors and needed to be kept intact by them, their children, and grandchildren through time immemorial, the nation's leaders and the Japanese people acting as one.

This philosophy was reinforced in the regular classes on morality *(shushin),* where Confucian ethics were taught. Many years before the boys would expect to be called up for military service, they were taught that as adults they should not fear sacrificing themselves for the good of the country. Such teachings had not been stressed in the early years of Japan's modernization; neither in the Sino-Japanese War nor in the Russo-Japanese War were such beliefs in evidence. As an extreme form of nationalism spread during the 1930s, however, Japanese education and the media emphasized the unique nature of the country's long imperial lineage, myths concerning the founding of imperial rule 2,600 years earlier, and the bonds between the imperial institution and the Japanese people. Although none of these could bear the scrutiny of historical inquiry, Japanese youths became increasingly inculcated with the notion that they had a veritable *duty* to die for the emperor. Even Otis Cary, son of an American missionary who was enrolled in a Japanese primary school in the early 1930s and became a navy language officer during the war, was impressed by what he heard in school, despite antidotes he received at home.

Universal military training for all young men, modeled on prevailing European practices, had been instituted as part of the Meiji period reforms. The Japanese government subsequently went far beyond this by also requiring preparatory military training in secondary schools, a practice unique to Japan. In 1925 a government ordinance instituted military training in the national school system under the direction of active duty officers. The goal was to promote glorification of the military at an early age and, not so incidentally, to provide jobs for officers when budgetary constraints required the elimination of two divisions. Retired senior sergeants assisted the officers. Military training began at the prewar Japanese equivalent of junior high school, normally with a captain in charge, although as the "China Incident" dragged on into the late 1930s, lieutenants were often substituted. Military training in the high schools and universities was headed by more senior officers. In the initial stages of training, boys were given close order drills using wooden rifles and physical fitness exercises. Already in their third year of junior high, at the age of fourteen or fifteen, they were issued obsolete rifles, bayonets, and model light machine guns. On average, four hours per week were dedicated to military training. This training became increasingly realistic and sophisticated as the boys progressed in school. It inculcated the message that this was serious preparation for induction into the army or navy and for the subsequent combat young men were likely to experience.

Indoctrination included instruction on the high place of the military in Japanese society, the emperor's leadership of the military, the need for absolute loyalty to military superiors, and the importance of unit cohesion. As one former soldier put it, they were indoctrinated to follow orders in all situations, "even when they could see that black was being described as white." The Japanese people's cultural predisposition to resign themselves to fate pointed the way toward giving over their future to their superiors.

Many veterans, especially those with some higher education, recalled their time in basic training as the worst period of their life. They could accept the strict hierarchy of military life as an extension of normal life within the family and society as a whole, but the daily abuses of the recruits, designed to accustom them to enduring all hardships and overcoming all obstacles, were something else again. As Suzuki Michiya wrote in a privately published memoir, every recruit was assigned to an older soldier with greater seniority. He was required to serve his senior in a variety of ways, including preparing his senior's food, washing his chopsticks, and taking care of his bedding in the morning and evening. Recruits raced to be the first to their noncommissioned officer's (NCO's) room to fold his futon when wake-up call came in the morning. They even took care of their senior's rifle, boots, and horse. But the most resented humiliation was the requirement to wash their NCO's underwear.[1]

Another disagreeable practice in the Japanese military was that of hitting subordinates for even the most insignificant transgressions, real or imagined. Soldiers could be physically abused for such failings as being too slow in answering a superior, not finishing work on time, even for showing insufficient enthusiasm. The custom of hitting recruits in the face, known as *binta,* was allegedly designed to harden the men for the rigors of combat. The weapon of choice might well be a hand to the cheek, but more often a slipper or boot was used, occasionally one with a steel plate on the sole.

Sugawara Yasuhiro, who survived combat as a navy fighter pilot, provided extensive information on these *binta* exercises. In the Japanese navy, nonofficial punishment in theory was not authorized but in practice was administered on an almost daily basis, purely on the whim of noncommissioned officers. No mistake, error, or accident was needed to provoke punishment; it was used to instill blind discipline, nothing more. Sugawara participated in fleet maneuvers at the Kure naval base in August 1942. On his first day he became convinced that all the rumors about *binta* were true, that training would be "hell." The navy frequently used the *ago* (chin) method that involved hitting the offender not only around the cheeks but also on his chin. It became a form of boxing, with, however, only one active participant. The results were predictable. Sugawara recalled having been knocked out ten times in his three years in the navy. Once he got into the naval air force, *binta* was prohibited because of concern that the practice might rupture an eardrum and render the pilot useless.[2]

Another Japanese navy practice was that of hitting recruits' buttocks with baseball bats. This punishment was often meted out when the recruit failed to complete an assignment within a fixed time. However, the exercise was stacked against him because the allotted time was so short that timely completion was impossible. Punishment could also consist of requiring the offender to stand on his head for thirty minutes or stand with arms extended for an hour. Such practices, it was said, were intended to sharpen the edge of pilot trainees destined to participate in dogfights with only two possible outcomes: victory or death.

Several former POWs recalled having to endure occasional group "lynchings." (For unknown reasons, the English word was always used, but not in its extreme American sense.) Often employed to deal with group transgressions, these occasionally featured hitting recruits with an eight-sided stick that was somewhat larger than a baseball bat. One former soldier recalled that the bat used to hit him was carved on one side with the appellation "Military Spirit Instilling Bat." On the other side was written, somewhat obscurely, "Roosevelt and Churchill breathe in and out before our very eyes," presumably to convey the idea that the recruits were in combat with the leaders of the Western powers. Group solidarity was fostered in these practices, along with endurance. If one member of a group broke a rule or caused his unit to lose in a competition, the entire unit might be subjected to a *binta* exercise or even a "lynching."

However brutal, childish, and absurd such training devices might seem today, they appear to have worked in solidifying blind loyalty to authorities, both immediate and distant, and a willingness to die whenever ordered. Most recruits fatalistically accepted the constant abuse as inherent in the system, something that could not be changed and from which there was no appeal. For recruits from the many desperately poor rural areas, military life might not have been much tougher than existence down on the farm. When these indoctrinated young men wound up in Allied prisoner of war camps, the contrast could not have been greater between what they had endured and assumed was the universal norm and their treatment at the hands of Western soldiers who had been trained in a very different way.

Recruits were kept so busy during basic training, day and night, that they had no time for recreation, either within the camp or in town. Besides, they often lacked the money to engage in frivolities. In the initial four months of training, recruits received two yen, seventy-five sen per month, the equivalent of sixty-five cents in 1936. There was hardly time even to write a letter home. The recruits learned that the military owned them body and soul. On the other hand, their honored position as soldiers and sailors in a status-conscious society was the highest the nation could bestow.

After basic training, the recruits might be returned to civilian life, but they remained subject to recall to active duty. Once the war began in the Pacific, those recalled to active duty often went straight to their overseas assignments without any additional training and frequently without home leave. Some thought that even the front lines might not be as bad as basic training, but those sent to combat zones in Southeast Asia soon realized they had been mistaken in that assumption.

The success of the indoctrination program on impressionable youths over a period of many years created new ways of speaking that reflected the new Japanese reality. When Japanese troops engaged in combat in the late 1930s and early 1940s, a special vocabulary was devised to mark the death of a soldier or sailor. Normal expressions of sympathy or condolence *(shusho)* were never employed. Instead, one of the following expressions was considered proper: "Congratulations on (his) having achieved the honor of a death in battle"; or, "This occasion was really one of honor"; or, "It appears that (he) attained the long-cherished desire of a soldier." The proper response for a family member of the deceased to a condolence expressed in this form was: "Thanks to your kind concern he was able to achieve the honor of a death in battle. He (the deceased) certainly wanted this above all else. For us as family members it is enough that (his) death could repay the emperor's great beneficence." To shed tears on such an occasion was viewed as shameful and inappropriate behavior toward the deceased.

The official imprimatur of the preexisting belief in "death before the dishonor" of becoming a POW came in the form of the army's Field Service Code *(Senjinkun),* released with an imperial sanction on January 7, 1941. Proclaimed by army minister General Tojo Hideki, half a year before he became prime minister, and released to the public with much fanfare the following day, the *Senjinkun* decreed that it was impermissible for Japanese soldiers to become prisoners of war. This document provided the only servicewide, authoritative statement on the subject. Under the heading "Regard for Reputation," the code stated: "Those who know shame are weak. Always think of [preserving] the honor of your community and be a credit to yourself and your family. Redouble your efforts and respond to their expectations. Never live to experience shame as a prisoner. By dying you will avoid leaving behind the crime of a stain on your honor." The use of difficult linguistic formulations and expressions common to official documents in prewar times lent a special aura to Tojo's pronouncement. It may not have been fully comprehended by the less educated, but the overall impact was awesome.

The timing of the *Senjinkun* was dictated, as noted above, by a perception of lax discipline among Japanese forces engaged in the "China Incident" and in the Battle of Nomonhan. Both conflicts involved what the Japanese high command considered an impermissible number of their soldiers being taken prisoner. The *Senjinkun* was not regarded by the general public as the announcement of a new policy but as the reaffirmation of an old one, even though it had never before been officially expressed.

The Japanese government accompanied the issuance of the *Senjinkun* with an extensive propaganda campaign extolling the heroism of those who had rejected all thoughts of surrender and had given their lives in Japan's wars. Four competing record companies held a joint pep rally and pop music recital on March 5, 1941, at Hibiya Hall, then the largest concert hall in Tokyo, and on the following day released the "Senjinkun no Uta" (Song of the *Senjinkun*) phonograph record to the general public.[3]

In March 1941, the China Expeditionary Force issued a secret summary of the *Senjinkun,* referring to "instructions concerning prisoners of war" and admitting that "in the course of our sacred war not a few Japanese soldiers had fallen into enemy hands and besmirched their honor." For the first time, the issue was brought out into the open within senior military circles. The summary ordered subordinate commands to come up with appropriate measures to deal with the problem without offering concrete suggestions for how that might be accomplished. It simply assumed that the subordinates would redouble their efforts to assure that their troops knew their duty to choose death over dishonor, with no alternative. It was apparently not considered necessary to amend military law to make becoming a prisoner of war a crime. Unlike the fanfare given the *Senjinkun,* no publicity accompanied the army's 1942 criminal code, which stated: "A commanding officer who surrenders his troops to the enemy in combat, even though he has done his utmost, will be sentenced to a minimum of six months imprisonment."[4] Nobody paid attention to this law. It dealt with a serious dereliction of duty but had only insignificant consequences that paled next to the *Senjinkun,* under-lining the reality that in governing, the Japanese accorded a much higher value to societal norms than to the law.

Equally curious was that the navy never did issue a parallel rul-ing. Some navy veterans averred that they never even heard of Tojo's *Senjinkun.* It made no difference. By the time it was issued, the spirit of the *Senjinkun* was already so deeply embedded in the national psy-che that it was more than a military directive to a single service. It had become an imperative not only for the military but also for civil-ians attached to the military and ultimately for all civilians, includ-ing even women and children. This was subsequently demonstrated on Saipan, which had large numbers of Japanese settlers, and on Oki-nawa. Many women and children on the two islands took their own lives rather than dishonor themselves by falling under American con-trol. On the occasion of ordering the final suicide charge, the top Japanese commander on Saipan, Vice Admiral Nagumo Chuichi, quoted the *Senjinkun* as a great moral statement that needed to be cherished and obeyed.

While postwar Japanese scholars have argued back and forth as to whether General Tojo's *Senjinkun* was a legally binding document, this question is ultimately of no consequence. During the late 1930s, the Japanese media produced romanticized accounts of suicide mis-sions that publicized the notion of "glorious battle deaths" as role models to be followed, and these had captured the imagination of the population as a whole.

In the period between Japan's seizure of Manchuria and the out-break of the Sino-Japanese War in 1937, intermittent but occasion-ally heavy fighting occurred between Japanese and Chinese forces on Chinese soil, especially in and around Shanghai, a center of strong anti-Japanese feelings. In order to divert the attention of disapprov-ing foreign powers from the birth of the new, Japanese-sponsored nation of Manchukuo, Japan's Kwangtung Army instigated what became known as the Second Shanghai Incident. The plotters paid a Chinese national to murder a Japanese Buddhist priest of the Nichiren faith. This provided the motive for Japanese forces already on the scene to launch a revenge action. A Japanese naval contingent led an assault against Chinese troops on the pretext of "protecting Japanese nationals." The passions of war rose to fever pitch in Japan.

When the ultimatum for the withdrawal of Chinese forces had expired, the Japanese attacked. One evening the Japanese were thwarted in efforts to take a well-fortified Chinese position "surrounded like a spider's net" with interlocking barbed wire fences nine feet high. The Japanese commander called on his engineers to solve the problem of breaching the barbed wire the following day. Lacking more conventional tools to do the job, he asked for thirty volunteers prepared to give their lives in the operation. The volunteers were organized in teams of three, each carrying a bangalore torpedo. In one sector there was complete success; in another, three teams were wiped out. Two reserve teams were ordered into action. Judging the approach taken earlier to be futile, one team leader proposed lighting the fuse before his team came up to the fence. The suicide mission was approved, and Japan had the heroes it craved. The team had only thirty seconds to run the forty meters to the barbed wire. The ensuing explosion had the desired effect of breaching the Chinese lines, costing the team members their lives. These exploits were extensively featured in the press, where those who had sacrificed themselves became known throughout the nation as the "three brave bomb warriors."

In another engagement around the same time, a Japanese infantry unit came under a withering cross fire from Chinese forces. The surrounded battalion commander, a Major Kuga, was in a desperate situation, with no relief able to come to his rescue. He had only thirty men left and had himself been severely wounded. Following a futile charge by a lieutenant under his command, only thirteen men remained alive. When a second lieutenant asked the major to authorize a retreat, Kuga refused. The two officers became separated. After numerous efforts to reestablish contact with Major Kuga evoked no response, the junior officer ordered the retreat and reported the major's death in battle. Survivors brought back some of the major's earthly effects but lacked evidence that he had actually died. A search party failed to find his body. In fact, Major Kuga had been captured and, in the cease-fire that ensued shortly thereafter, was returned to Japanese control in a prisoner exchange. As a senior officer, he had been well treated. Two weeks later, Major Kuga returned to the exact spot where he had been captured and committed suicide, leaving behind a poem that spoke of the "warrior's dishonor in having been taken prisoner of war."

The media again used the Major Kuga incident to underline the message that the officer had taken exactly the right steps to remove the stain of dishonor from his name. He became a role model for many of Japan's future soldiers and sailors, who died of their own volition in the belief that they followed not only the best but the only course open to men of honor facing the likelihood of becoming prisoners. Their heroism was also celebrated in poetry and songs. Typical of the overwrought glorification of combat deaths at the time was a song entitled "Matte Orimasu Kudan Zaka" (Kudan Hill Is Waiting for You), the hill at Kudan being the site of the Yasukuni Shrine in Tokyo dedicated to the memory and enshrinement of fallen soldiers and sailors. The song, as translated by Shinoda Tokohiko, went:

> *With you away at the battlefront*
> *on the emperor's command*
> *Our little son and I are alone with the moon*
> *But I refuse to cry out*
> *I'll be awaiting your meritorious service*
> *at Kudan Hill*

In wartime the distinction between outright suicide and the braving of enemy fire in order to secure an honorable exit from life became clouded for many Japanese. Especially toward the end of the war, when the tactical situation was often hopeless for Japanese troops, commanders in their final messages to higher headquarters reported that they were ordering a *gyokusai,* meaning suicide charge. Since the men were often emaciated, ill, and near their physical limits, such charges, made with inadequate weapons and ammunition, often amounted to little more than a suicidal way out, often with little or no effect on the military situation. On the rare occasions when the military unit carrying out a *gyokusai* was still intact and had enough ammunition, it was able to inflict heavy casualties on the enemy, as occurred in the desperate rearguard actions on Saipan.

Glorified examples of suicidal actions in the process of carrying out missions for the country's benefit fell on extraordinarily fertile cultural soil. Countless anthropological studies of Japan have noted the relatively large role played by suicide in Japan's arts. Indeed, in hara-kiri (or seppuku, as it is better known in Japan), Japan had perfected a ritualized form of suicide celebrated in numerous plays in the Kabuki theater, notably in *Chushingura,* the best-known and most beloved play of this genre. Japanese poetry dwelt at length on the transitoriness of life, which was often compared to the beauty and brief existence of the cherry blossom.

In the absence of any religious basis for condemning the taking of one's own life, suicide was seen approvingly as a response to irreconcilable conflicts involving the pull of personal passions and the limits imposed by social norms. In prewar years, the press gave extensive coverage to double love suicides, often achieved by jumping into the crater of the active volcano on Oshima Island near Tokyo. It was even rumored at the time that the government, in a futile effort to put a halt to the rash of suicides on Oshima, forbade the company operating the island ferries to issue one-way tickets. In fact, prewar Japanese suicide rates were not abnormally high compared to the incidence of suicide among Europeans and Americans. This suggests that in peacetime, Japanese may have been more enamored with the idea of suicide than with its actuality.

Motivation for suicidal behavior on the battlefield was clearly different from the various causes for suicide in civilian life. Already at the outset of Japan's war against the West, however, Japanese troops were more disposed than Americans and their Western allies to a pessimistic view of their chances of survival. Countless diaries and numerous statements by POWs testify to the fervor with which so many Japanese apparently embraced their impending death. At the same time, many of the captured diaries reflected a literary style that was poetic and sentimental rather than a realistic appraisal of the situation facing their authors. The religious belief that in their afterlife they would continue to fight on behalf of the fatherland was another significant factor that enabled them to view death with considerable equanimity. One soldier's handwritten pledge to Amaterasu, the mythical Sun Goddess and founder of the Japanese state, was typical of such strong feelings:

> *We vow to be first to die.*
> *We vow to be first to achieve glorious deeds.*
> *We vow to be first to follow orders.*

Another POW wrote of his longing for death in this stirring poem:

> *My comrades are crossing the seas*
> *To the Shrine at Kudan.*
> *But I, like a caged bird,*
> *Cannot join them.*
>
> *My comrades have been scattered by the wind,*
> *But they will bloom again as flowers of Kudan.*
> *My name was scattered too,*
> *But I cannot lose this five-foot body of mine.*
>
> *For my sovereign and my country,*
> *My name was lost on the battlefield,*
> *But I cannot lose this five-foot body of mine.*
>
> *The comrades I talked with yesterday*
> *Have become protective gods of the nation.*
> *I, alas, am not yet dead,*
> *And my carcass in enemy lands remains unburied!*

Despite the fact that most Japanese soldiers and sailors surrendered to the pressures and compulsions of their culture and chose death before capture, it is clear that more than a few, like most of mankind, would much rather have lived than died. This was reflected in the accounts of those who became prisoners of war. Some lacked the courage to take their own life, some thought it was foolish to throw one's life away, and some were induced to surrender by promises of good treatment. One POW felt that surrender needed to be a personal choice; another felt abandoned. Many expressed bitterness toward officers who fled to relative safety while leaving their troops to face continued hardships.[5] Even when Japanese soldiers and sailors said or wrote that they did not expect to return home alive, they were voicing the popularly accepted manner of commenting on their fate. Opinions varied as to whether they truly believed it. That which they were expected by society to believe and express *(tatemae)* often merged in their consciousness with their own truly held belief *(honne)*.

There is no question that Japanese, at least during wartime, were far more fatalistic than Americans in similar situations. They certainly would have missed the humor of an apocryphal American army story that had a sergeant telling his squad of ten men that they would be going out on so dangerous a mission that nine would not return alive. All ten of the men grieved deeply over the sad fate of the nine others!

During the first year of the war there was only a trickle of Japanese prisoners. Japan was still on the offensive, an uncommon time for prisoners to be lost to the enemy. One notable exception occurred during the Battle of Bataan in early 1942. Most of the members of three battalions of a Japanese regiment that landed on the peninsula's west coast as part of an envelopment maneuver were killed, but almost fifty soldiers were captured when incapacitated. Soon thereafter, they were liberated by the victorious Japanese. The officers of the misadventure were required to commit suicide, and the enlisted men were scattered and assigned to the most hazardous duties available in their new units.

Additional Japanese sailors and airmen were taken prisoner from sunken ships and downed aircraft when a Japanese naval task force was routed in the Battle of Midway in June 1942, but their numbers were still insignificant relative to the huge number of Japanese who perished in these operations. Although some of these prisoners had suffered injuries as well as hunger and thirst while drifting on the ocean for many days, they tended to be in basically good physical shape.

A different kind of prisoner came into Allied hands on the islands of the southwest Pacific, where the Japanese advance was eventually blunted and then pushed back at the end of 1942 and in early 1943.

On New Guinea, Australian and American counterattacks forced the Japanese to retreat over the Owen Stanley Mountains under extremely difficult conditions. American forces landed on Guadalcanal in the Solomon Islands and engaged several divisions of Japanese on some of the most inhospitable terrain of the war. These were the initial land battles in which Japanese unit cohesion ultimately disintegrated. Japanese troops sustained heavy American artillery fire, aerial attacks, and constant pressure on the ground; they also confronted impenetrable jungles, suffered a sharply rising incidence of disease, and endured dwindling stocks of food and munitions when American interdiction of supplies became increasingly effective.

An estimated one-third of all Japanese prisoners who fell into Allied hands were physically incapacitated by disease, wounds, or malnutrition and dehydration. Some were also mentally unhinged by intense Allied bombardment and the cumulative effect of trying to survive for a long period in the jungle. Conditions were so extreme that in a few instances Japanese soldiers resorted to cannibalism.

Allied patrols found a few men unconscious or asleep, but many more subsequently recalled having been unconscious at the time of capture. Many, it is believed, feigned unconsciousness or convinced themselves that they had fallen into a comatose state to avoid having to admit to themselves that they had not offered last-ditch resistance before being taken prisoner.

The majority were taken prisoner in a variety of ways. Some had simply come to the conclusion that they wanted to survive and decided to take their chances with the Allied forces, however hazardous that might be. Others harbored resentments against superiors because they felt mistreated or abandoned by their leaders. One prisoner mentioned that it was "not uncommon for officers to be shot by their own men," and others alluded to the same phenomenon. Many were left behind to die by their own hand but ultimately lacked the will to commit suicide. Some were captured by natives who delivered them to the Allies, and a few deliberately sought out natives to use as intermediaries, with a view to making the transition to POW status as safely as possible. Quite a few were persuaded to surrender by Allied leaflets or loudspeaker appeals, especially during the last stages of the war.

In many instances a combination of factors led to the decision to surrender. Sometimes there was not much deliberation, as, for example, when a small group suddenly found itself confronted by a much larger Allied force and realized resistance would have been futile. More often, two or three or four with similar doubts about the utility of further resistance discussed whether or not to surrender and came to the often painful realization that they wanted to live. In making that decision they faced a totally unknowable future and, as they saw it, much danger.

4

HONORABLE DEATH
OR SHAMEFUL LIFE

The spirit of the *Senjinkun* held fast among Japanese soldiers and sailors almost until World War II ended. As the war drew ever closer to the Japanese mainland in late 1944 and early 1945, more and more prisoners fell into American hands, although still in exceedingly small numbers, usually by ones, twos, and threes. Of the 5,000 Japanese who defended the island of Tarawa in late 1943, only 17 survived, along with 129 Korean laborers; 1,000 Americans died in the same battle. In late 1944, 65,000 Japanese soldiers died and about 5,000 were taken prisoner on the island of Leyte in the Philippines. Out of 250,000 Americans participating in the island's recapture, 3,500 died and 12,000 were wounded. Iwo Jima was defended by 14,000 Japanese soldiers and 7,000 sailors in early 1945; only 216 Japanese and a few Koreans surrendered. Many Japanese on Iwo Jima died in suicide charges, and all senior officers committed suicide. But, as the fighting on Okinawa wound down in the summer of 1945 and all Japanese hope of even a stalemated war faded, for the first time in the war some Japanese surrendered in small military units. Of the 170,000 defenders of Okinawa, 10,000 survived as prisoners of war.

When Japan surrendered on August 15, 1945, a total of 38,666 Japanese had been taken prisoner by the United States, Australia, New Zealand, and the United Kingdom, on battlefields and oceans stretching from the Burmese-Indian border to Attu in the Aleutians, Midway Island in the mid-Pacific, and Guadalcanal and New Guinea in the southwest Pacific. In addition, 4,554 Koreans and 4,487 Taiwanese, most of whom had been employed in construction battalions attached to the Japanese army, were also captured.

The ratio of Japanese POWs in Allied hands to the number of Japanese killed was phenomenally low compared with prisoners taken in the European/North African theaters. Japan had a total of 1,140,000 army and 410,000 navy personnel killed during the war, and just 26,304 army and 12,362 navy personnel taken prisoner. The number of POWs as a percentage of the number killed in action was 2.3 percent for the army and 3.0 percent for the navy.

Translated to specific battlefield locales in the South Pacific, there were 15,791 Japanese dead in Papua New Guinea, compared with just 350 POWs, a ratio of 45:1. On Bougainville, the Japanese suffered 16,497 dead, while 233 survived as POWs, a ratio of 71:1. In West (Dutch) New Guinea (now West Irian), Japanese military units were small, widely scattered, and minimally resupplied. This led to one of the lowest dead-to-POW ratios of the Pacific War, with 19,639 counted dead and 3,017 taken prisoner. Those captured included the 256 Japanese soldiers who, angered by their officers having confiscated all food supplies for their own use, surrendered en masse in September 1944 on the island of Numfoor off the coast of West New Guinea. To better effect their planned desertion, these Japanese split up into groups of 30 men each. The Numfoor captives, representing roughly one-sixth of the Japanese forces on the island, constituted the largest unit surrender until the latter stages of the war on Okinawa.[1]

In Western Europe, by comparison, military historians have calculated that, on average, a unit that suffered 25 percent casualties would give up the fight. On the Eastern front, German and Soviet forces had about an equal number of soldiers killed and captured by the enemy. In the early stages of the Russo-German war, hundreds of thousands of Russians surrendered to the advancing Germans in a single sector, and similar numbers of Germans surrendered to the Soviets later in the war. In the Battle of Stalingrad alone, about 250,000 encircled Germans—the entire Sixth Army Group—surrendered to the Soviets. Nothing even remotely comparable occurred in East Asia, where the Japanese normally fought on even when no chance remained that the outcome of the battle or the war would be affected.

It is hardly surprising that the Japanese quickly earned a reputation for willingness to fight until the last breath, even in hopeless
situations. Westerners were inclined to regard such extreme dedication to duty inhuman and attributed it to the unquestioning and complete loyalty of the Japanese to the emperor, and a facet of emperor
worship. In reality, such dedication to the emperor was generally far
from the minds of Japanese troops facing death. As reflected in the
testimony of survivors and diaries of those who died in battle, not
even love of country, let alone the distant figure of a god-emperor,
provided the chief motivation for Japanese behavior in combat. Such
alleged motivations were easily dismissed by the survivors as *tatemae,*
group orthodoxy, motivation more avowed than real. These were
not their *honne,* the true inner feelings of individuals, which were
revealed only under unusual circumstances to intimates, rarely even
to a diary, often to no one. U.S. staff sergeant Min Hara was interrogating Japanese prisoners on New Guinea when he asked a group
whether it was true that all dying soldiers shouted "Tenno Heika Banzai" (Long Live the Emperor). The response was unexpected. "Maybe
1 soldier in 10,000," said one prisoner, and another believed that "1
in 20,000 is too high." All they ever heard on the lips of dying soldiers was the word *okā-san* (mother).[2]

Writing and talking about the war and their capture many decades
later, Japanese veterans recalled that their thoughts at the time
focused mostly on their immediate family, especially on their moth-
ers, as well as on their community. This is what motivated them to
seek glory in death rather than the dishonor of surrender, even invol-
untary captivity. Their strong group identification made surrender
extremely difficult to talk about, let alone organize with others. To
contemplate flouting such deeply felt ties was simply unthinkable.
Soldiers shrank from considering surrender, knowing their comrades
would think them cowards. They recalled fearing Allied treatment,
including torture, and postwar punishment by what they assumed
would be a victorious Japan. Those who had witnessed or heard about
Japanese mistreatment of Allied prisoners believed that retribution
and revenge would be the obvious, inescapable Allied policy toward
any Japanese prisoners. At times an element of mass hysteria induced
Japanese troops to commit suicide even when capture was not immi-

nent. Finally, former POWs have made it clear that another very strong deterrent to surrender was their belief that they would be letting down comrades who had already paid the ultimate price.

Under the existing cultural conventions of the time, Japanese soldiers and sailors believed that their capture, if it became known, would have direct and dire consequences for their families. They felt certain that their shame would result in community ostracism of their families and close relatives. This was the worst fate possible in a group-oriented society. It could well affect a sister's chance of finding a husband and have an impact on parents, children, and siblings in a myriad of ways, including opportunities for higher education and good jobs. Above all, there was the fear of letting down *"okā-san,"* the strongest family bond of young Japanese men in uniform.

The Japanese disdain toward prisoners of war and their glorification of death in battle manifested itself in many ways. It began with the employment of midget submarines early in the war and continued with the use of small naval craft configured for suicide attacks and modified manned torpedoes. By far the largest number of Japanese deaths in suicide missions, however, occurred in the final, often massive, desperation charges by Japanese ground forces, when their forces were already decimated and weakened by disease and malnutrition. These final assaults, known as banzai (hurrah) charges by Americans, had the dual purpose of inflicting maximum damage on the enemy while at the same time ensuring an honorable death and avoidance of the shame of surrender. The act of achieving such an honorable death in a desperate, usually losing, tactical cause was known as *gyokusai,* or "shattered jewels" in Japanese. The term was derived from the *Book of Northern Chi,* a chronicle of the Chi dynasty in sixth-century China that spoke of men of strength, or heroes, who chose to become gems that break into myriad fragments rather than roof tiles living out their lives in idleness. In the latter stages of the war, the Japanese extensively used kamikaze ("divine wind") attacks by manned suicide aircraft against Allied warships. They derived their name from the typhoon that destroyed the Mongol invaders of Japan in the thirteenth century. The terminology spoke to the Japanese instinct for cloaking references to death in a haze of verbal romanticism.

Participation in a *gyokusai,* or desperation naval or aerial attack, would ensure glory even when it occurred in an utterly hopeless engagement. Most of those who took part fervently believed that it would earn them a place in Tokyo's Yasukuni Shrine, the pantheon of Japan's war heroes where, enshrined and deified, they would continue to fight alongside the living to protect the nation. They would become, as Japanese would put it, "gods." While this Japanese appellation lacks the sense of awe and majesty of the capitalized singular English word, it nevertheless denotes a superior spirit with the power to affect the material world. It was more than enough to provide a noble legacy for their families and descendents.

Despite the socially approved predilection for a glorious death, reality did not always accord with the ideal. The Japanese "grunt" always understood tacitly that in a hopeless situation the generals and other high-ranking officers would commit suicide first, followed by the rest of the troops. The generals often had the "luxury" of committing suicide in the approved traditional manner in which an assistant would cut off their heads with a sword after they cut open their belly. Enlisted men and lower-ranking officers did not have this option. They were expected to participate instead in a *gyokusai* charge, even when lacking weapons and ammunition. Having to face a hail of enemy bullets under such conditions was an understandably fearsome prospect. Some lower-grade officers who were expected to lead their men in the charge would have wanted first to fill themselves up with liquor, but that was seldom available. "Half crazed with fear and as in a dream," uppermost in their minds as they charged was the fear of having a finger pointed at them for failing to do their duty toward their unit and toward their country.[3]

The tenacity of the Japanese soldier and sailor contributed to establishing a more general code of conduct on Pacific battlefields. Japanese disdain for prisoners of war also induced the Americans and their allies to regard surrender as an unacceptable option themselves. The result was that combat in the Pacific theater of operations was one of neither giving nor asking for any quarter. Accordingly, Westerners regarded combat against the Japanese as more barbaric and merciless even than combat against the Nazis.

OBSTACLES TO SURRENDER

In these circumstances, the relatively small number of Japanese inclined to surrender faced enormous obstacles. As models for the conduct of their men, officers were in an especially difficult quandary when contemplating surrender. In the Japanese military, officers were not only leaders but also father figures for the men they led. There was no tradition in the Japanese army for officers facing a desperate situation and suffering unacceptably high casualties to surrender their unit to the enemy. Indeed, it was considered simply out of the question that officers might surrender, and hardly any field grade officers and few company grade combat officers did so. Until the last few months of the war, only a handful of officers ever surrendered together with the men under their charge. Many who did were survivors from naval vessels that had been sunk.

When a Japanese lieutenant emerged from the jungle and surrendered with fifty-nine of his men in the Marianas, it was such an exceptional act that special note was taken of it. Stressing form and decorum to the end, the officer had his men line up, count off, and salute before "turning them over" to the Americans, who transported them to a POW enclosure. The explanation accompanying the picture of this unusual scene in a Japanese book noted that the officer committed the act in the belief that his men did not become POWs, a dreaded word, but "disarmed soldiers."

While many enlisted POWs spoke approvingly of their officers, others expressed disdain during interrogations, attributing Japan's string of defeats to poor leadership. Accusations were rife about officers taking the best prostitutes available, keeping the bulk of scarce foodstuffs for themselves, and even abandoning their men to their fate while fleeing the battlefront to safer areas. Some officers clearly did not live up to the high ideals expected of them, and one POW even told his interrogator that "not all the bullets were fired by enemy forces." Rumors of this nature encouraged some enlisted personnel and even junior officers, left to their own devices, to desert.

Privates did not dare to confide in their NCOs about plans to surrender. One soldier could hardly bring himself to broach the subject with another, but often did so in an elliptical fashion. In the end,

those Japanese who made the conscious decision to surrender generally had to do so either on their own or in the company of just two
or three others. Once that decision had been made, they still had to
assure themselves that their own forces would not kill them while
they were trying to surrender.

After Japanese soldiers had succeeded in removing themselves
physically from the vicinity of their comrades-in-arms, usually under
cover of night, they had to find Western forces without getting killed
in the process. Waving surrender passes, written in English and Japanese, that had been dropped behind Japanese lines was helpful in
some cases. Others made up white flags, often fashioned out of underwear or a shirt, or raised their hands. Nobody had instructed them
in these procedures, but almost all had seen pictures and newsreels
of Western soldiers surrendering on Bataan or Singapore, and they
hoped such methods would work for them. As it turned out, however, even these widely accepted Western-devised symbols of surrender were not given full credence owing to the widespread belief
that the Japanese would take advantage of any ruse to kill their enemies. Understandably, Americans were often skeptical about a Japanese combatant's sincerity in wishing to surrender, knowing all about
the Japanese soldier's determination to fight to the last. They also
knew about instances of Japanese staging fake surrenders in order to
lure Americans to come out into the open, where they became easy
targets for snipers.

The first efforts to induce Japanese to surrender were made on
Guadalcanal, using leaflets and voice broadcasts. A process of trial
and error was required before these efforts brought results. Attempts
to induce surrenders by discrediting Japan's leaders or by attempting to prove that the army and navy had instigated the war in opposition to the emperor's will were ineffective. Far more useful were
leaflets and broadcasts that stressed the hopelessness of the situation
of those to whom the appeal was directed, the uselessness of being
slaughtered, and the promise of food and medical attention for those
who surrendered. Soldiers contemplating surrender had to be assured
that they could do so in relative safety if they followed American
instructions. To be effective, such appeals had to be directed into areas
where the position of Japanese units was precarious. Voice appeals

to the Japanese were preceded by requests to American combat forces in the area to cooperate with the experiment. Such extensive preparations were usually rewarded.[4]

Even when all else proceeded without incident, surrender was a tense matter. Only rarely did the Japanese know any English. When they did, their pronunciation was often so poor that the Americans could not understand them. In order to minimize the risk of misunderstandings, American forces were instructed to give the simplest possible commands to Japanese wanting to surrender. Unfortunately, some Japanese failed to make their peaceful intentions plain enough and were killed, and such cases served as a deterrent to others who might have been inclined to surrender. Inevitably, since Japanese-speaking Americans were not always available at the front lines to interpret, there were instances when the opportunity to take additional POWs was lost.

Only an estimated one-third of all Japanese taken prisoners had been actively seeking to surrender when captured. Various circumstances accounted for the remaining two-thirds. Some were too sick or wounded to offer further resistance when Western forces came upon them. Quite a few were utterly lost while retreating through the jungles of Southeast Asia and came unexpectedly upon Western forces. Some were captured by indigenous forces and delivered to the Allies, while in other cases local inhabitants simply told the Japanese that they would lead them back to their own lines, then took them to the Allies instead. American and Australian forces in such places as New Guinea regularly paid a reward to indigenous people who brought in Japanese soldiers. In the Marianas and on Okinawa, hundreds of Japanese soldiers were talked out of the caves where they were hiding, often together with civilians, by Japanese language-competent Caucasian or Nisei officers and enlisted men. Some Japanese prisoners were also persuaded to join in efforts to bring civilians and even combatants to safety.

The *Senjinkun* was issued by the army minister and technically could apply only to army personnel. While navy men fully recognized that they were equally bound to prefer death to the dishonor of surrender, it proved intrinsically more difficult for sailors to commit the ideal suicide. Naval officers and sailors were normally in much better health when captured, subject to combat wounds but much less to tropical diseases, malnutrition, and dehydration. They had not been provided with side arms, hand grenades, or other personal weapons, in accordance with routine aboard warships. Thus, when a ship was sunk, the men would launch life rafts when possible or jump into the sea to find driftwood to cling to or swim toward a distant shore. Seeking death did not immediately come to their minds. They would initially hope for rescue by the Imperial Japanese Navy, but this seldom came about. When their situation became more desperate they might have tried to drown themselves, but those able to swim discovered that suicide by drowning was exceedingly difficult as long as they retained the physical strength to remain alive. Besides, especially with no enemy in sight, it was almost impossible to resist the elemental human will to survive at any cost, and eventually most decided to wait and see what developed. If captured, they reasoned, the option to commit suicide at a later time would still be theirs.

More than a few naval officers and men captured at sea claimed they became prisoners while "unconscious." In most cases such assertions fly against the dictates of common sense. It is well known among lifeguards that an unconscious person in the water will soon sink; thus these claims can be understood only in the context of the intense shame felt by those taken prisoner, leading them to blame factors beyond their control for their misfortune. This is not to question the sincerity of those who made the assertion. Such were their strongly ingrained cultural values that they truly remembered having been unconscious even when the reality was otherwise.

Japanese pilots, both army and navy, tended to encounter a similar dilemma. Pilots and crews were normally not issued parachutes. Even those with parachutes disdained to use them, choosing instead a final chance to destroy an enemy target in a suicide plunge. When shot down or when an aircraft ran out of fuel with no worthy targets available, however, pilots generally tried to make a landing that would give them the greatest opportunity to survive, perhaps to fight another day. Also, like sailors on board ships, pilots lacked the weapons to take their own lives. A few tried to commit suicide by biting off their tongues in order to bleed to death but usually abandoned the effort when it failed to work.

Finally, there were those who succumbed, despite the *Senjinkun,* to the elemental human instinct to live, deciding to surrender either by passively waiting for the enemy to come upon them or actively seeking him out. Many of these men had been forced to endure all manner of incredible hardships for which even the rigorous training of the Japanese military had not prepared them. Their desperate fight to live despite a fear verging on horror of the consequences of capture provides the context for the following representative accounts taken from books, articles, and interviews of those fortunate few who survived the war in the central and southwest Pacific. Taken together, these accounts provide a snapshot of the general physical and mental state of Japanese soldiers and sailors at the time they became prisoners of war in Allied captivity.

ISHII SHUJI

Some of the Japanese soldiers facing the stark choice between life and death had the complicating burden of having considerable time in which to weigh their options. This was bound to be a wrenching experience, given the strong desire to live and the internalized horror of becoming a prisoner. One of those who wrote eloquently of these conflicts was Ishii Shuji, one of the few Japanese survivors of the Battle of Iwo Jima.[5] In his memoirs Ishii noted that, with the Americans in control of four-fifths of the island and his situation worsening daily until, at last, the end was plainly in sight, only then did he think of surrendering. At the same time, he felt that becoming a POW was "like obliterating oneself." He believed that imprisonment at the hands of the enemy was not an option for a Japanese soldier, but then he would think of the children he would be leaving behind. He also had the all too human desire to survive in order to tell the world what had happened on Iwo. For days on end his emaciated body and confused mind went back and forth. He realized that there was no realistic chance of escape from the island; meanwhile, increasing hunger and thirst were driving him ever closer to choosing between equally unacceptable options or losing all ability to choose.

As a medic, Ishii had often witnessed the killing of helpless men, either by their own hands or by those "helping" them to avoid the shame of surrender. He began to think that perhaps his military education had been entirely wrong. He was barely surviving in a cave along with others, only venturing out briefly at night to seek water and scraps of food. He began to wonder how long this life could go on and to ask himself what purpose was served by what he called, without any apparent sense of irony, further "resistance." Rationally, it made no sense, but the influence of the *Senjinkun* still exerted a tremendous pull on Ishii and his comrades.

At this critical point, Ishii learned that his commanding officer was planning to order subordinates to "accept U.S. protection," a euphemism for the unutterable "surrender." This was a rare instance of an officer seeking to deliver his subordinates from their moral dilemma. The senior medical officer assembled his staff of fifteen and told them that he would accept all responsibility for this step, saying, "Please place your lives in my hands." But the men doubted that the officer could protect them once they had been turned over to the Americans and, stone-faced, they refused to commit themselves one way or another. Some believed they should not take the advantage conferred on them by their medical status to save themselves. Gradually, however, the officer brought them around to his way of thinking. Clearly relieved to have the weight of decision making lifted from his own shoulders, Ishii fatalistically concluded: "If it comes to it, the matter could not be helped." Consensus had decided the issue. Only three senior NCOs balked at accepting surrender as their course of action, even after considerable pressure had been placed on them to conform with the group.

Those in favor of surrender found a way to disengage from the NCOs and placed themselves in a position to be found by the enemy, but when a small American unit appeared in front of their cave, Ishii's head was still in a turmoil of conflicting feelings. Part of him wanted to remain in the cave to die of hunger; another part felt that he had already given his all and had no more to give and that perhaps, while becoming a POW would not be pleasant, it might not be all that dishonorable.

After being taken into custody, prisoners were asked their names and unit designation by a Japanese-American soldier and then thoroughly stripped and searched. "Strangely," American soldiers offered them cigarettes, but the new POWs remained mute with eyes cast down. Taken by bus to a stockade, they marveled at the engineering miracles that had transformed the island into a formidable base for the aerial assault on Japan during the brief time they had been holed up in their cave. Huge mounds of war matériel, including aircraft and landing craft, as far as the eye could see, dotted the landscape. All this demonstrated to Ishii, as nothing else, the imbalance of power between the United States and Japan and why the struggle on Iwo Jima had ended as it had.

A sense of relief overcame Ishii when he saw that the POW camp already held dozens of his countrymen. Shame would be a little easier to endure when shared. In his memoir, Ishii went on rapturously about the cleanliness of the field hospital, the clean drinking water, soap, medicines, and his soft bed, while only hours before he had been starving and drinking his own urine simply to survive. Now he had food in quantities he could only have dreamed about earlier in the day. Then he smoked his first cigarette as a prisoner, a moment lovingly described. Truly, as Ishii wrote later, it was "the difference between heaven and hell."

KOBAYASHI SHIGEHIKO

Kobayashi Shigehiko's account of his final weeks trying to survive without surrendering on Saipan is similarly poignant.[6] As a graduate of Kyoto University's prestigious law department, he had found employment with the city government of Nagoya. On being drafted into the army's Signal Corps, he became convinced that he would not return alive. When American forces landed on Saipan, Japanese troops scattered and Kobayashi's unit lost contact with its higher headquarters. It absorbed punishing bombardment for days on end, continually retreated, and was hunted from cave to cave. Kobayashi felt that "only my body was still alive; mentally I was in a catatonic state."

Stumbling along in the jungle, occasionally stepping on a corpse, he knew the end was near. Finally, his unit received word that the division commander had given the order for a *gyokusai,* then committed suicide himself. Kobayashi thought that, except for his small band of stragglers, the remnants of his division must already all have died. The fifty remaining men of his unit, with a small number of others, heard the senior NCO express appreciation for their service amid great hardship and inform them that the command structure was now dissolved. They were now on their own, free to make their way to safety individually or in small units. The NCO's final words of advice were not to waste their lives needlessly; however, if they were going to die, "do it in the course of accomplishing a big task." Given the state of their bodies and minds, which no longer allowed even small accomplishments, this admonition was bound to be left unheeded.

Kobayashi's outlook on the future was entirely hopeless. He had nothing left physically, and felt himself going fast. He decided to drag himself no further. Just then, advancing Americans set the jungle ablaze with flamethrowers, and Kobayashi ran off with his last ounce of strength. He stumbled on a severely wounded Japanese soldier, who asked to be killed. Kobayashi did not have the stomach for it and walked away. Throughout the war he "had gradually discarded unnecessary things until there remained only my life to throw away."

Kobayashi was now completely alone. He had no one to consult and no one from whom he needed to disguise his innermost feelings. Alone as never before in his life, he somehow found himself ecstatic to discover a personal identity. He felt liberated from the physical and psychological pressures that had created his despondency of the past months and experienced a rush of spiritual reserves, which would allow him to surrender to the Americans a short while later.

Kobayashi still had a grenade and two bullets left. In his memoirs he claimed to recall that, as he was weighing for the umpteenth time the option of committing suicide or getting shot by the Americans, the Geneva Convention came to his mind and from that time forward dominated his thinking. There is an outside chance that he might have stumbled on a reference to the convention as a law student, but since the convention was never mentioned publicly in Japan at the time, it would be remarkable if this had not been a postwar addition to his thought processes. More believably, Kobayashi reasoned that he could do more for his country alive than dead, since Japan was sure to be defeated. There would always be time later on to consider whether or not to take his life. In any event, he came to the inescapable conclusion that Japan was going to lose the war. The enormous advantage of American firepower was too much for Japan's spiritual qualities.

When Kobayashi heard some Americans talking nearby, he threw away his rifle and readied the grenade so that he could pull the pin at the last moment, delaying his final decision until the very last second. He recalled that he jumped out from his hiding place, startling the Americans, who all shot and missed him. Thus, he "lost his life, his homeland, his race, his honor and knew shame. I had lost everything." Of his own free will he had decided to face an unknown world. Kobayashi's initial encounter with the enemy in that new world occurred when an American NCO gave him a cigarette, and Kobayashi thought he should say something, so he said in English, "Don't kill me; help me." Instinctively he realized that the Americans would not kill him.

He was placed on a truck for the trip to the POW camp, accompanied by a rifle-toting "Japanese" soldier. This turned out to be a Japanese American who had studied at a Japanese university and then returned to America. Kobayashi was assured not to worry about all the puzzling things that Americans might do. In the POW camp he was again surprised and relieved to find about two hundred Japanese who had preceded him on the path to captivity. He also noted carefully that Americans did many things differently from Japanese, and not only because they were rich.

YAMAMOTO TOMIO

Yamamoto Tomio had great difficulty attempting to reconcile his conversion to Christianity, while a student at Tokyo Imperial University, with his responsibilities as a signals officer in the Battle of Guam.[7] Because of his liberal education, he had been appalled by the excesses of Japanese militarism. This placed him in a terrible quandary: he knew that he had a duty to carry out his responsibilities both as an officer toward the men in his unit and as a Christian toward his family.

Yamamoto's odyssey led him from induction into the army in February 1942 to service in Manchuria and Guam, where his unit was decimated in an American attack in July 1944. Following a three-day battle, his commander decided that the time had come for a *gyoku-sai*. All documents were burned. Subordinate units were ordered to make the necessary preparations. Authorities in Tokyo were informed of the plan for the "decisive battle," an expression frequently used when it was clear that everything was lost, while leaving the impression that there was still hope. In any event, Tokyo was assured that if the "decisive battle" were lost, all were prepared to die. Tokyo's wholly unexpected response was that if the general attack was doomed, Japanese forces should instead wage a holding action as long as possible "by crushing the enemy's war fighting capability." Lacking all information on the location of their subordinate units, officers were clearly unable to carry out such orders, as Tokyo must have known. In the following three days, "the honorable way out" was taken in numerous uncoordinated *gyokusai* charges that made little or no military sense but fulfilled the moral obligation not to be taken prisoner. The senior Japanese officer still standing dispatched a message to Tokyo stating that he hoped the Japanese people would not be disheartened by news of their "honorable deaths" and promised that "all our spirits would forever protect this island and pray for our imperial nation's repose." But not all participated in these suicidal actions; that decision was ultimately left to the subordinate unit commanders.

The remaining officers and men scattered north and south, fleeing into the jungle, abandoning heavy weapons, and gradually losing what little physical strength they still had. Yamamoto witnessed severely wounded stragglers being given a grenade to end their own miserable existence; those too weak to accomplish it on their own were dispatched with a pistol shot.

After all organized resistance ceased on Guam in August 1944, Yamamoto's life consisted of periods of hiding out and, fearing detection, staying on the run. After the death of his last companion, Yamamoto was entirely on his own. He existed on a diet of fried copra, earthworms, slugs, snails, and lizards, supplemented by fruit growing in the wild. Extreme hunger was his constant companion. He drank water that collected in the holes of trees and in depressions in the soil. Leeches stuck to every part of his body.

Yamamoto finally reached such a state of malnourishment that he collapsed and lost consciousness. He was found by an American patrol and taken prisoner. Somehow, he had survived almost a year in the jungle, alone for over six months. His hair had fallen out, his eyes appeared shrunken, his stomach was distended, and the ribs protruded from his chest. Yamamoto was also afflicted with four festering wounds and the inevitable effects of malaria. He described himself as "looking like a ghost." *Life* magazine published a picture of the seventy-two-pound Yamamoto captioned "Live Skeleton."

Yamamoto resigned himself to anything that might occur. If he remained alive his spirit would have to lead him because his body was no longer able to move. In the end it was the sympathetic care and feeding of the American hospital staff that nursed him back to health.

KONOYE MAKOTO

Konoye Makoto was a medical officer on Leyte Island in the Philippines, where, in the spring of 1945, he felt like a hunted animal.[8] His unit had been largely decimated, and he was sick and exhausted by his bouts with malaria. In the beginning of his odyssey, he traveled with two others, but they died. He had seen medics kill ten to fifteen Japanese soldiers too ill or wounded to move deeper into the jungle. After wandering around in efforts to reach the coast, Dr. Konoye finally came upon an enemy encampment below him. It was "like nothing he had seen during his military service in China." At night the area was ablaze with lights, "as if the Americans had already won and had nothing to fear." Still indecisive, he found refuge in an abandoned school building. Too weak even to drink or eat, Dr. Konoye fell asleep. On awakening, he saw two Filipinos and managed to convince them that he was alone. They stripped him of his weapons, wristwatch, and pen and started to bind his arms behind his back. He explained in broken English that being killed while his hands were bound was the greatest shame for a Japanese officer, but instead of killing him, the natives brought him to an American camp. Compared to the jungle, the POW enclosure in which he was placed seemed like a first-class hotel.

Konoye was given a medical examination, a chocolate bar, and a cigarette and thought that his treatment was exceptional. He tried to eat, but the food would not pass his throat. Still, he was grateful for his "last supper." Put on a landing craft, along with a large group of Americans and Filipinos, he was still wondering why so many were necessary to kill just one emaciated Japanese officer, until he discovered that he was simply being transferred to a central POW camp.

MATSUBARA SHUNJI

Matsubara Shunji was one of those relatively rare individuals who had been influenced by Western professors at his university.[9] Among these professors quite a few had had missionary backgrounds that often included a streak of pacifist idealism. To some extent they imparted this to their students, who often shared their concern about the trend toward militarism in the 1930s. After graduating from Meiji University's Higher Business College in 1941, Matsubara entered the Hitachi Corporation. He took all the available deferments but finally entered the army in February 1942. Believing that his induction was probably equivalent to a death sentence, he successfully urged his mother not to come to the induction ceremony, because he did not want to see her cry.

In boot camp the recruits were routinely slapped around, even by privates first class. Matsubara's unit was made up chiefly of university graduates, so his unit's NCOs, who lacked higher education, gave them a very hard time. Matsubara wrote that he had to approach his master sergeant's room in the appropriately deferential manner with the food tray raised high, addressing the sergeant as *dono* (roughly equivalent to "esquire"). The NCOs got the recruits out of bed at all hours and hit them in the face with slippers ("so that it didn't hurt the NCO so much"), while informing them that they were thus being instructed in the "military spirit." Short rations and resultant hunger pangs were similarly deemed instructive.

Matsubara's auto maintenance unit was left without repair vehicles, sophisticated tools, or parts, and without weapons, ammunition, or food supplies, when their ship was sunk by American air attacks en route to the Philippines. Matsubara ended up on Leyte, anticipating a U.S. landing in November 1944. Since his unit no longer had any vehicles, he had by then been transformed into an infantry soldier, with no prior infantry training. Fewer than half the members of his unit even had a rifle. At one point his battalion commander berated Matsubara for withdrawing from his assigned position in the face of intense U.S. naval gunfire. The officer pointed out that had the American forces landed, a suicide charge would have been ordered. Although he managed to deflect the battalion commander from taking disciplinary action, the commander's determination to die in a *gyokusai* gave him a bitter foretaste of what was to come.

At one point a member of Matsubara's unit attempted indirectly to veer the commander away from courting certain death by asking him about his small children. The opening was brusquely rejected with the order to stop such idle talk. As the Japanese position on Leyte became increasingly desperate, another NCO approached Matsubara and bluntly asked that he not abandon the unit but somehow lead them to safety. Somewhat later Matsubara met a fellow "intellectual," a lieutenant, from whose cryptic remarks he gleaned that he, too, would try to avoid throwing his life away. A few more days passed while they huddled in defensive positions, and then they heard the unmistakable sounds of a *gyokusai* charge, followed by silence. Matsubara's men looked at him beseechingly, their eyes asking, "Will we be next?" Fleeing Japanese troops passed through their positions yelling at them to abandon their positions before it was too late.

Finally, the opportunity to surrender to a group of Americans presented itself. Matsubara shouted at them, "No resistance, no weapons." He was stripped of his insignia of rank and his wristwatch, then offered a Lucky Strike cigarette by a soldier who lit it for him. The American asked him for his Japanese cigarettes as a souvenir, trading them for a pack of the GI's Luckies. The Americans were understandably curious about this English-speaking Japanese, a rarity in those days, and asked him about his hometown and where he had learned his English. Matsubara, in return, asked similar types of questions. He felt that once communication between himself and the American NCO was established, the mutual desire to kill one another evaporated, if only for a brief time.

Shortly thereafter, however, the American tried to enlist Matsubara in finding other members of his unit, threatening to kill all the captured Japanese if this was not accomplished within fifteen minutes. Matsubara debated with a buddy about whether to comply with the order, die on the spot, or try to run for it. In the end, though, as he admitted in his memoirs, Matsubara had lost the combativeness of an Imperial Japanese Army soldier to the instinct for survival. He complied with the order to bring in additional Japanese soldiers.

Under guard, Matsubara was then returned to a village that earlier had been under Japanese control. It had become a different world. The mountain road, barely passable before, was now paved, jeeps whizzing by. Native women and children had come out of their hiding places. Another set of guards took over for the trip, led by a man Matsubara described as huge, with hair and face the color of the red earth, a veritable "devil." Matsubara was hauled on the back of an ancient Japanese truck that picked up other POWs along the way. All were tagged with a label secured by a rope around their necks; his was marked "Speaks English."

Some time later, Matsubara gesticulated to obtain water. A Filipino sergeant came up to him as if to kill him. Fatalistically he thought, "Well, this could not be helped"–the Japanese equivalent of "This is the end, and there's nothing I can do about it." He recalled what he had heard about an entire company of American POWs having been killed by their Japanese captors. The sergeant, whose face was contorted by rage, grabbed him by the nape of the neck and dragged him along until he fell. Other Filipino soldiers were placing bullets in the chambers of their rifles as if they were going to shoot. Matsubara's unspoken "last wish" was that news of his death be communicated to his mother, when suddenly a person speaking perfect Japanese and wearing an American uniform appeared. For an instant, Matsubara thought the man might be a Japanese traitor now working for the Americans. Then he learned that he was facing a Nisei officer. The Nisei told Matsubara that "something inexcusable just happened," attributing the lapse to the Filipinos' intense hatred of the Japanese. He was assured that it would not happen again.

Another Japanese language officer, this time a Caucasian, came by. He and Matsubara discovered mutual friends who had been at Meiji University. Another officer asked for his sword as a souvenir. Matsubara replied that he had left it in the house where he had spent the previous night. Asked to guide the way, he rode off with the American officer, "like two old friends." Matsubara was especially pleased that he did not hear any curses along the way. He felt as if the distinction between enemies and friends had already disappeared. His captors even asked him whether he preferred to be imprisoned in Australia or the United States. Not knowing how to respond to such an unusual question, he sought their advice. The language officers told him that Brisbane, Australia, might be preferable because that would allow him to be reunited with the American officer son of one of his old professors at Meiji University, and besides, anti-Japanese feeling was running high in the United States.

Matsubara was repeatedly asked which country would win the war. This placed him in a quandary. Realistically, Japan was losing, but at the same time Japan was calling it the one hundred years' war. Finally, he replied equivocally, "As a Japanese noncommissioned officer, I must believe that in the end Japan will win." He was taken to Ormoc POW Camp, where he was jammed in with other POWs in a small tent. There he felt utterly powerless, with no guarantees for his future, and sank into a deep depression.

AOKI TAKESHI

It was the spring of 1945, and Lt. (jg) Aoki Takeshi, a navy pilot in the Special Attack Corps (or Tokkotai, popularly known as kamikaze in the United States), and his copilot, Sergeant Yokoyama, were on a mission off Okinawa.[10] A "tactical misjudgment" caused their plane to plunge into the sea rather than into their intended target, an American warship. To avoid capture, they played dead, but their American rescuers were not fooled. Hauled on board by the crew of the warship that had been their target, they were immediately given plenty of food. Whether or not to eat was a difficult question for them because eating the enemy's food would constitute an obligation that might have involved a need to repay the kindness.

Aoki was filled with remorse about his failures. He had been strongly attracted to the military already as a youth. A visit to the German cruiser *Emden* and participation in a military parade at the famed Yoyogi Parade Grounds in Tokyo only confirmed his intention to make the military his career. He was so thoroughly imbued with the spirit of the *Senjinkun* that he regarded becoming a POW as a fate worse than death, but he also realized that he hardly had a choice in the matter since he lacked any weapons when he crashed into the sea. Aoki thought it prudent to await developments. Perhaps an opportunity to escape or commit suicide would present itself. Still, the reproving looks from Sergeant Yokoyama weighed on his soul. The two POWs received their flight suits back, all cleaned up, and a table was set up for them loaded with bread, butter, milk, and apples. The American fare looked far better than any Aoki had ever encountered during his military career in Japan. He took it all in and politely suggested to Yokoyama, "Since they went to all this trouble, why don't we try some of this food?"

MIYAMOTO MASAO

Miyamoto Masao was an Esperanto enthusiast active in Japan's prewar labor movement.[11] As a result of his trade union activities, he had been charged as a "spy" and given a two-year sentence. While imprisoned he had a *tenko* (conversion), meaning that he acknowledged the error of his beliefs. In his memoirs, he admitted a weakness for giving in to his ideological enemies. The army must have considered him an unlikely prospect, calling him to the colors four times and releasing him three times after brief service. The fourth time he was attached to a base maintenance unit in the Kerama Islands, off Okinawa, for a fleet of small "special attack" (suicide) boats. As "coolie" laborers and self-described bottom-of-the-barrel material, this unit's chief mission was to construct caves for the suicide boats.

Although he had not received a higher education, Miyamoto realized early in 1945 that Japan's defeat was inevitable. Dying under such circumstances, he was convinced, would be stupid. Such views could not be voiced, however, and when others speculated on the need to become guerrillas to continue the war, he remained mute. Although the word "surrender" never passed his lips, Miyamoto obtained what he thought was an unspoken agreement with a few of his buddies to seek POW status at an opportune moment.

In the waning days of the Battle of Okinawa, he later wrote, he felt totally nihilistic. He was unable to trust members of his own unit and even lost all sense of attachment to his wife and newborn son. Staying alive, against the odds, became his preeminent concern.

Miyamoto wandered around for days on the small island on which he was trying to survive, avoiding both Japanese and American troops while looking for a good place to surrender with a white flag. He subsisted on a little rice and dried bonito and any juice he could extract from the abundant sugarcane. While hiding out on a beach he heard an appeal to surrender from what he assumed was a Japanese officer on an American ship offshore. He watched while a Japanese soldier who tried to swim to the warship was killed by rifle fire from the shore.

Eventually, Miyamoto managed to surrender, ending what he termed his "tale that lacked any valor." Like many others, Miyamoto was more puzzled than chagrined to find a "Japanese" in an American uniform ordering him around. "Acting as if he was one of the victors," the Japanese American told him to follow along with several other POWs. At his initial examination Miyamoto was relieved of his wallet, watch, military notebook, and other written material. His rising sun flag decorated with Chinese characters, which he wore as a kind of protective charm around his waist, was "liberated" by souvenir-hunting GIs. The American soldiers then passed out cigarettes to the captives. These tasted better than the Japanese ones he was used to, and he began to feel a little more assured about chances for his own survival.

SATO KAZUMASA

At least the early period of life in the jungle was not especially problematical for Sato Kazumasa, a medical doctor who sought to avoid capture by U.S. forces on Guam long after all organized resistance had ceased.[12] Together with several others from his unit, he lived on the bounty of abundant breadfruit and banana trees, along with wild cattle and pigs that members of his small group shot and ate either raw or broiled over an open fire. Their vegetable intake was largely restricted to taro roots. Trading among the Japanese groups hiding out in the jungle was a common practice. Sometimes men crossed over the mountains to the sea to obtain salt, although the trip was arduous and dangerous.

Life was relatively tranquil in the beginning, except for the occasional American patrols through the area. Then, as the months passed, loudspeaker appeals for the Japanese to surrender became a daily event. Though accented, the appeals in Japanese "weren't bad" linguistically. The Japanese were ordered to strip to the waist and come out to a road where American tanks passed periodically. The war was over on Guam, the loudspeakers informed them; all organized resistance had ceased. The Japanese were assured that they had completed their mission, that further suffering and deaths were needless, and that rice, tea, and other good food awaited them. Sato was especially impressed by the fact that the Americans told the truth. When they announced via loudspeakers that there would be no sweeps for five days, the Americans invariably held to it, and at those times it would be safe to surrender. Those not inclined to surrender were urged to take special care during sweep days to avoid getting killed. Many Japanese, however, rejected these appeals outright, thinking they were merely tricks to lure them to their deaths. Some had seen, or claimed to have seen, Americans killing several Japanese soldiers who had come out into the open with hands raised high.

With the passage of time, Sato began to question whether remaining in the jungle "like a savage" served any purpose. Sooner or later he would have to give up. But the mere thought of surrender implied that he was serious about contemplating something disloyal and immoral. He finally managed to persuade himself that life as a prisoner of war would be better than a slow death, but he wanted, indeed needed, others to join him. He could not take such an awesome step alone.

One day, Sato's group unexpectedly received news of the outside world. They picked up a letter that an American soldier on patrol had accidentally dropped. The letter was from the soldier's mother, who wrote about the Battle of Okinawa and the fall of Iwo Jima. This piece of reality, clearly not propaganda, indicated that war was drawing nearer to Japan itself and lent much credence to loudspeaker claims that Japan had actually lost the war.

Suddenly the men in Sato's ragtag group realized they had a choice, but nobody felt able to talk openly about the possibility of surrendering. They fenced verbally, Japanese-style, attempting to discover the position of the others without revealing their own. Most important to them, whether they lived or died, was that they do it together. They would even be satisfied to perform forced labor in the wilds of Alaska for the rest of their lives, they decided, so long as they remained together. Gradually, a three-man informal leadership group became convinced they should surrender. Five others remained dubious. The group decided to give it three days, then get together again. Sato was consumed by fear—fear of becoming a POW, of becoming a POW only to be killed by the Americans, and of jumping into the totally unknown future. When the group reassembled, full agreement was reached to surrender.

There was great relief finally to have made a decision. On their last night in the jungle they feasted on all their hoarded food. One person sang a folk song from his native place. They remembered their fallen comrades with a prayer. Then they walked single file behind a white flag down to the tank road. They came upon a group of Americans led by a sergeant. They were immediately given food. Hardly believing their good fortune in finding the Americans so kind, they asked for cigarettes and received a whole carton. They were assured that they would not be killed. The tension went out of their faces and "one cursed a fate that had delayed their deliverance from the jungle for so long."

TAKAHASHI SHIGERU

In a privately published memoir, Takahashi Shigeru told one of the most harrowing stories of Japanese soldiers' sufferings as they sought to avoid both death and capture.[13] His unit managed to remain fairly intact until mid-June 1945, when their headlong flight on Luzon Island in the Philippines began. Takahashi had only two cans of food but had saved more salt than his comrades and traded some of the salt for more food. Pursuing Philippine guerrillas threatened the retreat of his battalion, whose strength had been reduced to just eighty men. They crossed innumerable mountain ranges on foot and, after several weeks, reached some of the native Igorot villages in the far north of the island.

There were always stragglers, Takahashi wrote, but the advantage of remaining with one's unit was that if one died, somebody would still have the strength to bury the body. With only emergency rice rations left, and losing men daily, the group faced almost certain death.

They were simply dragging themselves through another day with no ultimate hope. Poignantly Takahashi noted that "ordinarily the medics would have no reason to provide quinine (against the prevalent malaria) to a lowly private in the middle of the mountains, but in my case they gave me two injections." Two or even three days passed, sometimes without food. At night he was kept awake by the sound of exploding hand grenades as one after another weakened soldier chose to end his life. With no food left and the path strewn with the bleached bones of Japanese soldiers who had passed through the area before them, Takahashi thought only of surviving.

What remained of Takahashi's unit came under American control on September 20, 1945, five weeks after the emperor's surrender message. Word of the surrender had not reached them earlier. They marched down the mountain behind a white flag as Filipinos yelled curses at them. Takahashi thought that could not be helped; after all, the Japanese had burned down Filipino houses, stolen their food, and most likely killed some of their parents and siblings.

The Japanese turned over their remaining weapons to the Americans. Takahashi reflected that although the emperor had given them these weapons "as objects more important than their very lives," now they had turned into rubbish. Then their personal effects—watches and pens—were taken. He had thought that thieves existed only in the Japanese army, but victors in war "were all the same."

WATANABE NORIO

In a war of statistically infrequent surrenders, instances of actual desertion were exceedingly rare. Watanabe Norio not only deserted but also lived to write about it many years later.[14] He had arrived on Okinawa on June 1, 1944, ten months before the invasion by American forces. Watanabe had been trained to operate antiaircraft guns, which had to be used as antitank weapons once the Americans landed on the island. As an antitank gunner on Okinawa, he would have had scant opportunity to avoid death in the fierce fighting. Fate intervened, however, and he was transferred to a signals (communications) position, where he had access to information about developments in the wider world that ordinary infantrymen never had.

In his memoirs, Watanabe quoted some of his comrades' comments that if the war did not end soon, they would all be dead. They speculated that they might be better off if Japan were defeated; Japan might then become one of the states of the United States or a republic like France. The latter "option" especially appealed to the group. They also came into possession of air-dropped leaflets designed to encourage Japanese troops to surrender that also contained news stories in order to provide greater credibility. One of the leaflets showed a picture of a Japanese officer marrying an Okinawan girl in the POW stockade. That one caused some raised eyebrows (though it proved to be accurate), but "the rest of the stories were great": the death of President Roosevelt, Shirley Temple's marriage, and the return of night baseball in the United States.

In the last phase of the battle, while hiding out in one of the island's innumerable caves, Watanabe heard his section leader say, "I don't want to die a dog's death. Tonight, after leaving the cave, I plan to get away from the battlefront." This statement of intent was contrary to the strict orders to remain in the cave, and it came as a surprise to Watanabe, especially because the section leader had earlier reprimanded him for his lackadaisical attitude. Now the section leader frankly observed that if caught by the Japanese he would be shot, but added that: "In light of the alternative of dying in a battle I don't understand, I am determined to give it a try. It would be well if we all go together, but I understand there can be differences on the matter." Watanabe confessed that he had been thinking along the same lines. He had now been in the army for over a year, and while duty and loyalty had been pounded into him through physical punishment and intimidation, he had come to believe that loyalty to the emperor did not extend to participating in a final *gyokusai*. The future suddenly looked a little brighter. The section leader's earlier remarks about becoming a part of the United States or like France reflected his own real feelings and wishes for his country.

There was a moment of high drama when the section chief asked his men to choose. Watanabe and another soldier decided to go along with their leader. The four remaining group members failed to raise their heads. The leader placed additional pressure on the holdouts by invoking the Imperial Precepts to Soldiers and Sailors, the bible of Japan's fighting forces, which dealt with the duty to follow orders blindly, and so they all finally agreed to go along.

The prospect of being free of restraints was exhilarating but soon replaced by the men's realization that they faced immense odds against coming out of their course of action alive. They decided to head for the southern end of the island, find a boat, and head for Taiwan via the southern Ryukyu chain of islands. This was, as they already realized, an utterly hopeless plan in light of the unlikelihood of finding a boat and then avoiding American naval surveillance. Another vote was taken, and this time Watanabe and one other soldier chose to try their chances in the provincial capital of Naha, a city that at least they knew. The others would still seek to obtain a boat in the south. The two groups parted ways, wishing each other luck. Watanabe managed to get aboard a small sailboat in Naha, together with an old comrade and ten other soldiers and civilians, and in the night drifted through a major storm, thereby avoiding likely detection.

They were unclear where they were when they landed on Kume Jima, a small island west of Okinawa, where a small party of Japanese sailors soon found them and ordered them to come along to a navy communications station. When asked where they had come from, their answers were unconvincing, and they were charged with desertion. The ragtag group was put to work digging foxholes and making bamboo spears to repel the American forces expected to land on the island. After a while, the deserters were able to escape from the Japanese and found refuge among Okinawan natives, who told them that a small contingent of Americans had already landed on Kume Jima. Watanabe resolved to meet them; the others wanted to hang back until they saw how Watanabe fared. He approached the American encampment and was promptly greeted with a cheery "good morning" and a cup of steaming coffee. This was the first American he had ever met. The GI's attitude immediately melted whatever tension he had felt, and the wonderful smell of coffee convinced Watanabe that he was in touch with "truly civilized people." No real communication was possible since neither understood a word of the other's language, but then a middle-aged, Japanese-speaking American, who introduced himself as a *New York Times* correspondent (most likely Burton Crane, the *Times*'s prewar correspondent in Tokyo), appeared on the scene. Finding such a person who had lived in prewar Japan and could interpret for him further eased Watanabe's fears.

Watanabe was led to a tent, where an officer asked him about Japanese troop dispositions on Kume Jima. The next question concerned the religious affiliation of Watanabe and his sidekick, Takahashi, who had now also surrendered. Takahashi answered in a low voice, "Christian." The correspondent then asked them to pray, creating momentary confusion on Watanabe's part because he had only seen such behavior in movies. He managed to put his hands together properly, drawing only laughter from the assembled Americans. The next question was whether they "knew Hirohito." Watanabe politely replied that he might have heard that name before but could not place him. This was hardly surprising since Japanese never referred to their sovereign by his name, only by the more deferential appellation *tenno* or *heika* (emperor). The next question was whether Watanabe knew Tojo. He responded that he had heard of him. He was then asked whether he thought Japan would win or lose the war. Watanabe said that "unfortunately" Japan would lose. This concluded the "interrogation," and Watanabe became Kume Jima's Prisoner No. 1.

YOKOTA SHOHEI

Yokota Shohei was one of the fairly rare soldiers influenced by considerable socialist and communist ideology before the war.[15] Japanese authorities, who persecuted both wings of the leftist movement, seldom made significant distinctions between the two. In any event, this background made Yokota somewhat more likely to attempt to surrender. When the high command on Guam ordered a *gyokusai* attack, it was clear to all that continued defense of the island was a lost cause. Yokota himself had neither the weapons nor the will to continue fighting. He decided that if he just sat quietly and unthreateningly by the side of a road, it was unlikely that he would be shot. He realized, of course, that he was supposed to commit suicide but asked himself, "For what purpose?" He believed that the war was a necessary outcome of the capitalistic system under which Japan was ruled, saw himself simply as a pawn in that struggle, and no longer felt any fealty to Japan's rulers.

After mulling over the matter for a long time, Yokota was finally able to muster the courage to talk to a soul mate, friend, and fellow soldier about his true feelings. They discussed what becoming prisoners might be like. Japanese newspaper pictures of American POWs suggested to them that they would have to work. That would be a price worth paying if it freed them from the fear of aerial attacks and if they could get enough food and sleep to stop worrying whether they would get through each day alive. Even the anticipated boredom of POW life was better than being dead, they agreed. They were also sustained in the difficult decision to surrender by their belief that postwar Japan would move in the direction of socialism.

The two friends were convinced that if they had been forced to surrender to the Chinese, they surely would have been killed since the Chinese were bound to seek revenge for the cruelties the Japanese had inflicted on them. Fortunately, they thought, the Americans would not hate them because, for the Americans, "war was sort of like a job." So far as they knew, Americans were not especially warlike. The Americans' outlook was formed by a "weak sense of duty toward their country." They had read the report about Americans running over Japanese POWs with tanks, but their response to this story was a healthy dose of skepticism. (Rumors about such an event abounded within the Japanese forces at the time. It was either started by the Japanese authorities in order to keep their soldiers from surrendering or, more likely, arose when Japanese soldiers mistook for a mass murder the sight of Americans burying Japanese corpses in mass graves and covering them by using earth-moving machinery.)

The two Japanese soldiers spent considerable time planning their moves and examining their own feelings. They decided that their chief problem was how to distance themselves from friendly forces. To avoid being shot by the Japanese, it was best to proceed at night, but to avoid American fire it was preferable to move in daylight. They pondered what their comrades would think of them when they were discovered to have fled and cursed as "despicable persons." (The Japanese language lacks a rich vocabulary of swear words.) Since they would hardly chance to see them again, it would not much matter. Finally, when their officer told them that a *gyokusai* order was

The POW camp on Okinawa where Watamake Norio was held, 1945. Courtesy of Watanabe Norio.

Japanese marine surrenders to U.S. infantrymen during mopping-up operations on Saipan, August 1944. U.S. Army photo, courtesy of the National Archives and Records Administration (NARA) 111-SC-392361, box 116.

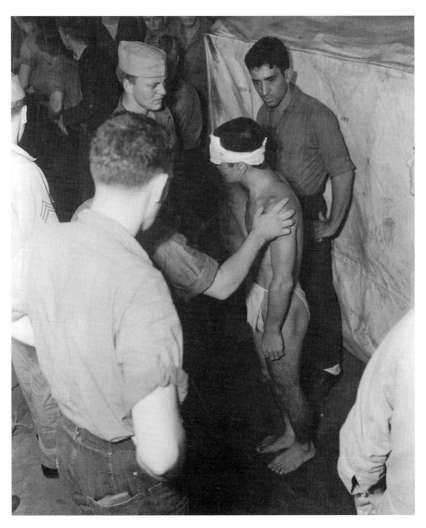

Japanese pilot POW brought aboard the aircraft carrier USS Hornet, *July 8, 1944. U.S. Navy photo, NARA 80-G-367226, box 1400.*

Pole inside Pen 6B, tent 6, at Paita, New Caledonia, POW camp where Japanese POWs hanged themselves (see page 183). Photo dated January 12, 1944. U.S. Navy photo, NARA 80-G-274896, box 919.

Japanese POW (eating) near the front lines, after surrendering in the mountains of Luzon, April 16, 1945. He was thankful not to have been killed and talked freely, wanting to know if Japanese troops had really landed in the United States. U.S. Army photo, NARA 111-SC-266-311, box 116.

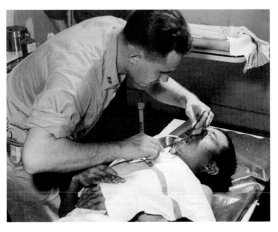

U.S. Navy surgeon operates on a Japanese POW's mouth and tongue after a failed suicide attempt, June 1944. U.S. Navy photo, NARA 80-G-333801, box 1255.

A POW provides information to U.S. soldier (with binoculars) concerning a possible target acquisition near Ipo Dam, Balacan, Luzon, Philippines, May 20, 1944. U.S. Army photo, NARA 111-SC-265805, box 116.

In Burma, British lieutenant Kostoloff interrogates a Japanese POW dressed as a native, February 1945. The POW provided accurate information on enemy forces. U.S. Army photo, NARA 111-SC-242884, box 96.

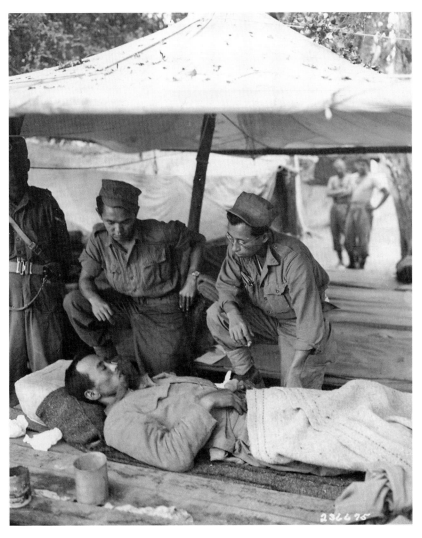

A wounded Japanese POW is questioned by Japanese American interpreters S/Sgts. Hinoki and Honuma on detached service with the British 36th Division in Burma, February 1945. U.S. Army photo, NARA 111-SC-236675, box 91.

S/Sgt Susumu Toyoda (at right) of G-2, 37th Division, instructing a POW on how to appeal by loudspeaker to the Japanese forces on New Caledonia to surrender, given the hopelessness of their position. March 26, 1944. U.S. Army photo, NARA 111-SC-237902, box 92.

U.S. 41st Division and 5th Air Force intelligence officers interrogating Japanese flight petty officer at Port Moresby, New Guinea, June 1943. U.S. Army photo, NARA 111-SC-236852, box 91.

A POW on Guam drawing a dragon picture for bartering with American GIs, September 1945. U.S. Navy photo, NARA 80-G-490276, box 2129.

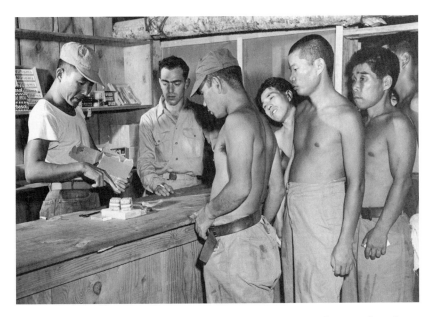

Japanese POWs buying supplies at the PX with money earned from work in the POW camp. U.S. Navy photo, NARA 80-G-490278, box 2129.

A POW officer marrying an Oki-nawan nurse, June 30, 1945. A U.S. Army chaplain conducted the service. U.S. Army photo, NARA 111-SC-245307, box 99.

Two POWs posing as geishas for a play in the POW camp, November 1944. U.S. Army photo, NARA 111-SC-272679, box 122.

Japanese surrendering at Neefar, New Guinea, May 3, 1944. U.S. Army photo, NARA 111-SC-258165, box 2.

Lt. General Robert L. Eichelberger, commander of 8th Army, wearing helmet, standing third from right, facing a Japanese POW on Mindanao, the Philippines, March 10, 1945. U.S. Army photo, NARA 111-SC-263744, box 114.

Japanese POWs on Guam hear the emperor's surrender message, August 15, 1945. U.S. Navy photo, NARA 80-G-490319, box 2129.

A Japanese POW behind barbed wire. U.S. Navy photo, NARA 80-G-333887, box 2129.

Group of ex-POWs get together in Japan, April 1999. Yamamoto Tomio, whose story is related in chapter 4, is second from left. Courtesy of Yamamoto Tomio.

Yamamoto Tomio with his daughter and four grandchildren. Courtesy of Yamamoto Tomio.

Yasukuni Shrine in Tokyo, June 2000. The shrine is dedicated to all Japanese soldiers and sailors who lost their lives in the service of their country. Author's collection.

likely on the following day, they decided that they had to stop debating and begin acting.

The surrender was effected smoothly. At the front lines Yokota and his friend were asked a few questions and then ordered to dig a hole. They feared the worst, but after being placed in the hole, realized it was merely a precaution to restrict their movement. Later in the day they were moved to a rear area where they were plied with food and cigarettes.

The Americans on Guam seemed admirable in their ability to let a tidal wave of machinery do the job for them. They never had to fear Japanese planes or warships and could, therefore, contemplate the world around them with a sense of superiority, even contempt, and not with the kind of fear that engenders hatred. The two Japanese friends concluded that those who "wage a superior kind of war can have the common sense to be magnanimous toward the beaten foe."

KOJIMA KIYOFUMI

Lt. Kojima Kiyofumi's writings include an unusually detailed account of the feelings and thinking processes leading up to the surrender and epiphany of a well-educated naval officer.[16] He had served as code officer on the battleship *Yamato,* but after the Imperial Navy's defeat in the battle off Leyte he was transferred to Clark Field in the Philippines. No sooner had he arrived there than virtually all the other naval officers, including all the high-ranking headquarters personnel, hurriedly flew off to the relative safety of Taiwan. The fifteen-thousand-man naval contingent in the area around Clark was left with only twelve hundred rifles between them, and virtually no food or medical stocks.

Kojima was ordered to the front as a platoon leader. All but fifteen of the men in his platoon had been killed in combat the day before he arrived on the scene, and all of his men had come down with malaria. A few days later he received an order to retreat, with the admonition to kill all those who were too sick or wounded to be moved, only one of whom fell into that category. As was common among Japanese at the time, that man had to be killed because of the concern he might be captured by the enemy and reveal intelligence on

Japanese forces, as well as to avoid the ultimate shame. Accordingly, Kojima was forced to wrestle with two unacceptable choices—either to kill the man or to face his own execution for failing to obey an order. Kojima was able to escape his moral dilemma when the man committed suicide by putting a rifle muzzle in his mouth and pulling the trigger with his toe. The man left behind a cigarette case on the back of which he had written "Tenno Heika Banzai" (Long Live the Emperor) and "I pray for the platoon leader's eternal military good fortune." This generosity of spirit shook Kojima to the very foundations of his being. The man had not even left a message for his own family.

Kojima felt that in his final moments the man had lived only by his *tatemae,* and while immensely relieved that he had been released from his terrible moral dilemma, Kojima believed that it was "inhuman" for the man to have acted as he did. When another one of his men could no longer go on, Kojima left him with some food and the admonition to rejoin the unit when he felt better, well aware of the risk that the soldier might fall into enemy hands. He was satisfied with this decision.

In time, Kojima was ordered to retreat further into dense wilderness, for what was to be a final stand and a *gyokusai* charge. When he and his men arrived at the designated area, they found it had already been heavily bombarded by the Americans. Loudspeakers were urging their surrender. His men had only the *Senjinkun* in mind, but Kojima was weighing other options; he believed the war might well be over in another month or two, and he thought it senseless to get killed needlessly when all was already lost. From his university studies, Kojima was well aware of the enormous disparity between American and Japanese economic development. Why and for whom should he still carry on the war? Not for the emperor, who for Kojima was just a human being like himself.

Kojima had read *All Quiet on the Western Front,* the well-known antiwar novel of the First World War. This best-seller accurately reflected the despair of men who wondered why they had to die just to gain a few feet of ground, when in actuality they were dying for leaders who wanted to hold on to power. From that angle, reasoned Kojima, it makes sense only to defend parents, brothers, and a sweetheart back in Japan, but he was not doing them any good in the Philippines, dying without even a weapon in his hands. Still, the *Senjinkun*'s admonition would not leave him. Talking to his subordinates about surrender, he felt, could even lead to his own death at their hands.

The matter had to be thought over carefully. Kojima had control of the fate of his men, some of whom still dreamed of a miraculous escape to the East China Sea. This was clearly a delusion. They were delivered from certain death when a group of Americans stopped to rest at a large rock behind which the Japanese survivors hid. Kojima looked at his NCO's face. If their eyes had met, he would have felt obliged to order an attack in order not to lose face, but it did not happen. Kojima's band prudently withdrew and resumed their pointless flight unobserved.

Its food stocks dwindling rapidly, Kojima's bedraggled unit lived for a month on roots, weeds, and occasional fruit found in the jungle. By that time, Japanese were even shooting each other for food. The longer they suffered in this manner, the angrier Kojima became at those in authority who were responsible for their predicament and all the deaths they had caused. He finally came to the conclusion that he had to get out alive in order to inform the Japanese public about all that had happened—and he was the one who had to act, since his men knew only how to follow orders.

By the time Kojima's group reached the East China Sea, it had grown to thirty-seven men, with the addition of other stragglers. Their situation was desperate. All food was gone. An army captain who had joined the group asked Kojima what he thought about "surrendering," carefully using the English word since the Japanese one would have been unacceptable to the men. The two officers convinced themselves that it was their duty to bring their subordinates to safety, even if they themselves did not survive.

The following day, the captain (a finance officer) told the assembled troops that the idea of surrendering was Lieutenant Kojima's, and he gave them an hour to think about the matter. Sensing that he might have been set up, Kojima went alone into a cave, waiting for the outcome with pistol at hand. At last all those who had been with him since the start came to him and, to his immense relief, said they would follow his lead. Shortly thereafter, they all walked down the mountain behind a white flag and surrendered to the Americans.

It was then that Kojima "received a big shock." He had known that the United States was a nation made up of many races, but to see this with his own eyes still amazed him. All along, he wrote improbably, he had thought that Japan was fighting for the people of the entire world. But on encountering the Americans he saw that the color of their hair ranged from blond to black, with all shades in between. Moreover, they claimed to be fighting not for their country or race, but for the liberty of all peoples. Kojima was treated well beyond all his expectations, even getting the same meals provided to American troops. Even more welcome, when Kojima asked a question of an American officer, the officer responded "Yes, Sir."

While the seeds of democratic ideas had probably been implanted in Kojima during his university years, it took the crucible of war to make them sprout. He realized the truth of the democratic principle that "the nation is us," not something or someone else, and that its citizens were obligated to take responsibility for its fate. The war affected different Japanese in different ways (and some not at all), but Kojima expressed most clearly and convincingly the changes that came over him from his experiences in war.

OOKA SHOHEI

Very few of those who eventually became POWs confessed in their reminiscences to having rationally debated the issue of whether to live or die while they were on the run from the Americans. One who did was Ooka Shohei, a graduate in French literature from Kyoto Imperial University and an intellectual who had found military life repellent.[17] He was in a force of about one hundred fifty soldiers, most of them over thirty-five, who were ordered to defend the small island of Mindoro in the central Philippines. When the Americans landed on the island on December 15, 1944, the Japanese melted into the jungle without contact having been made, hoping the war would pass them by. Higher headquarters, however, ordered his company to scout out American troop dispositions. The only result of this reconnaissance was that the Americans came after them with a much larger force.

In these circumstances, weakened by malaria, as were so many others, Ooka began to question whether any of what he was doing made sense. "To arrogantly choose a needless death" struck him as a form of self-deception, and Ooka, along with others, came to the conclusion that "sacrificing one's life in the pursuit of absurd tactics was simply insignificant, nothing more." His small group of compatriots hatched a rather absurd plan to escape Mindoro by infiltrating enemy lines in order to reach the coast, seize a native boat, and escape to Borneo and on across the South China Sea to China. He was dissuaded from this attempt by the argument that the group lacked both food and navigational skills. Ordered to withdraw further into the jungle, Ooka ultimately managed to remain behind with some of the sick and wounded, to await his fate at the hands of the Americans.

Though feverish with malaria, Ooka finally decided to leave the others and move to higher ground. While dragging himself, more dead than alive, through the jungle, he tried to kill himself with a grenade, but the pin did not release. He claimed that he tried many ways to seek death, even though doing so went against all his basic instincts. Finally, though, his efforts seemed to be rewarded; the pin released, but then the grenade failed to go off. (Ooka noted wryly in his memoir: "It appears that 60 percent of the grenades sent to the Pacific front misfired.") Later he realized that he could fix the grenade, but the very thought of doing something about it sent shivers down his spine. He tried to commit suicide by pointing his rifle at his head and moving the trigger with his toes. This, too, failed.

While engaged in this fashion, Ooka fell into a deep sleep from which he was awakened by an American soldier, who immediately realized that Ooka had no intention of resisting capture. Subsequently, as he was passed along from the front lines, Ooka recalled having often been asked by American soldiers whether he surrendered or was captured. He always lied proudly that he had been captured. "It was not that I was prejudiced against surrendering, but my personal pride did not permit me to submit in such a way to the enemy." Even though a university graduate influenced by communism who believed himself a rational human being, Ooka retained some elements of the *Senjinkun* to the end.

NAKAJIMA YOSHIO

A survivor of the Battle of Iwo Jima, Nakajima Yoshio recounted his miraculous survival in a privately published story of survivors and the family members of those who had died there.[18] Nakajima was manning an artillery battery on February 12, 1945, the day the American forces landed. Most of his comrades died in counter-battery fire from offshore naval vessels; Nakajima and two others found shelter in a cave.

At first the three decided to commit suicide using a dagger that a newlywed soldier had received from his wife. Then they seized on a better plan. The one man who had a grenade suggested that he place himself between the other two and pull the pin. It was agreed. Not wanting the Americans to find him in an untidy uniform, however, Nakajima stepped aside to make last-minute adjustments to his clothing, and at that moment the grenade exploded. His two comrades died a "heroic death." The grenade had apparently been triggered when hit by a shot from an American soldier firing an automatic rifle from the opening of the cave.

Nakajima recalled thinking, "Damn! How can one die in a place like this?" He had been slightly wounded by a fragment. The American soldier left, no doubt believing he had killed all the Japanese in the cave. Nakajima felt like a corpse already. He was totally alone, without even the strength to bury his fallen comrades. He had neither food nor water. With only a small opening to the outside, the cave became oppressively hot. Meanwhile, the battle shifted to the northern end of the island. After a few days alone, Nakajima started to hallucinate, thinking he saw his wife and brother, no longer able to distinguish what was real from what was imagined.

Half crazed with thirst, he finally managed to urinate into what had been a can of salmon. He drank his urine, which, he admitted, "even tasted good." He saved half of it but several hours later could not drink any more because it had putrefied, like everything else around him. Nakajima's sight began to fail and he thought his end was near.

Then he heard voices and a dog barking. He awaited his inevitable capture and death at American hands. An American soldier shone a flashlight on him, hesitated, and letting out a fearful yell, fled the cave. After a while, another GI came and called for him to come out.

Since he was going to die anyway, he thought he might as well do as he was told. He crawled out into the sunlight with the dagger, the last weapon he still had, but was temporarily blinded and found himself with his hands tied behind his back.

An overwhelming thirst induced him to ask his enemy for water, which was soon produced. Nakajima was asked the usual questions about name, rank, and unit designation and whether he was wounded. He was overwhelmed by the Americans' kindness in giving him a bandage and some medication.

En route to a POW holding pen, Nakajima was interrogated by a Nisei. Nakajima became teary-eyed on hearing Japanese again. He reached a barbed wire enclosure and saw three Japanese huddled in a corner. He was pretty sure that this was the place where he would be killed. The first night, totally exhausted, he slept soundly on an empty stomach. Nakajima was awakened in the middle of the night, but it was just an American who wanted to try out his minimal Japanese language skills. The next morning, after further interrogations, Nakajima's hands were untied and he was given American rations and cigarettes. Nakajima thought this was a major improvement over the stale bread the Imperial Japanese Army usually fed its troops.

Finally, Nakajima was brought to the island's central POW camp. He was reduced to skin and bones and wore only his shirt. One of the POWs approached him and said, "I don't know whether you are an officer or NCO, but here there are no ranks. You have to obey those who came here first." Nakajima had entered a new and unfamiliar world.

YOSHIDA OSAMU

A graduate of Keio University, Yoshida Osamu was drafted in December 1943, and seven months later was staring death in the face.[19] Word came down to his hideout in a cave on Saipan that his headquarters was going to order a *gyokusai* attack at midnight. A fellow law student came by to ask what he was going to do. Yoshida responded in a noncommittal way. It would be best to act in a manner that would not incur the risk of others laughing at him. Until then his mind had focused on the emperor, but now all of a sudden his focus shifted to his mother and the rest of his family. Fear welled up from the pit of his stomach. As if possessed he pulled the safety on his grenade, but he managed to wound only his shoulder. Perversely, this episode only made him want to live as long as he could.

Yoshida had just gotten himself out of the cave when he heard voices in the dark begging to be killed. He looked for his second grenade, but he had left it in the cave. He found himself surrounded by ten Americans and was taken prisoner. Relying on his schoolboy English, he told his captors that he was wounded, asked them to take care of him, but then, not much later, to kill him. The Americans took his wristwatch and cigarette case and gave him water and a cigarette. The Americans were kind to Yoshida. When a storm came up causing the poles holding up his tent to fall over repeatedly throughout the night, the Americans came to right the poles. To Yoshida it was significant that they went about their business as if it were the most natural thing to do, "not for the benefit of Americans but for fellow human beings."

While Yoshida was confined at the first stockade, a GI used to visit for a chat. "Joe" could never understand why the Japanese all asked to die. He would ask whether Japan would be helped by Yoshida's death, to which Yoshida had to reply, "I don't think so."

These accounts clearly highlight the fact that unit cohesion remained high among the Japanese troops even though they faced appalling privation and hardship when their supplies dried up and they were fleeing for their lives. Such recollections would not be complete, however, unless there were mention of a very different phenomenon that occurred in these circumstances. Evidence accumulated that when Japanese soldiers were literally starving, sick, and apparently abandoned to their fate, the comradeship within their unit and the habitual respect for officers would occasionally crumble. Interrogations revealed that as the troops scrambled to obtain food for their very existence, "accusations of cowardice, greed, and negligence" were often cited, especially against officers. In some cases, hatred was translated into direct action. Animosities that were latent in victory turned into raw hatred in defeat.[20]

Bitterness among the lower ranks welled up in the wake of undisguised withdrawals to safer areas on the part of senior officers as Japanese forces retreated. Some POWs believed this was part of a well-thought-out policy to conserve trained personnel and to avoid the special embarrassment of having officers fall into Allied hands. As a result, the troops could deduce that their fate was now in the hands of less-qualified, lower-ranking leadership. This feeling that they were victims of abandonment led to predictable outrage, especially given that in the Japanese societal setting the responsibility of leaders to their men was taken for granted.

Prisoners would cite examples of officers eating first and better than their men. They would accuse officers of having greater access to better prostitutes, reciting similar charges that are heard in many armies. The lower ranks were not just venting their traditional spleen against officers; their complaints about at least some army officers were validated by a "Top Secret–To Be Read by Officers Only" document dated October 24, 1944, from the vice minister of war that addressed this problem squarely. It noted that officers neglecting their leadership responsibilities adversely affected the morale of the troops. It had been noted that some "senior officers" serving in the southwest Pacific had "frequently applied for transfers to Japan proper. When their applications were disapproved, they became downhearted and lost all desire for war." In their distress, they had gotten intoxicated when air raid alarms sounded, disobeyed orders from above, and "even cut telephone wires so they could not be reached."[21]

Citing specific events, the memorandum told of a captain who, "driven by an irresistible yearning for his mistress, . . . without permission . . . returned to Japan where he indulged in a spree with her." The memorandum also mentioned cases of NCOs deserting and of large quantities of war matériel either lost or falling into enemy hands owing to poor leadership.

The personal accounts cited also provide insights into the variety of circumstances and considerations that impelled at least some Japanese soldiers and sailors to consider being taken captive, and the steps they took to carry out such plans. Many used Allied surrender passes that provided Japanese soldiers with a road map on how to carry out the process of giving themselves up. Americans began dropping such passes over enemy lines as early as 1942, but they were rarely effective until much later in the war. In fact, initially they were so poorly done that Japanese commanders did not even bother to prohibit their troops from collecting them. Objects of derision, the leaflets were usually thrown away. In time, the army used Japanese-American military intelligence personnel to develop less offensive, more productive language in writing these leaflets. Americans gradually learned to strictly avoid employing such offensive words as "surrender." Instead, it was thought far more effective in the Japanese text to use language along the lines of "come to an honorable understanding with the Americans." The English text of the leaflet, however, continued to use the word "surrender."

For its part, the U.S. Navy used cooperative POWs to help frame written surrender appeals in ways most likely to bring results. Among other advice, the Japanese suggested that leaflets should incorporate the name of a prominent POW who could verify that he had been well treated in American captivity. While the substitution of a colloquial form of Japanese for the more stilted, formal phrasings used at first was increasingly helpful to get the message across, most psychological warfare personnel recognized that it was the continuing American victories that lent validity to the leaflets. When resistance seemed more and more futile, Japanese increasingly came to understand that losing their lives in continued resistance was pointless. In Japanese parlance, the Japanese wondered, first in their own minds and later with a select few, whether one had to "die a dog's death."

Ruth Benedict, a member of the Foreign Morale Analysis Division that established promising themes for the leaflets, at one point floated the idea that Allied conditions for Japan's surrender should include a provision that no reprisals were to be leveled against returning prisoners. While this was certainly an approach that would have helped increase the number of POWs, it was never seriously pursued.[22]

Japanese were somewhat more likely to respond to loudspeaker appeals than to surrender leaflets. Hearing authentic Japanese voices provided more assurance than the leaflets that statements about good treatment in captivity would be honored. Broadcast appeals were most often used in the latter stage of the war in such locales as the Marianas (Guam and Saipan), Iwo Jima, and Okinawa when some Japanese troops hid out in the islands' abundant caves. The loudspeakers were most effective in persuading Japanese and native civilians, who were frequently intermingled with the soldiers, to come out of the caves.

When the capture or surrender occurred on land, the prisoner was often in the hands of frontline troops that might not have included Japanese language speakers. In some circumstances, the Japanese language speaker, normally a Japanese-American NCO, would come down to battalion level near the front lines in hopes of obtaining immediate tactical information from the prisoner. Sooner or later, the POW would be placed in the custody of the military police during his transfer to higher headquarters (normally at the regimental level), where the first systematic interrogation would take place.

Apparently, some Japanese prisoners on the way to rear areas were shot "trying to escape" by their MP guards. Such charges have been made by a few Japanese language officers and enlisted men, usually based not on direct evidence, but on scuttlebutt and strong inferences. Given the hatred of the enemy that consumed many Allied soldiers, especially in the battle zones, there is little doubt that such incidents did occur. There is no written record concerning such incidents and no POW guards were either charged or convicted of such cold-blooded murders.

Simple acts of defiance by Japanese who had not formally surrendered also led, from time to time, to their deaths. This was especially true after *gyokusai* charges resulted in high American casualties. Such an incident was recounted in a letter from Captain Benjamin Hazard, who commanded a military intelligence team on Saipan in July 1944. Hazard wrote that on the early morning of July 7, a Japanese suicide attack breached the perimeter of the First and Second Battalions of the 105th Marine Infantry Regiment, temporarily sweeping some of the American survivors along. The following day the 106th Regiment received several uncoordinated suicide attacks.

Several hours later, Captain Hazard followed some distance behind the right flank of the skirmish line, accompanied by an MP sergeant and two MPs from the POW interrogation unit. Hazard wrote:

> I noticed that two of the bodies in the trench in the foreground had more of a lifelike color than the other bodies that partially covered them. I called on them to stand up. They attempted to

continue to play dead and since I did not go away, they shook off the bodies that they had partially covered themselves with and stood up, an officer and enlisted man. The Marines in the vicinity halted and turned to face them. At this point they were not surrendering, but shouting "Tenno Heika Banzai!" in defiance. . . . They climbed out of the trench on the far side and turned to face me. The officer defiantly tore up some yen and they sat down on the edge of the trench still facing me. I suppose that since I had spoken to them in Japanese, the officer may have thought that I would understand and appreciate what he was about to do. The officer began to commit hara-kiri with his drawn sword, when the MP sergeant cut them both down with his submachine gun. He said that he didn't want to give them the satisfaction of committing suicide. With the casualties that we had taken over the past couple of days, no court martial would have convicted him.[23]

The navy necessarily handled POWs differently from the army. Naval ships did not have Japanese language personnel on board for interrogation purposes, although some of the larger ships carried individuals trained in interception and decoding of Japanese military messages. When American surface warships or submarines sank Japanese ships and there were survivors on life rafts or clinging to driftwood, they would usually allow themselves to be rescued and taken on board. In some instances, the Japanese sailors would try to swim or paddle away in a clear attempt to avoid surrendering. They were usually shot. Those who became prisoners would be confined to a small area of the ship and treated very well. Their first interrogations generally took place when the ship returned to Pearl Harbor, but occasionally the prisoners were taken off the ship at some intermediate port.

Once securely in Allied hands behind the front lines, POWs gradually realized that they would not be killed. They were prepared for the possibility of being killed; they were much less ready for the process of interrogations that followed. Nothing had prepared them for meeting either Caucasians speaking their language with considerable fluency or Japanese Americans, who looked like them but wore the enemy's uniform.

5

AMERICA'S SECRET WEAPONS: THE ARMY AND NAVY JAPANESE LANGUAGE SCHOOLS

During the war, the Japanese depended on secret weapons in the form of so-called "spiritual qualities" together with suicide weapons designed to wreak havoc on the enemy. The Americans had secret weapons of their own to meet this threat. By employing language and other skills to break Japanese codes, interrogate Japanese prisoners, and translate Japanese documents and diaries, Americans were able to obtain information vital to the Allied war effort. To accomplish these tasks, however, the American government had to mount a major effort to train thousands of Americans to become conversant in the enemy's language.

When war broke out, the foreign languages taught at American universities were predominantly those of European countries. Only a few universities offered Japanese language courses, including courses needed to enable graduate students to read ancient texts. Such courses would not have prepared them to converse with ordinary Japanese people or to read contemporary Japanese writing, let alone allow them to interrogate prisoners of war. Courses dealing with contemporary Japan were in fact remarkably scarce in prewar times.

An obvious way for the military to find Japanese speakers after the attack on Pearl Harbor was to recruit from the ranks of Westerners who had spent time living in Japan. But the number of potential recruits from this source was limited. The entire Western community in Japan at any one time—primarily businessmen and missionaries along with a few diplomats, journalists, teachers, and other professionals—had never exceeded several thousand before the outbreak of war. Except for the missionaries, language competence across this group was not impressive. They knew enough to speak to servants and get around the country, but very few could read Japanese, let alone carry on a sophisticated conversation, especially on political or military subjects. Almost all Western businessmen in prewar Japan worked in Western companies and relied on their Japanese staff to interpret and translate for them. In those days it was rare for Western men to marry Japanese women, eliminating yet another way in which they might have made more of an effort to learn the language. Social contact between Japanese and Westerners was quite limited, for cultural and language reasons. Most Westerners believed that Japanese was simply too difficult to master, and very few even tried. Missionaries, especially those who lived outside the metropolitan cities of Tokyo, Yokohama, and Kobe, had to have language competence to accomplish their work. Some of their children who attended Japanese kindergarten and perhaps a few years of Japanese primary school before transferring to Western schools were among the best Japanese speakers available in the Caucasian community.

In prewar times it was practically unheard of for Westerners to educate their children in the Japanese school system, let alone in a Japanese university. Only one white American, Donald Gorham, ever accomplished the feat of graduating from the prestigious Tokyo Imperial University, and his was a most unusual case. His father was a senior employee of the Nissan Corporation and had lived in Japan most of his adult life. Gorham's parents became so enamored of Japan and its people that they renounced their American citizenship to adopt Japanese nationality, but Don remained an American citizen despite having received his entire education in Japan. He was still living in Tokyo in the fall of 1941 when he was contacted by the naval attaché at the American embassy, who advised him that relations between the United States and Japan were deteriorating rapidly and urged him to return to the United States. He made the voyage on one of the last passenger vessels to cross the Pacific before the outbreak of war. After Pearl Harbor the navy showed a strong interest in obtaining Gorham's services. He was required to undergo numerous security checks to assure the navy that his views differed markedly from those of his father. When he finally passed muster, he was assigned to some of the more highly classified operations, including interrogations of the highest-ranking Japanese prisoner of war brought to the United States, navy captain Okino Matao (discussed in chapter 7).

Before the war, the Departments of State, War, and the Navy created, through two specially designed programs, only a small pool of Japanese experts trained in the language. The State Department's program was the more modest of the two because diplomatic business in prewar times was conducted almost entirely with the Japanese Foreign Office, whose officers spoke excellent English. Our army and navy attachés at the embassy needed Japanese language capability because their opposite numbers could rarely communicate in English. All of these experts were Caucasian. Given the racial climate at the time, the government, with exceedingly rare exceptions, would not even have considered employing Japanese Americans for sensitive government positions. But as tensions were building in East Asia during 1941, both military services recognized America's grave shortage of personnel having proficiency in professional-level Japanese, let alone a good understanding of Japanese culture, and both resolved to meet the need.

The people of the United States, however, generally had no appreciation of the value of knowing the enemy's language. In the summer of 1942, when Frank Tenny, a son and grandson of missionaries in Japan, was slated to enter one of the army's early Japanese language programs, he prepared for induction by enrolling in an intensive Japanese language program at Columbia University. When his number came up and he presented himself to the draft board, the board's chairman uncomprehendingly asked: "What the hell are you studying Japanese for? We ain't talkin' to them bastards. We're shootin' at 'em. You might as well be studying ancient Hungarian."[1]

The army's intensive Japanese language program was launched in the fall of 1941 at the Presidio of San Francisco with sixty students, of whom fifty-eight were Japanese Americans and two Caucasians. Ironically, the school was located near the headquarters of the Fourth Army, whose commanding general, Lt. Gen. John Dewitt, was to order the evacuation of all persons of Japanese ancestry from the West Coast, stating contemptuously, "A Jap is a Jap." The forty-three Nisei who survived the rigorous course were able to graduate and looked forward to their assignments, although unlike Caucasians, who were invariably commissioned upon graduation, Nisei graduates were only given the rank of corporal. Many subsequently earned sergeant's stripes, but the discriminatory system continued to rankle, even after a few Nisei were commissioned beginning in 1943. Ten of the best students were chosen to become instructors of the many Nisei who were to follow in their footsteps. They represented the core of the far larger number of instructors for the Nisei who entered the Military Intelligence Service Language School (MISLS) programs in Minnesota, first at Camp Savage and later at Fort Snelling. When the war ended, some fifty-seven hundred Nisei had received Japanese language training.

The program that began at the Presidio was the last to include both Japanese-American and Caucasian students. Once the war started, students were separated by race. Moreover, the school soon had to be relocated to Camp Savage, a former CCC (Civilian Conservation Corps) camp. The move became necessary when the instructors at the school, all of whom were Japanese Americans, faced the likelihood they would be forcibly rounded up and sent to the inland internment camps.

LANGUAGE TRAINING FOR ARMY CAUCASIANS

The number of Caucasians brought into the army's intensive Japanese language program grew to around two hundred in each semiannual class. When the program closed its doors in the summer of 1946, a total of 780 Caucasians had passed through the army language programs at the Presidio, Camp Savage, the University of Michigan, and Fort Snelling. The first few classes were composed largely of students who already knew a fair amount of Japanese, including those who had lived in Japan for many years; a small number had picked up the language through extensive contact with Nisei on the West Coast who still spoke it at home. Owing to pressure to get linguists into the field, the early classes were given just six months of training. Subsequently, students received one year of training in basic Japanese at the University of Michigan, followed by six months of concentrated study of specialized military language training at Fort Snelling. The entire teaching staff, all civilians, necessarily had to be Japanese Americans; most were recruited from the internment camps. Only eighteen had ever taught before. They came from varied backgrounds and included lawyers, a caterer, an insurance salesman, a Buddhist priest, and an accountant.

The newly minted teachers were glad to get out of confinement and into the relatively more liberal atmosphere of Michigan and Minnesota. Ann Arbor was then a small and somewhat provincial town in which the arrival of as many as forty-six Japanese language teachers created a stir. The initial antagonisms, evidenced in the Nisei's difficulty in finding adequate housing, eventually dissipated. Relations between the Japanese-American instructors and the Caucasian students were generally good, but there were exceptions. George Totten, who became a professor of Japanese politics after the war, began his Japanese language studies with some typical prejudices acquired in growing up on the West Coast. Decades later, he ruefully recalled that at first he naively suspected the teachers would teach wrong Japanese words as a way of undermining the American war effort.

The massive effort to teach Japanese to selected soldiers was supposed to be kept secret to prevent the enemy from learning about the effort, but it was an open one. The local paper ran a number of articles on this strange breed of soldiers who spent their time walking around town while "drawing" Chinese characters in the air in their unrelenting effort to get them down pat.

The army's Japanese language students came from a wide spectrum of the society. They included a fair number of college graduates, as well as men whose advanced academic training had been interrupted by the war, but a college background was not considered essential. High school graduates who had no idea why the army had selected them somehow mysteriously managed to get around the army's high standards for entry. Some students had earlier received as much as a year of Japanese study under the Army Specialized Training Program (ASTP) before they were selected for the MISLS. The ASTP Japanese language program, conducted on a number of university campuses, was of roughly the same size as that run by the

MISLS; its graduates were not commissioned and normally were not assigned to combat intelligence positions, but during the Occupation many were used in military government positions.

In some instances, having learned a few phrases of Japanese was enough to convince army personnel officers to assign these students to the MISLS program. One of these recruits was James Wickel, a high school graduate from Detroit. (He was the author's classmate in the program and later a colleague at the embassy in Tokyo.) Wickel got into the program because he had memorized a few Japanese phrases that proved sufficient to awe a recruiter whose own language capability was even more minimal. He performed moderately well in the language program, but his ability in Japanese blossomed after he arrived in Tokyo early in the Occupation. He soon met and married a Japanese woman, made it a point to speak only Japanese in the home, and continued to study the language long after leaving school. In due course, Wickel created his own shorthand for note taking while interpreting and pioneered in the development of simultaneous interpreting from Japanese into English and vice versa. He became the State Department's foremost American interpreter and served as the ambassador's voice in Tokyo, for many years regularly interpreting at functions involving the Japanese prime minister and foreign minister.

The language students had a powerful incentive to study hard. Those who failed to keep up would be sent to the infantry, not an appealing possibility, especially while the Battle of the Bulge was raging in Europe. Some students, however, simply could not take the pressure of daily learning and retaining a dozen Chinese characters. Some who lacked the aptitude for a language considered among the most difficult for Westerners to learn were released.

Although a few officers went through the army's intensive Japanese language course, most of the students remained enlisted men until the end of the program. Then they were normally assigned to units in the Pacific upon receiving commissions as second lieutenants. Most of these Caucasian linguists were given duties other than interrogating prisoners. In teams with Nisei enlisted men and a few Nisei officers, they translated personal and unit field diaries, letters and other personal papers, military documents and orders, and maps and charts. They also prepared propaganda and psychological warfare material, including leaflet and broadcast appeals to surrender. Those who worked on POW interrogations headed teams made up of Nisei enlisted men whose language competence, with rare exceptions, was superior to that of their officers.

At first, there were hardly any prisoners to be interrogated. One reason was that the American and Australian troops in the field were disinclined to take prisoners even when that rare opportunity arose. Hatred of the enemy was intense, and there was little confidence that a Japanese soldier with hands held high could be trusted to keep them there. Conventional wisdom among the troops was that there was little or no likelihood that the fanatical Japanese would divulge anything of military value, resulting in little motivation for taking prisoners. The few Japanese language officers with the Marine Corps on Guadalcanal had had minimal exposure to the Japanese language and were initially unable to establish meaningful contact with the handful of POWs captured.

LANGUAGE TRAINING FOR JAPANESE AMERICANS

The army eventually trained some six thousand Japanese Americans in intensive Japanese studies programs at Camp Savage and Fort Snelling. The six-month programs were designed to brush up what was assumed were existing language skills learned at home and in after-school Japanese programs. In fact, Nisei language skills varied greatly. After Pearl Harbor, Japanese Americans understandably became loath to speak Japanese in public and wanted to underline their patriotism by talking little in their parents' native tongue even in private. On the whole, Nisei from Hawaii were more conversant with spoken and written Japanese than those from the West Coast. After a very slow start, the training of Nisei language personnel was greatly accelerated in late 1943 when the need for their skills became manifest.

Along with other Americans, Japanese Americans had become subject to the draft in 1940, and hundreds were already serving in the army when the Japanese struck Pearl Harbor. Their treatment then differed, depending on where they were located at the time. In the hysteria that engulfed the West Coast, many Nisei soldiers who happened to be in that part of the country were summarily discharged over the next months. At an airfield in California, Nisei were stripped of their weapons and no longer even allowed to look at P-38 fighters. Many were made permanent KP, assigned to peeling potatoes and washing dishes. Akira Nakamura was at Fort Lewis, Washington, and together with other Nisei draftees at the post, was relieved of all duties and restricted to an isolated area of the base. Soon after, Nisei soldiers were marched to the front of the base headquarters, escorted by military police. The base commander, who treated them as if they were POWs, warned them that "if any of you soldiers make a suspicious or false move or engage in suspicious activities while under my charge, you will be shot on sight."[2] All Nisei in Hawaii's Territorial Guard were discharged when Washington learned that Honolulu had been guarded principally by "Japs" ever since the attack on Pearl Harbor. Some Nisei soldiers were sent off to labor battalions, while others in the Midwest and East continued to serve their country in the same functions as before Pearl Harbor.

When Nisei again became subject to the draft, the army was inclined to group them in the all-Nisei 442nd Regimental Combat Team rather than assign them to language and intelligence training. This unit earned the highest marks for its "Go for Broke" spirit in the Italian campaign, ending the war with more decorations than any other army unit of its size. Although the Congressional Medals of Honor these soldiers earned were not awarded until the fall of 2000, when the army made amends, their unquestioned patriotism and sacrifices undoubtedly led to the decision that ultimately allowed large numbers of Japanese Americans to participate in the intelligence effort in the Pacific War.

Only Nisei who already knew some Japanese were admitted to the army's language program. Their study load was heavier than that prescribed for Caucasian students. John Aiso, the strict head of training for MISLS, threatened Nisei that he would send letters to the parents of those failing in their studies. At the time, this was a threat that was taken seriously given the strong family system in the Japanese-American community. Many had developed an ear for the language by hearing it spoken at home and most could speak it well.

It was fairly common among the Issei (first generation Japanese

Americans) in the 1930s to send their children to supplementary Japanese language schools. Some met every Saturday, but more rigorous ones held classes every afternoon for several hours. Nisei children were often unenthusiastic about attending school at times when their Caucasian classmates were playing. Obedience to parents, however, was still deeply ingrained in the second generation, so they attended, albeit reluctantly. When the army finally opened its gates to Japanese language training for Nisei, many wished they had paid more attention to these studies. The army provided six-month courses for Nisei—normally enough to brush up on the language and to learn the special vocabulary used by the military. Nisei had inevitably absorbed a great deal of Japanese culture and values in the home, whether or not they themselves subscribed to the values, and this knowledge, as much or more than language skills, proved invaluable in dealing with POWs and even in translating documents.

The most prized group of Japanese Americans in intelligence work had spent part of their youth in Japan. These individuals were called Kibei, meaning individuals who had returned to the United States from stays of various lengths in Japan. Issei sent sons and daughters back to the homeland for various reasons, at times to accompany a parent fulfilling filial duties to an aging parent. Some American-born Japanese dutifully returned to Japan when one of their parents died; others went to live with relatives. Not a few Issei parents were uncomfortable with the values adopted by their children and believed that a dose of Japanese discipline, education, and language, administered in the ancestral homeland, might prove useful in future.

Kibei subsequently faced a double dose of suspicion at home when war broke out. Extensive time spent in Japan was initially considered a clearly negative mark, among many others, when Nisei were considered for induction in the army. The complex questionnaire used by draft boards to determine Nisei eligibility for service consisted of fifty questions. Anyone who had traveled to Japan more than once earned three minus points, and for each two years of residence in Japan one point was deducted. Three years' attendance in a Japanese language school in the United States or any postgraduate work in Japan earned a Nisei two minus points, the same as membership in the Communist Party. Plus points were earned by such factors as having embraced the Christian faith, having been employed by an American company doing business only in the United States, and membership in the Boy Scouts and Masons. If the Japanese American "reads, writes and speaks Japanese good[*sic*]," two points were deducted.[3]

Despite routine discriminatory treatment, Kibei eventually overcame doubts about their loyalty to become teachers of other Nisei in the MISLS program and to render distinguished service at the front. Their years in Japanese schools had made them bilingual to the point of being able to read even the extremely difficult cursive form *(sosho)* of Chinese character writing. Diaries and hurriedly written military field orders were often written in this form. Since few Caucasian language officers ever managed to decipher such writing and even Nisei educated in the United States had considerable trouble in this regard, the contribution of the Kibei was special.

The not uncommon practice by Issei parents of sending their children back to Japan for some schooling resulted in yet another difficulty for the Kibei. When the Japanese attacked Pearl Harbor, some of their brothers and sisters were caught in Japan for the duration of the war. Although they were American citizens, Japanese authorities chose to treat them as Japanese nationals. The men were drafted and required to serve in the Japanese armed forces. Some even died while serving in the Japanese military.

Harry Fukuhara was one of those Kibei. Born in Seattle, he had accompanied his mother and three brothers to Japan after their father's death. They settled in the parents' hometown of Hiroshima, where Fukuhara attended high school. He returned to the United States in 1938 to attend college. In 1942 he volunteered for the army from one of the relocation centers. The outbreak of war, however, had caught the rest of his immediate family in Japan. His oldest brother was killed in the atomic bombing of Hiroshima, in which his mother survived but suffered from the effects of radiation for many years. Two other brothers had been drafted into the Japanese army and were stationed on Kyushu, awaiting an American invasion. During the war Fukuhara served with great distinction on Saipan and Guam, and after the war remained in the army until his retirement as a full colonel.

Phil Ishio was a member of the first group of Nisei selected for military intelligence training at the Presidio, and his experiences were fairly typical of those of other Nisei. Born and reared in Salt Lake City, where his parents ran a laundry, he had completed his first year at the university when his grandfather retired and decided to return to Japan. Ishio agreed to accompany him. In Japan, he honed his already impressive language skills by attending Waseda University for a year. In April 1941 he was advised by the American embassy to return home and promptly did so. Shortly thereafter he was drafted. Upon completing the six-month Japanese refresher course at Camp Savage, Ishio was in a group assigned to Fort Leavenworth, Kansas, where instead of enjoying a warm reception, Nisei soldiers were marched to the fence of the nearby federal penitentiary. Their military police guard threatened them, saying "that's where [they] would end up if [they] did anything against the United States."[4] On another occasion, Nisei were ordered to clean out horse stables while the rest of the troops were mustered out to pass in review of visiting President Roosevelt. Ishio recalled that it was parental admonitions to remain loyal to the United States that enabled his group of Nisei soldiers to put up with such humiliations and insults.

When Ishio and a group of similarly superb interpreter-translators reached the southwest Pacific in early 1943, they were initially assigned menial jobs. Their commanders failed to understand how they could be of any help against the Japanese. When finally attached to a forward unit on New Guinea, Ishio chanced upon and translated captured documents that provided information on Japanese unit identifications, their code numbers, and strengths. He also translated documents that detailed plans for a retreat from northern New Guinea that enabled Allied forces to thwart the effort. In addition to translating documents, Ishio also interrogated prisoners in both New Guinea and the Philippines. Some he induced to return to caves and other hiding places to persuade other Japanese soldiers to surrender.[5]

The emphasis on translating documents was typical for both Nisei and Caucasian language personnel at least until late 1944, when the number of POWs increased sharply. Written material provided a treasure trove of information. Confident in their view that Caucasians find the Japanese language impenetrable, and certain that the United States would never trust Nisei enough to employ them on the battlefields of the Pacific, Japanese authorities failed to treat sensitive material with care. Seemingly all Japanese kept diaries to which they confided information on military operations and methods, including the location and objectives of various units; but of equal value were the psychological insights and indications of morale they provided. Letters and personal papers carried by prisoners or found on the corpses of Japanese soldiers also included useful information on political and economic developments, as well as pay books and military postal savings books that the soldiers used to make deposits and withdrawals.

Fate would conspire to create some unforgettable encounters between Kibei and persons they had known when living in Japan. Higa Takejiro was a Kibei who had lived for fourteen years in his ancestral home of Okinawa, returning to America only in 1938. He went ashore on Okinawa on D day, April 1, 1945, with a unit of the Ninety-sixth Division. A few days later, Higa was called on to question a suspected imposter and was thunderstruck and overjoyed to discover it was his seventh and eighth grade teacher, Nakamura Sensei. Several months later, two rather shabbily uniformed young men were brought before him to be interrogated. As they responded to the standard questions on name, rank, and hometown, Higa realized they had been his junior high classmates. He asked them about Nakamura Sensei and what had happened to their classmate, Higa Takejiro. Surprised at their interrogator's familiarity with those names, they replied that Higa had returned to Hawaii. They were not sure they could recognize him if they saw him. Higa could not hold back any longer. He exploded: "You idiots! Don't you recognize your own old classmate?" The Okinawans stared at Higa in total disbelief and started crying because they had been certain up to that point that they would be shot at the conclusion of the interrogation. Realizing now that their lives would be spared, they cried with happiness and relief. Higa, too, was overcome by his emotions at finding his classmates alive.[6]

The extent of the Japanese Americans' dedication to the war effort can only be measured against the background of widespread fear and suspicion of anyone with a Japanese name and face. This prejudice was deep-seated and had been long in coming on. Beginning in 1908, West Coast states had passed far-reaching legislation that restricted the economic activities of Japanese and other East Asian immigrants, including prohibitions against their acquisition of land. As many as five hundred discriminatory laws were placed on the books at the state level. Having to live with such institutionalized racism was, for Japanese Americans, one of the prewar facts of life. At the national level, a so-called "Gentlemen's Agreement" between the United States and Japan terminated the immigration flow from Japan. The Oriental Exclusion Act had originally targeted only Chinese immigrants, but in 1924 Japanese were added to the list. This act barred the immigration of persons who were ineligible to become citizens and effectively ended further immigration from Japan.

Legally barred from ever becoming U.S. citizens, the Issei, first-generation Japanese Americans, more than most immigrants continued to retain affection for their homeland. Most lived on farms or in ghettolike urban enclaves and made only modest socioeconomic progress. Their children, however, by virtue of birth in the United States, had automatically acquired citizenship. Thanks to American schooling, of which they took full advantage, West Coast Nisei in particular began to integrate into the broader society. At the same time, as members of a minority that was discriminated against, they had to live up to a higher standard, and because of their cultural heritage, feared bringing dishonor on their families.

Following the attack on Pearl Harbor, some Caucasians remained calm and sympathized with the minority Nisei, but popular agitation hounded the West Coast Japanese Americans. Declarations of loyalty by Japanese-American organizations fell on deaf ears. The federal government succumbed to the pressure and issued Executive Order 9066 of February 1942, calling for the rounding up of over one hundred twenty thousand Japanese and Japanese Americans from California, Oregon, Washington, and Arizona and their "relocation," a euphemism for incarceration, to inland camps. Although the order was written so as to target nationals of all enemy countries, there was never any intention to incarcerate German and Italian aliens, let alone Americans of German and Italian ancestry. Only Japanese and Japanese-American evacuees were ordered to appear at collection points and transported under armed guard to their new "homes." They had to leave behind whatever possessions they could not carry with them. Most stores and small businesses had to be sold at fire sale prices; a few good neighbors offered to care for their property until their release from imprisonment.

A strong feeling of impotence overcame the evacuees in their new environment. Camp housing consisted either of old Civilian Conservation Corps shacks or shabby, hurriedly constructed new quarters with only a bare minimum of amenities. Without exception, camps were located in areas of harsh climate, where the wind whistled through the thin walls and heating was often inadequate. In the desperate early years of the war, most Americans either never heard of their fellow citizens' mass incarceration or were too preoccupied to try to correct the injustice. Congress rescinded the Oriental Exclusion Act only in 1952, at last removing the impediment to the naturalization of first-generation Japanese.

The ill treatment of Japanese and Japanese Americans was an odd, geographically defined phenomenon. It did not apply to Hawaii because Japanese Americans constituted one-third of the territory's population and were essential to the continued operation of our key Pacific base and surrounding civilian communities. Suspicions of Nisei working in defense jobs in Hawaii ran high, and rumors, charges, and hearsay abounded accusing Japanese Americans of disloyal activities. Pursuant to a congressional resolution authorizing an investigation of the Pearl Harbor attack, President Roosevelt appointed a commission headed by Supreme Court Justice Owen J. Roberts to look into all aspects of the Japanese attack. While the Roberts Commission found substantial Japanese espionage activity under the overall direction of the Japanese consulate in Hawaii prior to the attack, it could not find a single instance where Japanese Americans participated in any of these activities. None of the rumors implicating American citizens of Japanese descent was substantiated.[7]

The relatively small numbers of Japanese Americans then scattered throughout the Midwest, Mountain States, and East Coast were also unaffected by the relocation order. West Coast Nisei residents fortunate enough to "escape" to colleges, friends, or relations in the

East were able to live the more or less normal wartime lives of all other Americans.

Although Japanese Americans were treated decently outside of the West Coast, a national poll conducted in March 1942 showed that 93 percent of the American public approved of the removal of Japanese aliens from the Pacific Coast. Almost 60 percent condoned as well the wholesale incarceration of Japanese-American citizens who had lived on the West Coast. As late as April 1945, a poll demonstrated that 32 percent of the American people believed that at least half of the Japanese-American citizens "would try to do something against the United States if they had the chance," while only 19 percent replied "practically none of them" to the same question.[8]

Even when anti-Japanese prejudice was at its height, a significant majority of Nisei never wavered in their intense loyalty to the United States and their determination to find opportunities to demonstrate that loyalty. They had been raised in this country, had gone to school here, and felt totally at home in America. Like children of immigrants from other countries, they had conflicts with their parents, who were less acculturated to their new surroundings. Japanese immigrants, made less welcome than other nationalities, generally tried to inculcate Japanese values into their children and introduced them to Japanese religious beliefs and Japanese martial arts. Not a great deal of this stuck, however, because of the pull of American culture.

An ill-advised and poorly phrased government questionnaire that all residents in relocation centers were required to complete only served to stoke the anger of the evacuees and to sharpen existing tensions within the Japanese-American community. Designed to assess degrees of "loyalty" and similar to the questionnaire used by draft boards, it asked about attendance at Japanese language schools, affiliation with churches, Shinto shrines, and Buddhist temples, participation in traditional Japanese martial arts, and the like. Worst of all, it asked whether the individual responding to the questionnaire was prepared to renounce his allegiance to the emperor and affirm loyalty to the United States. Nisei not only felt insulted by the question but also asked how they could renounce something they had never believed. The question posed problems of another sort for the Issei. Through no fault of their own, they had been denied the possibility of becoming American citizens and therefore remained Japanese whether they liked it or not. Incarcerated, they retained little hope of attaining citizenship after the war, so that renouncing their loyalty to Japan would mean becoming stateless, thereby losing what little protection they might still have had. The very question posed by the questionnaire epitomized a situation that never should have come about and ensured that respondents were left with a choice of unsatisfactory options.

It was only after the few Nisei allowed to participate in intelligence work in the southwest Pacific more than proved their worth that the army realized it would need to vastly expand its Japanese language program. The increasing pace and scale of Allied offensive operations in the Pacific would provide fresh opportunities to use Nisei for POW interrogations, document translations, and code work. All of a sudden, the attendance at weekend Japanese language schools that had been considered a black mark against Nisei became an asset and, once again, Japanese Americans became eligible for the draft. When the number of Japanese POWs increased sharply and the few Nisei on hand in the Pacific fully justified the confidence of their Caucasian officers, the army began to funnel large numbers of Nisei into the language programs at Camp Savage and Fort Snelling.

Almost immediately, new fissures were created in the Nisei relocation centers. A majority of young Nisei, motivated by the patriotic appeals of the Japanese American Citizens League to join the army, responded favorably to the new opportunities opening up. A minority, however, took the constitutionally principled but "politically incorrect" position that they could not accept being drafted or volunteering for military service from within a barbed wire enclosure— that if allowed to leave the camps as free men, they, like other Americans, would eagerly serve their country. In the end, the so-called "draft evaders" served prison sentences of up to three years, while their brothers and friends seized on the ticket for release from the camps and served with great distinction in both the European and Pacific theaters. When internee Hank Gosho volunteered and went off to war with the famed Merrill's Marauders in Burma, a minority of bitter opponents to cooperating with the American war effort stoned his mother's house in the relocation center. The divisions thus created between and within families did not heal for another half century.

Tensions also inevitably arose between the generations. Most Nisei welcomed the opportunity to demonstrate loyalty to their country of birth, also viewing military service as a way of protecting their parents, who necessarily still held Japanese citizenship and felt very much at risk. The parents generally gave their blessing when sons volunteered for military service or were drafted. They understood the second generation's attachment to the United States and told their sons to serve proudly and not shame their parents by shirking their duty. Others were less forgiving. In the middle of the war, the Issei could not be sure they would not be repatriated to Japan at some point, and they were bitter about having lost their property in the wave of racial discrimination. Many saw no future for themselves in America, and now their sons were going off to fight against their native land. These wounds, too, took a long time to heal.

The absurdity of the relocation centers was underlined when young Nisei returned to them in uniform, on leave prior to shipping out for overseas duty. Those heading for the Pacific were not allowed to tell their families where they were going. The fact that Japanese Americans would henceforth be employed in the Pacific was kept secret to avoid letting the enemy know that we had a new weapon in their backyard. The Japanese propaganda campaign had gleefully taken full advantage of the manifestations of anti-Japanese racism on the West Coast and never suspected that the American government had shifted its policy on the employment of Nisei in the Pacific.

Nisei intelligence personnel fanned out through the Pacific theater, serving with every American combat division, as well as with selected Allied units. This exposed them to the unique and constant danger near the front lines that a member of their own forces might shoot at someone who looked like the enemy and ask questions later. Nisei had the added burden of knowing that their fate would be worse even than that of a Caucasian if they were captured by the Japanese. Nisei attached to Australian units were believed to be especially endangered because Australia was then pursuing a "White Australia"

policy that had permitted no Oriental immigration. Nisei were provided with a special pass, signed by a senior Australian officer and
bearing its owner's photo, that declared they were Americans to be
given access to all facilities extended to Australian troops. Since experience had proven that passes provided insufficient protection, army
commanders ordered that at or near the front lines, Nisei soldiers
were to be accompanied by a military policeman at all times. Despite
such precautions, several Nisei were shot and killed by their own forces.

Nisei were involved in a number of heroic exploits while serving with Merrill's Marauders in Burma. Seven West Coast Nisei who
volunteered from the concentration camps and seven Nisei from
Hawaii who were never affected by the relocation order joined this
elite ranger unit. Roy Matsumoto was with the Marauders' Second
Battalion in northern Burma when his unit came across a Japanese
telephone line that linked the headquarters of the Japanese Eighteenth
Division with component units further north. He climbed a tree,
tapped into the line, and gained information about the location of
an ammunition dump that his unit promptly destroyed. Matsumoto
also learned a great deal about the enemy's troop dispositions in the
area, allowing his behind-the-lines unit to evade far stronger Japanese forces. A month later, his battalion surrounded by the Japanese,
Matsumoto infiltrated behind enemy lines under cover of night close
enough to overhear discussions of the enemy's plan to attack First
Lieutenant Edward McLogan's platoon at dawn. The platoon booby-
trapped its own foxholes and moved further up the hill. When the
Japanese charged on schedule, the Americans held their fire until the
enemy reached the line of abandoned foxholes. The second wave of
Japanese hesitated in confusion. At that moment Matsumoto stood
up in plain sight of the enemy and gave the order to attack in Japanese. This so startled the enemy forces that they obeyed the order
and were mowed down by the well-prepared American forces. Matsumoto's extraordinary act of bravery allowed the platoon to break
the siege and defeat a more powerful enemy force. The action contributed to the eventual reopening of the Burma Road. While perhaps the most spectacular example of the Nisei's direct involvement
in combat, it also underlined that the work of Japanese language personnel was not restricted to interrogations and document translations.

Occasionally they found themselves in situations where they had to use their weapons. Some Nisei even served behind enemy lines with OSS (Office of Strategic Services) units.

One of the most successful intelligence coups to which Nisei contributed in large measure took place on Bougainville Island, northwest of Guadalcanal. In early 1944 the U.S. Thirty-seventh Infantry and Americal divisions were defending a key airbase on the island, from which attacks were mounted on the area's biggest Japanese base at Rabaul. The Japanese Sixth Infantry Division, which had participated in the Rape of Nanking (1937), sought to recapture the airstrip. A language team consisting of two Caucasian officers and seven Nisei enlisted men led by Sus Toyoda, attached to the Thirty-seventh Division's intelligence (G-2) section, had spent a good deal of time trying to convince front-line troops that, while the Nisei looked Japanese, they were really "good guys," able to process valuable documents and interrogate prisoners of war in ways that could save American lives. Combat troops were asked to extend humane treatment to any prisoner taken, in the hope and expectation of a payoff in intelligence obtained.

The team's first break came in late February when a regiment of the Thirty-seventh Division returned from a firefight with a prisoner in tow. The preliminary interrogation produced combat intelligence of immediate value. A second interrogation at division level indicated that the prisoner had become fed up with the constant harassment and humiliation he received in the Japanese army and was ready and willing to provide whatever information he had. Although the prisoner was a low-ranking enlisted man, he had learned that his regiment was conducting probes to prepare for an all-out attack on the American perimeter. He was not privy to the date of the general attack but had heard it would be soon. The Nisei were aware that the Japanese military was prone to carry out general attacks on Japanese holidays, and the one coming up was March 10, Japan's Army Day.

This information was conveyed to both the division staff and the American XIV Corps. At the corps level a third interrogation took place. There the prisoner surprised Roy Uyehata, one of the Nisei interrogators, by anxiously asking whether he would soon be taken off the island. This unusual question strongly suggested that the prisoner might be fearful of being recaptured when the Japanese attacked. As a result of these warnings, perimeter defenses were doubled and tripled in the ensuing two weeks. As anticipated, a Japanese regiment with three thousand men of the Fourth Division struck with full force on March 10 and were decimated by withering American fire, leading to a temporary lull in the fighting.

Late on the afternoon of March 23, the Nisei team received a load of captured documents. In the screening, they found a tactical map of the Japanese 129th Infantry Regiment, an element of the Sixth Division. The bloodstained map provided detailed information on a planned attack on American defenses, showing the assembly area, line of departure, and line of attack. All it lacked was the date of the planned attack. Since the Japanese had been probing American lines every other night at eight o'clock and the map had been captured two nights earlier, the Nisei inferred that the attack would come that very evening, March 23, 1944. As it happened, this again coincided with a Japanese holiday–the All Imperial Ancestors Day that fell on the vernal equinox. On this occasion, artillery fire killed virtually all of the enemy troops. These twin victories resulting from intelligence successes secured Bougainville for the Allies. The island proved to be one of the most important early stepping-stones of the war on the road to Tokyo.

In a somewhat similar but less dramatic episode on Saipan, Hoichi Kubo, a Nisei attached to the Third Battalion of the 105th Infantry Regiment, received a tip on July 4, 1944, from a civilian employee of the Japanese navy's seaplane base about an impending Japanese attack. The attack was scheduled to coincide with the date of the Tanabata (the star Vega) festival on July 7. On the afternoon of July 6 he interrogated a prisoner who confirmed that the attack would take place at midnight. Acting on this information, the regiment and its battalions embarked on intense preparation for the anticipated *gyokusai* by digging trenches, clearing fields of fire, and siting machine guns, 37 mm artillery pieces, and mortars along the defensive line. Reinforcements and tanks were requested from higher headquarters, but the request was turned down, presumably because the division and corps doubted the reliability of the intelligence. This decision resulted in a heavy cost in men and matériel to the already weakened American First and Second Battalions bearing the brunt of the *gyokusai* launched early on the morning of July 7.

Senior officers who knew most about the Nisei contributions to the American war effort held them in the highest regard. Col. Sidney Mashbir, who commanded the Allied Translator and Interpreter Section (ATIS) in the southwest Pacific, stated that MIS language and intelligence personnel "saved thousands of American lives." But the Nisei felt that their contributions were not fully valued, despite their dedication to the war effort. While Caucasian Japanese language students routinely received commissions, better qualified Nisei were generally not commissioned until late in the war. Moreover, Nisei failed to receive medals they believe they had earned. The army's Nisei linguists attached to the navy and marine units were denied medals on the grounds that they belonged to a separate service. Most bitter was the reality that helping their country in important ways did nothing to get their families released from concentration camps. The more sensitive Caucasian officers with whom they worked were sympathetic but felt unable to change the inherent injustice of the situation. It is striking, however, that this undercurrent of disaffection never carried over into their work environment. It was wartime and everybody soldiered on.

JAPANESE LANGUAGE TRAINING FOR NAVY PERSONNEL

The U.S. Navy's intensive Japanese language program was considerably smaller than the army's and, if for no other reason, could be more selective in its recruitment. The navy chose young men who had grown up in Japan or spent sufficient time there as adults to get at least a start on the language. Preference was given to university students who had either acquired a smattering of the language or taken enough advanced Latin, French, or German to establish a presumption that they could also handle Japanese. Some Americans who had grown up in China were brought into the Japanese language program on the not unreasonable presumption that a knowledge of Chinese characters would give them a leg up on learning written Japanese.

The navy's language program began at the University of California at Berkeley, but the removal of Japanese Americans from the West Coast had necessitated its transfer to the University of Colorado in Boulder. The program's one-year course stressed reading over con-versational skills because the navy (excepting the marines) did not expect to find many Japanese prisoners to interrogate but hoped to pick up a considerable number of military documents for transla-tion. Like their army counterparts, students were housed in univer-sity dormitories, met four hours a day in classes of five to six students, and were required to memorize ten to twelve Chinese characters a day. Unlike the army's language students, those in the navy contin-ued to wear civilian clothing at all times and received no military training while in school.

The classes combined students of roughly equal language com-petence; weekly examinations that included dictation determined whether a student remained in his section or moved up or down the skill ladder. Both the army and navy language schools enhanced their instruction with occasional Japanese movies that had played in the Japanese quarters of urban areas in Hawaii and on the West Coast. They were at best B movies with excruciatingly boring story lines. The army language school's prize possession was *Shina no Yoru* (China Night), which it showed so often that students memorized all the best lines. Set in wartime China, the hero was a Japanese naval officer who successfully convinced his Chinese lady love that Japan was fighting on China's behalf. The luminous beauty of the female lead, Yamaguchi Yoshiko, who appeared in several postwar Holly-wood movies as Shirley Yamaguchi, made it all worthwhile.

Navy instructors came from various backgrounds, including a few Caucasian academics, former missionaries in Japan, and some Nisei, most of whom had been released from relocation centers.

Upon graduation from the navy's Japanese language program, some of the Boulderites were commissioned in the Marine Corps, and many saw heavy combat in places like Tarawa, the Marianas, and Iwo Jima. The experiences of the marine language officers were similar to those of army officers. One veteran of the First Marine Division on New Guinea later recalled that he did not have a great deal to do in his role as a Japanese interpreter. Prisoners taken were so few, so low in rank, so long separated from their units, so sick and lacking in useful military information, that they were simply sent on to division headquarters, then shipped to rear area camps. Once the navy embarked on its island-hopping campaign in the mid-Pacific, marine units on such places as Tarawa, Saipan, Guam, and Iwo Jima interrogated many more prisoners.

The majority of Boulder graduates, however, were commissioned as navy ensigns, and many were initially assigned to the Joint Intelligence Center Pacific Ocean Area (JICPOA) in Hawaii. The translation section at JICPOA alone had two hundred or more language officers engaged in document translation, radio intercepts, code work, interrogation of POWs, and other intelligence functions. One of the more significant tasks at JICPOA was the translation of top secret Japanese hydrographic charts that revealed the location of Japanese mines around Japan's main ports. This information had immediate tactical interest for American submarines. Other strategic documents included a manual for antiaircraft defense and planning for the defense of Kyushu, the target for an American landing in the fall of 1945. From time to time, JICPOA personnel were temporarily assigned to duty with marine units that fought from Tarawa and the Marshall Islands to Okinawa. Most landed in the third assault wave and interrogated prisoners and wrote summaries of documents, while others found their way to subordinate naval commands.

The navy, including the marines, remained lily-white throughout the war. No effort was made to recruit Japanese Americans to supplement Caucasian Japanese language personnel, even after Nisei had proven their loyalty and competence in combat with the army. Navy language officers assigned to warships had few chances to come upon Japanese POWs. Marine units, however, were similar to the army in eventually having substantial opportunities to interrogate Japanese prisoners and to come into possession of Japanese documents. In time the marines realized they needed help and requested the army to provide them with Nisei linguists. Nisei thereafter fought alongside the marines in all their major battles, including Iwo Jima and Okinawa. Still, during the war, uniformed Nisei were not allowed on the premises of the navy's Pearl Harbor command headquarters. More than a half century later, the memory of such racist practices still rankled.

Despite its exclusionary policy, the navy assembled an impressive group of Caucasian Japanese language officers in Hawaii to deal with the initially small influx of Japanese POWs that grew steadily after the war at sea heated up. POWs captured in Admiral Chester Nimitz's Central Pacific Command were normally channeled through JICPOA and eventually to the American mainland. Lt. Comdr. Frank Huggins headed the officers dealing with POWs in Hawaii. He had acquired his superb language skills before the war in the navy's special program and a subsequent tour as assistant naval attaché at the embassy in Tokyo. He impressed POWs with his fluent, often coarse Japanese, having learned the salty language used by Japanese sailors and naval officers.

Navy lieutenant Otis Cary became Huggins's deputy in Honolulu in February 1943. Born of missionary parents in the city of Otaru on Hokkaido in 1920, Cary had attended Japanese schools through the fourth grade and regarded Japanese as his mother tongue. He accompanied the Allies' first Pacific offensive operation of the war in the retaking of Attu in the Aleutians. In that operation, twenty thousand American troops opposed sixteen hundred Japanese defenders. Only twenty-six Japanese were taken prisoner; all the rest perished. As luck would have it, the first prisoner Cary interrogated happened to come from Otaru, which provided the ideal basis for the establishment of instant rapport. The prisoner gave Cary detailed information on the situation on nearby Kiska, the island that the prisoner had visited shortly before his capture and the next island on the American agenda. Another bit of good fortune was the discovery of mounds of Japanese foodstuffs. These were "liberated" and became the first really good Japanese meal Cary had had in many years.

Cary's next combat mission was on Saipan, where relatively large numbers of prisoners were taken. His chief activity, however, was the rescue of Japanese and native civilians hiding in caves along with soldiers. He succeeded in persuading one prisoner to return to a cave and convince terrified civilians there that they would not be shot if they came out.

Cary's success with POWs rested not only on his ability to use familiar, slangy Japanese rather than the more formal, schoolmasterish Japanese favored at the language schools, but also on the unassuming, thoroughly decent, humane ways he dealt with prisoners.

As he put it, "Japanese were used to being coerced and knew how to take evasive measures; if treated humanely, they lost the will to resist."[9] Cary was determined to treat prisoners not as enemies but as human beings, individuals who deserved to have a bright future aiding the reconstruction of a new, democratic Japan. He initiated and led the effort to recruit a group of POWs to assist in drafting surrender leaflets and similar pro-Allied activities, convinced that by cooperating in such tasks they could hasten the day of Japan's liberation from the militarist yoke and bring about the dawn of a democratic era. This small group of men was willing to take the risk, in their mind, that the United States might betray its own lofty principles and reduce Japan to a colonial status. One of the volunteers in this idealistic task wanted to make sure their motivation was understood. He told Cary: "We are doing this for ourselves. It's not for your side and we are not going to become your pawns. Don't misunderstand us."[10]

Many years later, when Japanese wrote up their wartime experience in prison camps, Otis Cary's name was the only one cited repeatedly. When the war ended he brought messages from his incarcerated "friends" to their families, assuring them their loved ones were still alive, and remained in contact with many of them throughout his long postwar career in Japan, where he taught at Doshisha University in Kyoto. Shortly after the war, Cary had the opportunity to meet the emperor's younger brother. He successfully used the occasion to suggest to Prince Takamatsu that he urge the emperor to begin getting to know his subjects by traveling among them. Shortly thereafter, the emperor started doing just that. Cary's superb language skills were such that he wrote his memoirs on his experiences with Japanese POWs in Japanese. For the many Japanese who either knew him personally or through his writings and media appearances, Otis Cary typified what was best in American society.

Caucasian language officers had one advantage over the Nisei in dealing with the POWs. Understandably, Nisei felt that they were under constant scrutiny in their relations with the prisoners, especially during the early stages of the war; consequently, they tended to be careful to maintain strictly businesslike contacts with the POWs. Caucasian army and navy language officers, however, felt no such constraint. Many sought out the prisoners in their enclosure just to test out or improve their language skills or because they were curious to learn more about the prisoners' mysterious home country. Nowhere was this easy social intercourse more prevalent than at Pearl Harbor. Eschewing the normal venue for interrogations, Commander Huggins, for example, even dressed up a trusted Japanese warrant officer in civilian clothes and took him out to share a beer at a local tavern to pursue their discussion about the capability of guns on the battleship *Mutsu* in more convivial surroundings.

A just possibly apocryphal story making the rounds of JICPOA at the time illustrates the close relationships that navy language officers established with some of their prisoners. It had Admiral Nimitz asking for some information from his chief intelligence officer, who then telephoned the language officer in charge of the Japanese prisoners. The voice answering said that the officer was unavailable as he was out buying sports equipment for the POWs. Nimitz's chief intelligence officer then asked to speak to the deputy officer in charge, only to be informed that this individual was also out of the office, taking some of the prisoners to the movies in Honolulu. Becoming quite annoyed, the chief of intelligence asked to talk to the only other Japanese language officer there but was informed that this officer too was regrettably unavailable as he was purchasing phonograph records that he thought the POWs might enjoy. Now totally exasperated, the senior officer wanted to know to whom he was speaking. "Major Tanaka, Imperial Japanese Army, Sir," was the reply.

With prisoners willing to cooperate actively with the American war effort, such free and easy relations were possible at the special POW camp in Hawaii. Occasionally, however, they went awry, as Lt. Bill Amos, who had grown up in Japan, later related. He had befriended a Japanese navy lieutenant who had been shot down and rescued after the Battle of Midway. Amos believed that they had found much in common as both were navy reservists caught up in the war, but none of these conversations produced much of intelligence value. The POW was sent to the mainland. Amos subsequently learned from an American senior officer that his "friend" had been a regular navy lieutenant commander who had participated in the raid on Pearl Harbor. None of the information the "friend" provided turned out to have been accurate. Amos's rueful comment was that he had been taken for a ride.

Nisei language personnel rarely came up with stories about developing personal ties with POWs, at least not until the war had ended. In one case, however, such a relationship developed with a peculiar Japanese twist. In 1944, Sergeant Spady Koyama interrogated Petty Officer Takayama Yoshio on New Guinea. Before he was sent to a stockade in Australia, Takayama asked Koyama for his name and address so that he could express appreciation after the war for the many kindnesses Koyama extended to him and many other prisoners. Koyama explained that he would not provide this information because it might jeopardize his family members living in Japan, but that he would find a way to reestablish contact after the war. Koyama was wounded on Leyte, but when he arrived in Japan, he managed to trace Takayama through Japan's Demobilization Bureau. Then living in Tokyo, Koyama sent money to his wartime acquaintance so that he could make the trip from Kyushu. At their reunion, Takayama offered to become his servant as repayment for Koyama's helpfulness. Koyama turned him down on the grounds that Takayama had a family to take care of. A week later, Takayama's eighteen-year-old relative Hirano appeared at Koyama's door as Takayama's "replacement." After extensive negotiations, Hirano finally agreed to a solution that involved Koyama's finding him a job in Tokyo and Hirano's doing odd jobs around Koyama's house in his spare time.

In 1989 Takayama and Hirano both visited Koyama at his home in Spokane. Koyama had also invited his good friend Sam Grashio, who had been an American POW of the Japanese in the Philippines. Takayama and Grashio exchanged stories about the very different treatment they had received at the hands of their respective wartime enemies. As this encounter came to an end, Takayama, stating that he was "representing his entire nation," formally apologized to all those Americans mistreated during the war. Grashio graciously accepted the apology, and the two aging men declared themselves friends.

6

THE INTERROGATIONS

Frontline troops were not easily persuaded of the wisdom and utility of taking prisoners when they themselves could expect no mercy from the Japanese. Hatred of the enemy was intense, and there was little confidence that a fanatical Japanese soldier holding his hands high above his head could be trusted to abide by the Geneva Convention in the process of surrendering. Senior officers opposed the taking of prisoners on the grounds that it needlessly exposed American troops to risks, and this attitude was conveyed to the men under their command. According to the troops' conventional wisdom, there was little or no likelihood that the fanatical Japanese would divulge anything of military value.

Army captain John Burden had spent years as a plantation physician in Hawaii ministering to Japanese immigrant laborers, was fluent in Japanese, and brought keen insights into Japanese psychology to his tasks as a Japanese language officer in the southwest Pacific. He was one of the first graduates of the Fourth Army Intelligence School, organized in September 1941. Burden was the first Japanese language officer in combat operations on Guadalcanal in December 1942. Following the American conquest of the island, Burden was ordered back to language schools in the United States to lecture on his observations of Japanese POW interrogations.

Captain Burden also wrote a lengthy report on his experiences. It was remarkable in that it blamed the American officers he had encountered for the paucity of Japanese POWs. In one instance, Burden noted, a regimental commander censured a lower unit for bringing in prisoners, saying, "Don't bother to take prisoners; shoot the sons of bitches."[1]

In his report on the Guadalcanal POW interrogations, Burden also noted that on "several occasions word was telephoned in from the front line that a prisoner had been taken, only to find after hours of waiting that the prisoner had 'died' en route to the rear. In more than one instance there was strong evidence that the prisoner had been shot and buried because it was too much bother to take him in."[2]

Burden also complained that the troops had no idea of the value of Japanese documents. American soldiers were primarily interested in obtaining souvenirs. Since diaries were "usually well illustrated with sketches and maps, and the hieroglyphics held all the intrigue of the Orient," very few were turned in to intelligence personnel who might have turned them to good use. Burden further took the military to task for their failure to allow Nisei language personnel in combat areas, because their superior language capabilities would help extract intelligence from POWs. In wartime, taking on one's senior officers in that fashion took a great deal of courage.

Burden immediately embarked on a campaign to convince senior officers that taking Japanese prisoners could be fruitful. He even managed to get cooperative commanders to offer three-day passes and ice cream to anyone bringing in a POW. That resulted in an immediate response, and Burden's team scored some of the war's earliest interrogation successes. Burden also pioneered the use of surrender leaflets and loudspeaker surrender appeals in the Pacific War.

The missionary efforts of army Japanese language officers like Burden eventually convinced senior officers, and through them the combat units, to take prisoners of war, even to assume a certain degree of risk in the process. The navy needed far less persuasion, given the different circumstances under which it was able to take unarmed prisoners from ships sunk at sea.

With little motivation for taking prisoners during the war's first year, few Japanese prisoners were available to be interrogated. When Japanese did become POWs and were in sufficiently good physical condition to respond to questions, it was believed advantageous to interrogate them immediately. Prisoners might well have time-sensitive information that could affect the course of ongoing or impending battles. It was also initially thought that the sooner prisoners were interrogated, the less the chance of their concocting plans with fellow POWs to give false information. In short, the Americans hoped to obtain as much accurate information as they could get, as fast as they could get it.

When the unthinkable occurred and Japanese POWs were confronted with the reality of facing an interrogator all alone, they reacted in many different ways, making broad generalizations impossible. An extensive perusal of interrogation reports and the recollections of those who interrogated the POWs indicate that a majority of POWs provided information if they had any to give. Not having been indoctrinated about dealing with enemy interrogations, Japanese POWs were at a distinct disadvantage when confronted with a friendly face that offered them a cigarette. Most of the lower ranks, with some exceptions, were not in a position to provide intelligence of any value. This was especially so for those with a limited education in prewar Japan (four to eight years of primary school), who constituted 87 percent of the prisoners in the Pacific. Some prisoners gave information only in response to questions, but at least as many others talked freely and even occasionally revealed information that had not even been solicited. There were POWs who initially gave false information and subsequently volunteered corrections or amended their stories when discrepancies were brought to their attention. Many were clearly uncomfortable with lying, and when they did, were seldom successful. Some prisoners tried to safeguard what they believed was sensitive intelligence by keeping mum or concocting something. One POW imaginatively made up information that covered twenty pages in the report on him, but interrogators concluded it was all a lie when the information did not conform with intelligence on the same subject that had already checked out.

Japanese POWs, however, had little understanding of what, specifically, most interested the Americans. One POW made no apparent efforts to evade responding to questions, but when caught up in contradictions burst into tears, protesting that he was telling all he knew to the best of his ability. Another POW apologized for his ignorance of military matters, explaining that he had been in uniform only a short time.

Japanese propaganda had stressed both Japan's uniqueness and the inability of foreigners to understand the country and its people. When Japanese-speaking interrogators demonstrated what to the prisoners was a surprising amount of knowledge of their country and even specific intelligence about their own units, POWs became confused. They often assumed that their interrogators already "knew everything," so that by giving information they were not really providing anything new. In fact, interrogations often consisted of attempts to obtain corroborative or confirming information. Japanese were found to be very receptive to the idea that they should help their interrogators get the information straight. It was almost as if they were back in the classroom again, taking satisfaction from giving correct answers and perhaps even telling the teacher, an authority figure, something he had not known before. Japanese prisoners hardly ever stood mute, refusing to engage in conversation. They probably thought it impolite, or may have believed that they were obligated to reply to questions from someone in authority, even if he was the enemy.

In their approach to interrogations, Japanese POWs often did not keep uppermost in their minds the protection of possibly sensitive information. By far their greatest worry was whether news of their capture would be relayed to their families. Prisoners were routinely asked, in accordance with the Geneva Convention, whether they wished to have the Japanese government, and through it their families, informed that they were alive in captivity. Only a tiny minority of prisoners accepted the offer. For most of them, this was the last thing they wanted. Some even volunteered to tell their interrogators anything they wanted to know in return for a promise that their status as POWs was *not* made known to their families. Such promises were normally given in good faith but were difficult to keep. Once the prisoners reached the rear areas and representatives of the International Committee of the Red Cross insisted on getting their names, in accordance with the requirements of the Geneva Convention, these names were routinely passed to the Japanese government. The Japanese authorities, in turn, kept the information from the POWs' families, assuming that the next of kin would not wish to know about such shame having befallen their loved one. In any event, owing to the widespread use of assumed names in the prison camps, of which the Japanese authorities may well have been aware, the American breaches of trust did not necessarily affect adversely either the prisoners' fate or their families in Japan.

In his report on interrogation techniques, Captain Burden stated that a threat to send prisoners' names back to Japan was a most effective weapon in the hands of interrogators. Aside from the Burden report, there is no anecdotal or other evidence that such threats were used. Otis Cary, the navy interrogator at the Joint Intelligence Center Pacific Ocean Area (JICPOA) in Hawaii, stated that although there were plenty of rumors about pressuring prisoners, such methods were foreign to his camp.[3] As Cary had pointed out, the Japanese were accustomed to evading coercion but could not resist when treated humanely.[4] Former prisoners' autobiographies make no reference even to implied threats of this nature, and a large sampling of American interrogation reports does not indicate that such threats were made.

Even though the Americans did not use anything like force to make Japanese POWs talk, on one occasion serious consideration was given to using sodium pentathol, popularly known as "truth serum," in interrogating a senior noncommissioned officer. This question was discussed at length among intelligence and headquarters personnel of the Fortieth Division in the Philippines, including all of its medical, legal, and ethical aspects. In the end it was decided not to try it.[5] Moreover, it hardly proved necessary.

Some prisoners, at least initially, demonstrated overt hostility toward their American interrogators. But such recorded cases were relatively rare and repeated contacts with Americans usually led to a lessening of such enmity.

Almost inevitably, unless they committed suicide, the indoctrination of the *Senjinkun* left the prisoners with little alternative but to seek a future in another direction. By the act of becoming prisoners, they felt that they had, in effect, ceased to be Japanese. They had therefore lost their homeland, and, by extension, their families. They feared the dire consequences of their status becoming known to their families and neighbors. The Japanese government, by totally ignoring, indeed tacitly denying, their existence, confirmed the prisoners' belief that their country no longer wanted to have anything to do with them. Consistent with these policies, no letters or packages from home were ever received by the prisoners.

When first brought before an interrogator, the typical prisoner harbored two contradictory but very real fears. One was that he was about to be killed. While widely expressed by POWs, there is no indication that this fear was instilled in him by indoctrination. Since the *Senjinkun* mandated that there would be no Japanese POWs, the Japanese government could hardly suggest what would happen to a prisoner upon capture. The apprehension was, rather, the result of experiences gained in China, where it was believed that Japanese in the hands of guerrillas were tortured and then killed. From China such stories spread through the entire armed forces, and the Japanese government did nothing to discourage them. Veterans of the China campaigns also knew well that Japanese forces had treated Chinese POWs and civilians with utmost brutality, as if their lives were worthless. They had killed, raped, and used them for bayonet practice and for bacteriological experiments, and they feared the Western Allies might want to exact revenge.

The POW's other fear was that the enemy might *not* kill him but would allow him to live out his life in shame. In his despair, a POW's first words often conveyed a request to be killed. He was expressing what the system he had grown up under expected of him in such a predicament, and there is little doubt that many genuinely felt a need to die; however, not all prisoners really wanted to, or felt they had to. This much some former POWs later admitted.

In a few instances, Japanese-American interrogators became so annoyed with repeated requests from POWs to be killed that they invited the prisoner to make a run for it. The prisoner was told that if he really wanted to die, he would be shot by the MP guard while "attempting to escape." Interrogators were virtually certain a POW would not take up the offer, and they were proven correct. In one instance, an exasperated interrogator told the prisoner to start digging his own grave. When unable to do so in the hard soil of a coral island, the prisoner was ordered to try it again, and again he failed to reach the desired depth required for a grave. Eventually he became so tired that he gave up the effort and agreed to proceed with the interrogation.

CONDUCTING THE INTERROGATIONS

At first, the army was not inclined to send Japanese Americans into combat zones, lacking confidence in their loyalty. The first Nisei linguists to arrive in the southwest Pacific theater were two sergeants with excellent ability in Japanese. With no prisoners to interrogate, however, and lacking the protection that the presence of a Caucasian language officer might have provided, they soon found themselves far from the battlefront, driving trucks in Tahiti and Tonga. It was only a chance encounter with Admiral Halsey on Fiji that enabled top linguist Captain Burden to inveigle immediate orders for Guadalcanal for himself and several Nisei. This eventually resulted in the first permanent deployment, on Guadalcanal in December 1942, of an army language team composed of Caucasian officers and Nisei enlisted men close to the front lines. Although the skepticism about using Japanese Americans was initially shared by Major General Alexander M. Patch, commander of U.S. forces on Guadalcanal, he subsequently became the Nisei's strongest supporter when, as commander of the Seventh Army in Europe, he commanded the all-Nisei 442nd Regimental Combat Team. Racial fears and prejudices among the troops were soon overcome as most GIs simply assumed that the Nisei were Chinese Americans.

Caucasian language officers conducted some interrogations in the field themselves, but normally they had Nisei on their team to serve as interpreters. Nisei also conducted many interrogations themselves. Prisoners were frequently unsure about the nationality or race of the Nisei interrogator. They asked whether he was Chinese, Korean, Taiwanese, even Malayan, never guessing that the interrogator was a Japanese American. In a few instances, the prisoner was so confused that he assumed his interrogator was a Japanese national who had found new employment with the Americans. The interrogator saw no pressing need to enlighten him. Occasionally prisoners initially resented having a "traitorous Japanese" interrogate them. But when it was explained that the Nisei interrogator was

American born and possessed American citizenship, the antagonism evaporated.

Employment of Japanese Americans in the interrogation of POWs was one of the main keys to American success in this field. In addition to their language skills, most also retained from their home environment an understanding of Japanese cultural values that could not be achieved by study. It was, however, a long, hard road before their outstanding contributions to our intelligence successes in the Pacific were truly appreciated.

When the interrogations began, an estimated half of the prisoners used false names to ensure that their families would never hear of their disgrace. They apparently used any name that came into their heads at the time of the interrogation, without a great deal of thinking about their choice. Most popular was the name of a friend or deceased comrade, or a slight alteration of their own name. Some became rather inventive in choosing a new name. A remarkably large number used the name of Hasegawa Kazuo, the reigning male movie idol of his time. Other popular adopted names were Miyamoto Musashi (a famous swordsman of the seventeenth century), Inano Kantaro, a well-known fictional *yakuza* (member of a mafia group), and Kondo Isamu (a well-known nineteenth-century samurai). The prize for most amusing name would go to Kondo Katsuzo. When Otis Cary heard the name, which means "next time victorious," he thought it was surely fictional. But when he looked up the prisoner with such an unlikely name, he found a grandfatherly type from the Tohoku region in Japan's north. It turned out that Next Time Victorious really was the name given him at birth.

Lacking a great deal of cultural background on Japan, many Caucasians would probably miss such historical, literary, or linguistic allusions, but they did not escape the notice of Japanese Americans, especially those who had lived for some time in Japan. While phony names are often mentioned in autobiographical accounts by Japanese POWs, the obvious aliases somehow do not appear on the interrogation reports, no doubt because they were easily spotted. The names of prisoners, in any event, made no difference to the Americans, who were much more interested in whether other information the POWs provided was accurate.

The use of aliases ultimately proved more problematical to the Japanese than to the Americans. A few promptly forgot what name they had given themselves. Some prisoners recalled having used one made-up name for the interrogation and another for their fellow prisoners in camp, whom they also wanted to keep in the dark about their true identity. This sometimes led to embarrassing situations when they forgot which name they had used with which people.

POWs also sought to ensure anonymity by falsifying other personal data, such as place of residence, unit designation, and rank. There were those who looked for cover by assuming a rank lower than their own; others may have attempted to secure special privileges by passing themselves off as having a higher rank than the one they actually held. The latter strategy, if uncovered, could later create problems for them, since fellow prisoners resented anyone trying to secure privileges to which they were not entitled. Moreover, since officers and NCOs were assumed to have had a better-than-average chance of possessing information of intelligence value, they became special targets for the interrogators.

Sergeant Sus Toyota devised a clever way of dealing with officer POWs suspected of seeking to hide their rank. In an interrogation on the outskirts of Manila, two prisoners were brought in, both claiming to be superior privates. By his demeanor, one of the POWs appeared to be an officer. Toyota brought two stools into the enclosure, sat down on one, and waited to see what might develop. As expected, one of the prisoners promptly offered the seat to the other, thus establishing the rank difference between the two. The lower-ranked soldier was taken away, while Toyota proceeded to interrogate the higher-ranked one on the stool. He gave him a hard time for lying about his rank. Toyota pointed out that by removing the other POW, he had avoided making the officer lose face in front of his subordinate. The officer promptly confessed his status and admitted the other prisoner was his orderly.

Interrogators generally sought to put the prisoners at ease by initially avoiding any semblance of a formal questioning. A good start was to offer the POW a cigarette, which few could resist, and it set the mood for the "conversation" that followed. The prisoner might be asked whether he was being well treated, whether he was getting enough food, and whether he had any physical discomfort. Interrogators were usually successful in getting prisoners to talk about familiar subjects, such as their hometown and neighborhood. Such friendly banter was an unobtrusive way of getting the prisoners to start talking. The more they revealed about themselves, the better the chances they would eventually disclose information of interest to the interrogator. Although interrogators were provided with a checklist of subjects to cover, starting with name, rank, and serial number, the good ones would only get around to such matters after they had succeeded in establishing personal rapport.

The unsuspecting prisoner would not normally realize the interrogators already had, or would later receive from other prisoners, information that either corroborated or disproved anything he might say. Interrogators would sometimes discover a diary on the POW or find his real name sewn on his uniform. More often than not, a prisoner who had lied initially would later become extremely apologetic and remorseful, opening up even more to the interrogator than would otherwise have happened.

Some of the initial interrogations in the Pacific used techniques developed by the British in interrogating German prisoners of war. These stressed the utility of adopting a "tough" approach, but interrogators soon discovered that what worked in Europe was most unlikely to be productive in the Pacific. Japanese prisoners tended already to be very hard on themselves for having surrendered and regarded the enemy's physical and verbal abuse as justified. The tough approach, therefore, only worked to strengthen any remaining determination to observe the strictures of Bushido. Even the "good cop, bad cop" scenario so familiar from Western movies was unlikely to produce results.

Interrogators in the Pacific were far more likely to achieve success with Japanese prisoners if they adopted a soft approach. Sometimes they even told prisoners that they would never pressure the POWs for information or put a bayonet to their throats in order to get them to appeal to their comrades to surrender. Such assurances would go a long way toward easing the prisoners' uncertainties. The gentle approach was especially effective with the lower ranks, by providing a clear contrast with the way they had been treated by superiors in the Japanese military. The fact that humane treatment came as a total surprise only added to its effectiveness. It placed the Japanese prisoners in the context of an entirely new relationship, for which they had neither guidance nor experience, and it made them vulnerable to exploitation for intelligence purposes in ways not disallowed under the Geneva Convention.

A Japanese POW captured in Burma, Shinoda Toshikazu, told his captors that he believed it would be best for him to die a "beautiful death." He recalled his own brutality during his service in China and could not comprehend any treatment at Allied hands other than equally brutal treatment, which appeared "fearfully unattractive."[6] His ultimate perplexity was that Americans, at that stage of the war, treated POWs as human beings, as they would have wanted the Japanese to treat any Americans held as POWs.

Most prisoners came into captivity alone or in very small groups. Virtually all believed at first that they must be the only ones to have fallen into such disgrace, often leading them to provide false information. Once they learned, to their immeasurable relief, that there were other prisoners and that they would be well treated, their willingness to provide accurate information increased markedly. For this reason, contrary to initial American practices, it was found that allowing prisoners to mingle with others who had been in captivity for a longer period served to ease their fears and improved the success rate of interrogations. This was one of many examples where procedures based on American common sense had to be revised to take into account the need to deal with POWs who had been raised in a completely different culture.

The first interrogation normally took place at battalion or regimental level, close to the front lines. At that level, interrogators focused on gaining combat intelligence of use to their own units. They wanted to know about the identity, size, and equipment of enemy units facing them, the orders given them before they were captured, and other information that could relate to enemy plans. These initial interrogators were not even required to obtain "name, rank, and serial number," but routinely noted such information anyway. The interrogated prisoner would then be moved to rear areas as soon as possible to avoid any possibility of recapture by the Japanese and to allow higher headquarters to reinterrogate on their particular subjects of interest. Depending on the prisoner's willingness to talk freely and the amount of intelligence in his possession, he would be interrogated again and again as he was moved through rear area division, corps, and army headquarters, and ultimately to permanent POW camps in the United States, Australia, New Zealand, or India. Along the way he would be questioned on a much wider range of topics, including the location of specific Japanese military units in the area, topographical features, industrial and communications targets in Japan, troop morale, effectiveness of Allied weapons, capabilities of Japanese weapons, and the identities of senior Japanese officers.

The autobiographies of Japanese POWs generally give very short shrift to the painful and stressful interrogations to which they were invariably subject. Some war memoirs cover their interrogations in a sentence or two, generally asserting that they provided no information of military value to the interrogator. Ooka Shohei's 480-page book mentions an interrogation lasting a half day conducted by a Nisei on Leyte, and when it was over, he reports, the POWs were allowed outside for picture taking and fingerprinting.[7] Although Ooka provides a detailed description of his wartime experiences, no more is said on the subject of interrogations. Moriki Masaru, a wounded army sergeant captured on New Guinea, heard about interrogations from fellow prisoners who had also been wounded. He resolved "to say nothing that could benefit the enemy or harm Japan."[8] This fairly typical way of dealing with the issue in memoirs revealed that the prisoners believed they really knew what would and would not benefit the enemy. It also suggests that they probably covered a broad range of issues in discussions with their interrogators. Moriki noted that there was a fellow by the name of Yabuchi at the hospital where he was recuperating. None of the POWs knew where he came from, but it was widely believed that he was receiving special treatment from the Australians, and it was rumored that he was a Japanese defector. Yabuchi went around suggesting ways other POWs might deal with the interrogations in ways pleasing to the Australians. If the interrogations did not go well, Yabuchi said, he would find a way to inflict punishment. Some of the POWs were swayed by Yabuchi and followed his orders, Moriki reports.

Ensign Toyota Jo, a graduate of the naval academy, two-thirds of whose 1940 graduating class was killed in the war, was one of the relatively few who attempted briefly to analyze his own behavior under interrogation.[9] Shot down near Guadalcanal in April 1943 and drifting on the ocean, Toyota believed he had five unpalatable choices, including getting eaten by sharks. But the fate he most feared, he writes, was that of becoming a prisoner. Toyota was eventually rescued and brought to Pearl Harbor, where he was repeatedly interrogated by Lt. Comdr. Frank Huggins. Initially he was evasive, his replies liberally laced with "I don't know" and "I can't remember." While under interrogation, he came to believe that a POW is no longer in the Japanese military because it was impermissible to become one in the first place; by the same token, he was not even a Japanese anymore. By virtue of his new, self-designated status, he had become a man without a country and no longer connected to the military. Such an individual should not be questioned about military matters, he thought. On the other hand, having already surrendered, perhaps any other acts deemed disloyal might be considered less culpable. Besides, Toyota pondered, the *Senjinkun*'s precepts might not have been intended to apply to the "extreme situations" on the battlefield.

Toyota recalled that Huggins repeatedly sought to discover the route he had taken from Japan to his destination in Rabaul. Toyota provided some general information and evaded specifics, thereby avoiding, he believed, becoming a "traitor" to the country he appeared no longer to acknowledge as his own. Huggins was polite. He reassured Toyota by telling him that many other Japanese had become prisoners. He plied the prisoner with cigarettes and urged him to be thankful to the Americans for saving his life. Toyota countered that this argument was unreasonable, pointing out that he had not asked to be rescued at sea and had no reason to feel obligated to the Americans. Huggins said that he knew all about the Bushido code of honor, which led him to inquire why Toyota had not killed himself. Toyota replied that he had tried to swim toward an island in order to fight another day. He also admitted in his journal that he had a strong desire to live and a growing curiosity about how the war would end.

Toyota believed more than anything else that he needed to find a reason for his continued existence. He had not wanted to betray his fatherland, but by surrendering he had already done so. At other times he had the feeling that answering the interrogator's questions might be a worse betrayal of one's country than becoming a POW. Toyota's impulses at the time and his memory of events that transpired in this period of immense stress and despair were clearly contradictory. This fact, however, gives it the strong ring of truth. That so many others could recall so very little about one or more such painful episodes as interrogations only testifies to humankind's ability to repress what it wants to forget.

Matsubara Shunji was the well-educated 1930s liberal (portrayed in chapter 4) who did not entirely hide from himself his desire to avoid dying a needless death. Almost immediately after surrendering, he had felt the sense of enmity drain from him, to be replaced by a human bond with his captors. Newly arriving captives at the Brisbane (Australia) POW camp where Matsubara was interned generally feared the interrogations. It was rumored that prisoners would be extensively questioned and that those who had to stand trial for war crimes never returned to the camp. Until interrogations were concluded to the satisfaction of the Allies, therefore, no prisoner could breathe free. Matsubara was blindfolded, transported to another location, and placed in a small cell, his only human contact the Australian guard who brought him his meals. He failed in efforts to contact other Japanese POWs whom he presumed to be in the same structure.

The resumption of interrogations, contrary to Matsubara's fears, brought him a sense of relief by reestablishing a human bond with his interrogator. In passable Japanese, an American lieutenant offered him a seat and gave him a welcome cigarette. The American "amazed" him when he wrote down the Chinese characters for his unit's designation. What they discussed were "not serious matters," but the interrogations went on daily for over a week. Matsubara was so depressed by his living space that he asked whether he might not be released to the permanent POW enclosure by his birthday. To his great surprise, the wish was granted. On his return to the camp, the Australian commander pulled him aside and presented him with gifts from his interrogator—toothpaste, Lucky Strike cigarettes, cake, chocolate, and an English-Japanese dictionary, together with wishes for a happy birthday. Forty-five years later he still had not forgotten the emotional impact of that gesture.

POWs not yet interrogated gathered around Matsubara to ascertain what sorts of questions he had been asked, but Matsubara does not, in his memoirs, inform his readers what they were. He provides no further details on this matter except to write that American interrogation methods were effective, using one means after another until they found out what worked, "rather like American military tactics generally."[10]

One survivor of Iwo Jima, Ishii Shuji (see chapter 4), surmised that the interrogators at Pearl Harbor only asked questions to which they already knew the answers.[11] This interrogation technique was often used to establish the veracity of information interrogators were getting from other sources, but it hardly followed that Americans limited all questions this severely. Ishii concluded, however, that it made no sense to hold back information since the Americans already had all the answers. Evidently concerned that he might have gone too far in his narrative, Ishii concluded this "explanation" of his reaction to American interrogation by assuring his readers: "Even though Japan might be on its last legs, I would not have hastened the day of its defeat." While conceding that his becoming a POW might have been unfortunate, Ishii felt that since Japanese power had already been drastically reduced by then, soldiers who had been barely hanging on to life should express their appreciation to the Americans who had contributed to their survival.

Ishii also writes about his interrogation experience at the supersecret Camp Tracy in California, but only in passing. It was already August 1945 by the time he arrived there. His responses to questions were noncooperative or were wisecracks intended as unresponsive replies. Besides, they related to such mundane topics as whether he personally knew any Japanese politicians and whether the Korean railways were single or double track. Although life at Tracy was strangely liberating because the prisoners could purchase goods from a PX, the fact that the room he shared with another man was locked at all times caused him to think that something fishy was going on in that facility. As it later turned out, he was not mistaken.

The artillery NCO on Iwo Jima, Nakajima Yoshio, who hid in a cave until his suicide attempt failed (see chapter 4), was another one of those brought to Camp Tracy.[12] Within a few days his interrogation began, conducted by a man who called himself Coleman and claimed to have been a businessman in Kobe for thirteen years. Nakajima astutely deduced that he must be in an intelligence facility. He was puzzled as to why the Americans would want to interrogate him since surely POWs of higher rank must have been available. The questioning continued an hour a day for at least a week; his total stay at what he ironically called the "hotel" was three weeks.

Coleman asked him for detailed information on the specifications of Japanese warships, using a large, detailed drawing. Nakajima wondered whether this made any sense since he was aware that most of the Japanese fleet had already been sunk. He had decided to clam up when the interrogation started, but in the end he apparently responded to all questions, as implied when he admits, in his memoirs, that he felt a "great deal of shame." Later on he worried that in his naïve way he had succumbed to Coleman's "gentlemanly" interrogation technique and betrayed his country. Clearly, the isolation that enveloped him contributed to his declining morale. Although later given a roommate, Nakajima adopted a rather reserved attitude, not entirely trusting him. When they parted company they did not even exchange addresses.

On one occasion, Coleman "slipped up" and referred to an earlier discussion with Nakajima that the latter could not recall having had; with his roommate, Nakajima figured out that the Americans must be surreptitiously listening to what was being said in their room. They failed to find listening devices but were certain the room was bugged. On Nakajima's final day in camp, Coleman reviewed all the subjects they had previously covered during his interrogation, probably to check the accuracy of his information. The ever-courteous Coleman then effusively thanked Nakajima for his troubles and bid good bye to "Nakajima-san." Nakajima was astounded by the courtesy of being addressed in such a polite way, considering his rather humble station in life.

In the first years of the war, American interrogators found that some POWs remained entirely uncooperative, sullen, and arrogant but that even they often came around to talking more freely when the interrogators had enough time to spend with them. Almost invariably, POWs reacted favorably to the good medical treatment and ample food they received. Americans realized that interrogating an enemy with such a totally different cultural background had to be learned through trial and error. Preconceptions had to be abandoned along the way for new ideas that showed greater promise.

Marine Corps major Sherwood F. Moran, who had grown up in Japan and spoke Japanese fluently, laid out the criteria for a really good interrogator.[13] Moran had learned the importance of dealing with each prisoner on a "human-to-human" level rather than treating him simply as the "enemy" or "prisoner." The prisoner must be pitied, not hated, and it was insufficient to adopt such a pose; it was essential that one really feel it sincerely because the prisoner "will know the difference." An American who had lived in Japan had the advantage in being able to talk about places, events, and people familiar to both, and to note the pleasant times he had spent in the prisoner's country. Empathy with the prisoner was the key to establishing rapport. All else was likely to develop more easily after that.

Instead of following a prescribed checklist of questions or topics that the higher-ups had thoughtfully prepared, Moran found it more effective to ask questions to which the prisoner could easily respond. As Moran phrased it so cogently, "Make him [the prisoner] and his troubles the center of the stage, not you and your questions of war problems. Know where the prisoner is psychologically and focus on his wounds and other needs." Then, as one of Moran's prisoners did, they would be apt to ask, "Won't you please come and talk to me every day?"

Following the routine interrogations on tactical and strategic matters of interest, a select group of prisoners was also extensively queried on wide-ranging political, societal, and economic issues. POWs selected for this intensive exercise were often well-educated university graduates who had demonstrated some degree of willingness to cooperate with the Americans, at least to the extent of stating their views frankly and without reservation. One of the POWs thought the Americans wanted to obtain a kind of broad public opinion survey in order to prepare for the occupation of Japan, and he probably guessed right. These interrogations covered topics such as views on the emperor and the imperial institution generally, the education and political systems, the *zaibatsu* (corporate conglomerates) and leading financiers, prominent politicians and ultranationalist organizations. Prisoners were also questioned on their personal histories and on the morale of the Japanese armies in China and Manchuria. In an atmosphere made as collegial as possible by the interrogators, the Japanese often expressed astonishment at the depth of American knowledge concerning Japanese institutions and practices.

Among interrogators, navy lieutenant Otis Cary had an unexcelled knack of penetrating Japanese reserve and limiting the gulf that separated a POW from his captor and an enlisted man from an officer. He instinctively knew how to put people at ease so that they felt comfortable in his nonthreatening presence. This was not simply the result of a persona specially created for the occasion of an interrogation; it was Cary's personality, and he put it to good use on days he greeted the new prisoners at the POW stockade in Hawaii.

Cary was the first officer to address new arrivals at the Iroquois Point POW camp in Hawaii. Years later, many prisoners recalled with delight their first introduction to Cary. After relaxing them with introductory remarks that stressed they would not be harmed or harassed, Cary had them line up in a long row. He asked all privates first class to take one step forward, then the next higher rank two steps forward, and so forth. After he reached the rank of navy lieutenant or army captain, there was usually no further movement, but Cary persisted in calling out all the officer ranks in proper order. When he reached the rank of four star general/admiral without a response, he would say with mock surprise, "What, no generals or admirals?" With that, Cary won his audience. The men burst out in prolonged laughter at the absurdity of thinking that persons of such august rank would ever become prisoners.

Cary had the ability to use almost any of the many levels of Japanese politeness in his choice of language, but he deliberately used the coarser, more colloquial tone as a means of breaking down what he considered the excessively rigid rank structure in the Japanese military. He felt constrained to observe the Geneva Convention requirements concerning separating POW officers from enlisted ranks, but with that exception, he treated all men the same. His goal was to promote camp leadership by those of an independent mind with natural ability that had been repressed by the emphasis on rank.[14]

Cary won the admiration of the prisoners not only for his command of Japanese, knowledge about Japan, and understanding of the Japanese psyche. He received their respect for his evident humanity. Following lengthy discussions, many eventually also found persuasive Cary's argument that the prisoners had given their all in the service of their country, had nothing to be ashamed of, and should look forward to contributing to the reconstruction of a postwar Japan.

The other notable interrogator at JICPOA was Lt. Comdr. Frank Huggins, who received high accolades from prisoners for always being a "gentleman," even if he did occasionally swear and yell at them. As a career navy officer, Huggins had one asset that Cary lacked. He could bark questions at the awed prisoners using the vocabulary and rough phrasings used by Japanese officers in addressing enlisted men. Some prisoners then responded reflexively with the ingrained Japanese desire to have the right answers.

More commonly, though, it was the "soft" approach that paid the best dividends. Japanese POWs hardly knew what to make of the "nice" way they were treated. "Weren't the interrogators still the enemy?" The enemy's unwillingness to assume the proper "enemy role" made it difficult for the prisoner to adopt the correct role prescribed by the Bushido code. This led one former staff member of Japan's Combined Fleet to readily inform Huggins under interrogation that he had served on the super-dreadnoughts *Yamato* and *Musashi,* details on the armaments and other capabilities of which were among the highest intelligence targets for Admiral Nimitz's headquarters. The Americans knew only about the existence of the two battleships but not whether they had even been launched, or when they might be. Since the Americans believed that the batteries on these ships were likely to outgun those on the newest American battleships, information on their armaments was of the greatest interest. Huggins got at least some of the information he was seeking.

EXTRACTING INTELLIGENCE

Japanese prisoners identified as having had access to significant technical and strategic information, particularly individuals with a background in radio communications, code work, intelligence, or key industrial targets were eventually brought to one of two supersecret facilities built especially for the extraction of intelligence from POWs. Late in the war, the eligibility criteria for interrogation at these centers became much less selective. The two intelligence-gathering centers built in the continental United States were based on a pioneering British model. The British government had briefed American military experts on the concept in the latter half of 1941, before America's entry into the war. An American study of the British example confirmed the utility of intensive interrogations by trained personnel at a central facility. It was believed that more strategic intelligence could be gained in this manner than was normally collected shortly after the prisoner's capture.

Ubiquitous wiretapping was the key feature at the two facilities. Interrogations were recorded, unbeknownst to the person being interrogated, so that material could be reviewed and analyzed at leisure. In addition, when two or more prisoners were confined to a cell, their conversations were recorded. Overheard opinions on interrogations just concluded often provided important clues about the reliability of information the prisoners had just given.

Under the aegis of the Provost Marshal General and the Office of Naval Intelligence, the first facility was built at Fort Hunt off the George Washington Parkway in Virginia, near Washington, D.C. Indicative of the priority it was given, construction began in May 1942 and was concluded just three months later, with all microphones, recorders, and transcribers in place. This facility was used for German and Italian prisoners, although at least one senior Japanese naval officer was interrogated there near the end of the war. An identical facility began operations in 1943 at Byron Hot Springs (Camp Tracy), California, in an isolated area west of Stockton. The Camp Tracy facility was used mainly for Japanese prisoners and for an overflow of Germans.

Great care was taken to ensure that knowledge of the facilities was strictly limited to those with a need to know. In internal documents they were not classified as POW camps but as "temporary detention centers." This ensured that the International Committee of the Red Cross and third-party diplomatic protecting powers did not get

wind of their existence. Angel Island near Tiburon in San Francisco
Bay was the holding station and "cover" for the intelligence operations at Camp Tracy. All POWs destined for Tracy and their records
were routed through Angel Island.

Camp Tracy could accommodate 44 prisoners. Its table of organization called for 80 officers and 104 enlisted personnel, a ratio of
Americans to prisoners that indicates how much effort went into the
operation. All Americans at Camp Tracy used aliases. (One of the
Japanese Americans on the staff went by the name Tojo.) Roughly
half of the interrogators were Nisei, the other half Caucasians. The
daily roster indicated that interrogations lasted an average of forty-
five minutes, with some as short as twenty minutes and the longest
lasting two hours. As many as twenty interrogations took place in a
single day. The last interrogation at Camp Tracy took place on October 1, 1945, six weeks after the war had ended.[15]

In its first year of operations, Camp Tracy processed more German than Japanese POWs because there were so few of the latter.
The number of Japanese POWs at Camp Tracy increased from just
71 in 1943 to 921 in 1944 and 1,121 in 1945. In the summer of 1945,
many of the Japanese diplomats and military attachés taken prisoner
in Europe were also temporarily quartered and interrogated at Camp
Tracy. Close to half of the roughly five thousand Japanese POWs
who ended up in the continental United States at the time Japan surrendered appear to have been interrogated at the Byron Hot Springs
facility. It is not entirely clear whether such an exceptionally large
effort was merited, or whether valuable information was gained that
might have been acquired through more conventional intelligence-
gathering means.

At Camp Tracy the pattern of interrogations largely duplicated
experiences obtained nearer to the front lines; prisoners initially
unwilling to talk were gradually won over. Given that much more
time was spent on preparations for the interrogations at Camp Tracy,
that interrogators had ample opportunity to pursue various leads,
and that the veracity of statements could be easily cross-checked with
other information on the same subjects, the success ratio may have
been quite high. An assessment at Camp Tracy concluded that "one
in two or three prisoners provided information that showed dis-

crepancies relative to previous interrogations or otherwise known information. Generally, information became more reliable over time at the hands of skilled Nisei and Caucasian interrogators."[16]

Overall, the intelligence success rate was mixed. Some reports indicated that the information gained was of no value because the prisoner had had little military experience or lacked powers of observation.[17] On the other hand, the interrogations of four medical officers on March 27, 1945, yielded data on Japanese biological weapons capabilities and the existence of the Biological Experimental Center in Harbin, Manchuria. Similarly, two navy enlisted men gave their interrogators much information on training and ships in the Japanese fleet, including armaments, tonnage, cruising speed, and maximum speed. They also provided information on Japan's two super-battleships, including specifications on their main and secondary batteries, range finders, and fire control locations. Another talkative POW, captured on Iwo Jima and described as a well-educated intellectual, provided information on Japanese radar installations on the island, various munitions plants, and the organization of the 109th Division. He even spoke freely about a Japanese intelligence unit that specialized in radio intercepts and provided the code names for certain army units.

A navy paratrooper from the Karashima unit interrogated at Camp Tracy provided extensive information on Japan's largest naval base, at Yokosuka, including detailed sketches of its fortifications, gun emplacements, munitions storage, and training areas. A petty officer spoke freely about the Sasebo naval base on Kyushu, identifying munitions depots, warehouse locations, radar installations, barracks, and experimental torpedoes.[18] A seventy-six-page document produced at Camp Tracy reported on the Japanese mammoth submarine I-1, sunk by a New Zealand corvette on January 29, 1943, off Guadalcanal. The report was based on documents captured at the time of the sub's sinking and on interrogation of its three surviving crew members and covered the complete record of the ship's cruises, capabilities, and tonnage.

An interrogation officer at Camp Tracy or Fort Hunt normally required three hours of preparation for every hour with the prisoner. The prisoner was called in after it was ascertained that no significant

138 · THE INTERROGATIONS

conversation was taking place in his room. Case reports were then based on direct interrogations of the prisoner, together with relevant documentary material, conversations recorded after the prisoner returned to the room, and, at times, information provided by a stool pigeon.

Nisei linguists played a crucial part at Camp Tracy. They were needed for interrogations of high-level prisoners where accuracy was crucial, and for transcription of conversations among Japanese, which featured a good deal of colloquial language. The presence of Nisei at Camp Tracy had to be kept secret even from civilians living in the surrounding areas, not only because Japanese Americans were barred from California at the time but also to avoid tipping off the Japanese about the nature of the intelligence operation there.

A limited sampling of composite reports based on overheard room conversations of Japanese POWs at Camp Tracy suggests that despite the time and effort devoted to such surreptitious listening, this novel means of securing information produced relatively little of value. One of the reports, dated January 1945, notes that in evaluating the information, the difficulty of monitoring overheard conversations should be taken into account, suggesting that the technology was still rudimentary. This once secret report itself contained snippets of information on a large number of topics, including military units, shipping, aircraft, and equipment, that themselves were of little value. Examples of rather pointless intelligence included "Trains stop at Shirakawa for 10 minutes," or "We were constantly drilled in bayonet practice and rowing," or "Our new type airplanes are extremely fast and maneuverable." Slightly more interesting was a report covering room conversations during a week in early June 1944. At that time POWs were still confident about the course of the war. Few POWs dared talk about the possibility of Japan's losing, but prisoners expressed the unanimous determination that they would commit suicide in such an unlikely event. What the files now reveal seems inconsequential. It can be argued, however, that it is in the nature of intelligence operations that substantial effort is required to extract small nuggets of vital intelligence from huge amounts of sludge.

The Provost Marshal General's Office was responsible for assuring that the provisions of the Geneva Convention relating to the POW

Information Bureau were properly applied. It seems clear, however, that the two special intelligence facilities in the United States (as well as three others established in France, Italy, and North Africa) either violated the letter of the Geneva Convention or came very close. The Japanese government had not ratified the convention, and a large number of Japanese prisoners failed to provide their true name, rank, and serial number as required by the convention. The U.S. government may therefore have believed it was justified as well in flouting or at least skirting the convention in the case of Japanese prisoners. Indeed, whether the United States as a member of the convention had any responsibilities toward a state that had failed to ratify it is at least arguable. Prisoners at Camp Tracy were deprived of some of the rights provided for in the convention, such as ample exercise time. On the other hand, life there had extra benefits. Prisoners received exceptionally good food and had access to the PX, where large selections of alcoholic beverages, cigarettes, books, magazines, and newspapers were available. Although life in the controlled atmosphere at Camp Tracy could be boring, it did feature relatively relaxed interrogation sessions.[19]

The Geneva Convention sought to protect prisoners from divulging information as a result of physical and psychological threats. The technological advances that made it possible to overhear talk among prisoners who probably believed they were speaking in private were not foreseen. Thus, the convention did not specifically outlaw the practices employed at Camp Tracy, although a case could be made that these practices violated its spirit. A brief Provost Marshal General report on the two interrogation centers judged that "eavesdropping, while possibly repulsive, was seen as an essential, new weapon of total war" and did not attempt to analyze any further whether the centers were violating the convention.

Corroborating the interrogation records preserved at the National Archives are the recollections of the army and navy language personnel who interrogated Japanese prisoners that, sooner or later, most prisoners cooperated. Low-ranking enlisted men usually had little of intelligence value to give, and only some noncommissioned officers were really informative. Exceptions included a civilian laborer with a construction battalion (possibly an ethnic Korean), who was described in an interrogation report as "uneducated, very talkative, and intelligent." He provided exceptionally detailed information on a variety of subjects and was even knowledgeable on the names of senior officers and on military equipment. Most surprising, he had sophisticated views on economic and political conditions in Japan. The interrogators provided no hint that this prisoner might have deliberately downgraded his position in society or in the military.

Another exceptional instance of a low-ranking soldier who provided an immense amount of information was Ogino Seiichi (alias Hagihara), who was described as "extraordinarily garrulous" and endowed with a "brilliant memory." An intelligence corporal, he had been captured in the Bougainville area and subsequently spent twenty-two months at the Allied Translator and Interpreter Section in MacArthur's Brisbane headquarters getting debriefed on a host of topics. In that time span he was interrogated approximately six hundred times, resulting in twenty-five reports. He was deemed so eager to be helpful that his imagination occasionally took over, but his information proved largely correct. Much of his information pertained to industrial plants in the Kansai area around Osaka and Kobe in western Japan, an area of special interest to offices concerned with strategic bombing.

Most NCOs were protective of information that pertained to their own units. This was understandable in that Japanese loyalty often was restricted to their immediate group. They were far more willing to provide intelligence on all other matters and appeared quite unaware that talking freely on such matters could be damaging to Japan's national security.

POWs who belonged to the same unit often had sufficient cohesion even in captivity to be able to concoct mutually supportive misinformation that was fed to the interrogators. Such situations arose when sailors from the same naval vessel were incarcerated together. They had known each other and learned to trust each other over extended periods of time. Army personnel, on the other hand, were seldom captured in any sizeable numbers, and they appeared less capable of organizing themselves to tell convincing tales during interrogations.

Technical intelligence on weapons was a high-priority item, and a good deal of it was acquired from Japanese POWs. With their exceptional talent for drawing, Japanese prisoners were often pleased to be asked to supplement their verbal statements with detailed drawings on such subjects as military aircraft and warships. A fine example was the large drawing of the mammoth Japanese submarine I-24.[20]

Although officers were expected to be better informed than enlisted personnel, by no means did all have much significant intelligence to provide. Medical doctors, who constituted a relatively high percentage of officer POWs, usually could provide little more than information about the state of health of Japanese soldiers in their units, although that sort of information proved valuable at times. Of particular importance was the detailed information on significant subjects gleaned from a relatively small number of commissioned and noncommissioned officers.

Overall, the United States learned a great deal more from German than from Japanese prisoners, but given the 70:1 ratio of German to Japanese POWs in the United States at their peak, the intelligence successes against the Japanese were not insignificant. Moreover, at the outbreak of war, the United States knew less about Japan's troop dispositions, arms plants, and other matters of key interest than it did about those of Germany. In Europe, we could rely on the intelligence the British had been accumulating, and we had in-country espionage operations and extensive aerial photography. It was only in the last half year of the war that extensive aerial photography operations could be mounted over Japan, and in-country espionage was never feasible in wartime Japan.

WHY THEY TALKED

For Americans, one of the biggest surprises of the war was that the Japanese, who had fought so fanatically that few were taken prisoner in good physical shape, would provide us with any information at all, let alone give us liberally whatever information they possessed. A combination of many factors produced this unexpected result.

Japanese were not indoctrinated to any significant extent concerning the need to safeguard classified information. They were lax about the kind of written material, including diaries, that they had on them and naive about using their language in plain text to transmit military information. This laxness was directly traceable to the

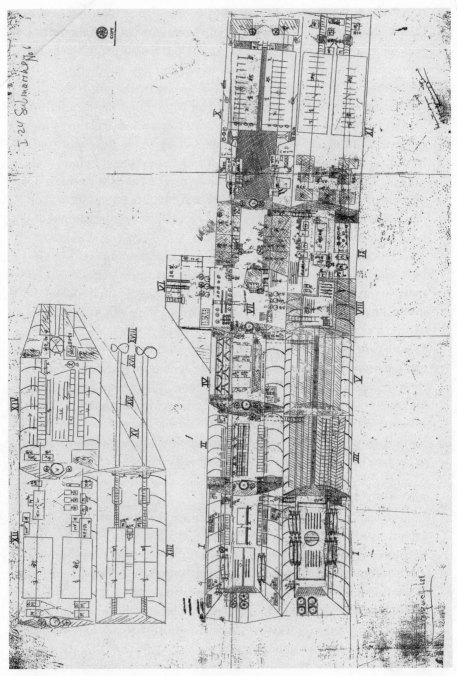

Sketch provided by a POW that identifies (in Chinese characters) armaments and other items of intelligence interest on Japanese submarine I-24 (detail of submarine midsection)

belief that foreigners could not possibly master Japanese. Since they knew that the U.S. government had incarcerated not only Japanese nationals but Japanese-American citizens as well, they were equally sure that they were not facing America's best Japanese speakers on the battlefield.

Hardly any Japanese knew about the Geneva Convention covering the rights and responsibilities of prisoners of war. As their country had not ratified the convention, almost none knew that it required only that prisoners provide their name, rank, and serial number. After that they were entitled to remain silent. The Geneva Convention, an international treaty drafted by Westerners, places prisoner and captor in a legal relationship that reserved certain rights to prisoners. Japanese, however, had no background for defining relationships in such legal terms. Seeing themselves as abject prisoners of war who had failed their country, they would not have thought it possible to have any rights at all.

Silence is by far the best weapon a prisoner determined to divulge no information can wield. It seems clear, however, that virtually none of the Japanese POWs availed themselves of it. Japanese have traditionally been uncomfortable in purely legal relationships and instinctively search for some more "human" ties. When they first met the Americans, they expected not to understand them or to make themselves understood. Some prisoners were keenly aware of how little they remembered of their school English. When the interrogator addressed them in Japanese, however poorly, they felt a strong sense of relief, impressed that a foreigner had taken the trouble to communicate with them. Perhaps unconsciously, it was their first intimation that they might live. They were no longer totally alone and at sea. They might be informed what would happen to them next. They might even ask for a drink of water.

POWs grew increasingly curious to learn more about these Americans. Prisoners who had wandered through the jungle for weeks and even months, often alone, were buoyed just by communicating with a fellow human again. Unquestionably, the Nisei's advantage of looking just like the prisoners facilitated an even freer flow of conversation. Their excellent language skills helped even more. Cpl. Ryu Itsushi was delighted to be communicating with a Nisei when taken prisoner in Burma: "Sharing the same Japanese blood, you Nisei have common feelings with me and you therefore understand my feelings."[21] Whatever the accuracy of these assumptions, they surely created the right atmosphere for a successful interrogation.

Once the Japanese prisoners opened themselves up to casual conversations with interrogators, they were at a distinct disadvantage in fencing with the interrogators' often well-disguised quest for intelligence. The prisoners often fell into the trap of believing that the Americans knew a great deal more than they actually did. Interrogators asked questions in the form of requests designed simply to confirm what they already knew, and many Japanese were only too anxious to provide the right answers. Such confirmations could help in providing yet another small piece in a much larger puzzle or in evaluating the reliability of the prisoner's statement. As soon became apparent, few Japanese prisoners resorted to outright lies, and this, too, was an important clue.

Traditionally, Japanese have lived in a society that highly prizes the reciprocal giving and receiving of favors, including those exchanged between superior and inferior. Once drawn into a "human" (that is, emotional) conversational relationship with their interrogators, the prisoners realized that they had already received many favors from their captors. They had generally been treated decently. Of particular importance to the Japanese, they had not generally been insulted or humiliated. These Americans did not look down on them with contempt. In almost all instances recorded by former prisoners, Americans had readily given them a cigarette, often more than one. The offer of a cigarette, highly prized in wartime, was a gesture of friendship that the Japanese gratefully accepted. Prisoners had been given chocolate bars and fed with K or C rations, often the first decent meal they had had in weeks or months. In one autobiography a former POW ruefully commented that when his feces disappeared in a slit trench, it represented his last possession from the time he served in the Imperial Japanese Army. Now all he had, even including the clothes he wore, came from the Americans.

In addition to all the material benefits they had received, some prisoners mused, the Americans had given them their life, if only by not killing them. For the Japanese, this huge imbalance of "favors" granted and received represented a serious problem. Many solved it by giving the Americans the only thing they had to give–answers to seemingly innocuous questions.

While Japanese prisoners were impressed by the material things the Americans shared with them, they were deeply affected by the more personal touches. They could not easily cast these aside saying the "rich Americans" could afford such things. It was not only that the Americans readily took out a cigarette from their own pack; more significant for them was that they were prepared to do so within plain sight of others. A few former Japanese POWs noted in their memoirs that they might have had the chance during the course of their military service to slip an American POW a cigarette. Now that the roles were reversed they were ashamed that they had lacked the courage to overcome the Japanese convention of the time, that all POWs of any nationality properly deserved total contempt. Prisoners so badly wounded that they could not even light or hold a cigarette were overcome with inexpressible gratitude when an orderly lit the cigarette and passed it from his lips to theirs.

Of all the many unfamiliar things the Japanese encountered in the prison camps, probably the most astounding was their medical treatment. They could hardly believe that prisoners received treatment identical to that accorded their captors. They would find themselves in hospital beds adjacent to beds occupied by their "enemy." Even more astounding, American medical orderlies deigned to lift them up with their own hands and even clean them when they soiled their bed. That Americans gave officer status to nurses often amazed the Japanese. That these nurses would not only treat lowly enemy enlisted men but also at times give them a smile astounded them even more.

Discovering that they received the same food and in the same quantities as their captors surprised them as well. For a status-conscious Japanese prisoner who viewed himself as beneath contempt, such recognition of a common humanity left an abiding impression. In this sense, the whole atmosphere of the prison camp became conducive to maintaining a civil, personal relationship with the Americans. While not designed for the purpose, in some instances this could only further American efforts to gain intelligence.

Another apparent factor in Japanese POWs' behavior, of which they themselves might well have been unaware, was that they truly believed they were now without a country, with no hope of returning to their homeland. At least one prisoner even maintained that his parents would demand he take his life once they learned he had been taken prisoner. When POWs were asked where they thought they might want to go once the war ended, they replied that they hoped to remain in Australia or in the United States. It clearly never occurred to them that, given the public's hostile feelings toward Japanese, Western allies would hardly allow them to remain in their countries. Many seriously thought of Manchuria, probably because POWs from the Nomonhan Incident had been settled there. Some even aspired to emigrate to Africa, a place representing the farthest imaginable from Japan. Having broken all human contact with their families in their mind, they were psychologically prepared in the prison camps to begin building new human ties, using whatever information they had.

What had linked the Japanese prisoners to their homeland were essentially the human bonds, the strongest being their ties to their parents and their neighborhood. Though they fervently loved their country, they viewed the emperor as one who institutionally embodied the nation's history and uniqueness. The sort of personal feelings that a British subject had for the king or queen, or the adulation the Nazis expressed for Hitler (even the ubiquitous "Heil Hitler" greetings used between ordinary people) were foreign to the Japanese mind. In contrast with the Japanese, German prisoners never believed that by the act of surrendering they had lost their country. On the contrary, the true believers among them were sustained in their captivity by their strong faith in the ideology of Nazism. The Japanese had no equivalent ideology, only the inadequate *Senjinkun,* to see them through the rough road of captivity.

ATIS personnel in Australia commented on this contrast. They had interrogated the crew of a German submarine raiding Allied shipping in the Indian Ocean. Most of the crew were described as "typical arrogant Nazi ideologues," contemptuous and hard-core enemies to the end. In interrogations they insisted on all their rights and obdurately refused to answer all questions. True, this was the report on the officers and men of only one German submarine and an elite crew at that, but similar descriptive language cannot be found in the interrogation reports of Japanese prisoners.

If any Japanese were consumed by passionate personal hatred of the enemy, of the kind common among Americans and other Westerners in Japanese captivity, it was seldom if ever evident among Japanese in the stockades. This could well have reflected their education in a society where the display of hostile personal feelings was frowned on. Questioned about their attitude toward Westerners in general, Japanese POWs tended to give Americans and the British high marks, especially as compared with fellow Asians. One might doubt the sincerity of such responses and believe that the Japanese simply wished to ingratiate themselves with their "new masters," but it seems at least equally likely that the POWs viewed their situation in starkly pragmatic ways, dealing with the unexpected as best they could. Even the survivors of the various "uprisings" of Japanese POWs in Allied prison camps took pains to emphasize that they had not meant to harm the "enemy" guards, although this was an inevitable outcome.

Although Japanese had a wartime reputation for deviousness, their interrogators maintained that by and large the Japanese they encountered were very poor liars. While many POWs revealed less than they knew, it was relatively rare for a POW to attempt to provide the interrogators with complete falsehoods.

From the Allied perspective, many interrogations succeeded in producing hoped-for results, while many others failed to do so. In the familiar "fog of war," some remained mysteries. Such a one was the interrogation of an unidentified Japanese first lieutenant.[22] We know nothing about him except what is contained in an intriguing American intelligence report that left many questions unanswered. According to the report, the lieutenant was in a group of three officers and one enlisted man of the Japanese Thirty-first Army's intelligence section who, under cover of night, buried key intelligence documents within hours of the American landings on the west coast of Saipan on June 15, 1944. The group was in the Garapan area,

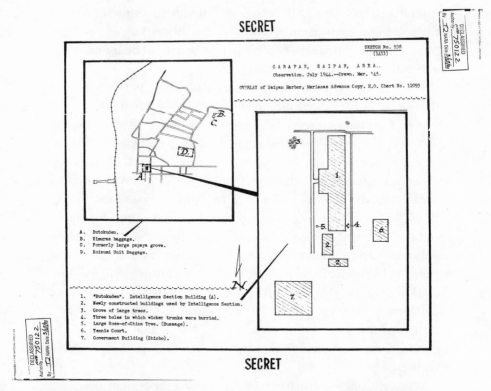

Sketch drawn by unidentified Japanese lieutenant of the location of an alleged treasure trove of secret intelligence documents buried near Saipan harbor. Document declassified 3/13/01.

approximately five miles north of the landings. The chief of the intelligence section, a Major Yoshida, supervised the burying of three trunks containing sensitive documents, the trunks wrapped in waterproof canvas to protect them from moisture damage. Before leaving the area, the four men burned down the nearby building that had housed their unit.

During the ensuing heavy fighting, Major Yoshida, Warrant Officer Sato, and an enlisted man were killed. The fourth person in the group, the otherwise unidentified first lieutenant, was captured by U.S. Army personnel on July 17, 1944. In the course of his interrogation, the lieutenant drew a detailed map that identified the precise area where the intelligence documents were buried, stating that they included an army code book, about forty maps of the Bonin

Islands, information on fortifications on Japan's home islands, books dealing with intelligence matters, and the military yearbook of 1943.

The discovery of such a treasure trove of intelligence material would have represented a major coup for the American interrogators. Yet there appears to be no corroborative evidence that it ever existed. Moreover, eight months were allowed to pass between the lieutenant's date of capture and the date it was reported by an American army intelligence organization. This gap in chronology, plus the fact that the lieutenant indicated that the three other witnesses of the burial of the alleged documents had died, suggests that the lieutenant might have attempted to perpetrate a hoax. One is left to wonder why Japanese intelligence officers would bury the documents rather than ensure their destruction by burning them, and why a Japanese intelligence officer would have wanted to present the enemy with such immensely valuable material. Was he attempting to ingratiate himself with the Americans? Perhaps the detailed maps he drew were part of a plan to ambush Americans trying to recover the documents. Did the Americans ever follow up, with or without the Japanese lieutenant in tow, to see what they might find? Like so many unanswered questions of the war, we may never learn what really happened.

Mysteries of this kind aside, evidence from both Japanese and Allied sources points to the conclusion that Japanese prisoners of war represented an important source of intelligence, sufficient to hasten the end of the war–truly remarkable considering the relative paucity of prisoners, especially those of higher rank who would have known more about what was going on.

7

A FEW VERY SPECIAL POWs

THE ADMIRAL WHO CHOSE TO LIVE—SORT OF

With so few high-ranking Japanese officers taken prisoner during the Second World War, it is hardly surprising that special circumstances attached to their capture. The most bizarre story is that of the capture of Vice Admiral Fukudome Shigeru, chief of staff of the Imperial Combined Fleet under Admiral Koga Mineichi. On March 30, 1944, the two officers were on board their flagship, the battleship *Musashi,* in the harbor of Palau Island (east of the southern Philippines), where they were planning the defense of the Marshall and Caroline Island groups and the Philippines against an American assault. Anticipating an early attack, the admirals and their staff disembarked before the *Musashi* left port. On the following day Combined Fleet Headquarters decided to relocate to Davao on Mindanao in the southern Philippines and ordered the naval base on Saipan to provide three transport aircraft to fly them there. The senior officers of the Combined Fleet left hurriedly that same evening by air without taking time to refuel.

The first plane, carrying Admiral Koga, encountered a typhoon and was never heard of again. The third plane, carrying lower-ranking staff members, reached Davao without incident. But due to the effects of the typhoon, along with equipment malfunction, the plane carrying Vice Admiral Fukudome was thrown off course until it was still one hundred sixty sea miles north of Davao. Figuring that the aircraft did not have enough fuel either to reach its destination or get to Manila, the pilot changed course to Cebu, an island in the central Philippines, which had a seaplane anchorage. While flying north along the east coast of Cebu in pitch-dark conditions, however, the crew mistook the Japanese-owned Onoda Cement plant for the lights of Cebu City and prepared to land in the water. But because of the pilot's faulty altitude estimate, the aircraft plunged into the ocean from a height of one hundred fifty feet.

Nine persons of a combined total of twenty passengers and crew were thrown out of the plane upon impact and survived, including Admiral Fukudome. The others perished in the flames that engulfed the plane. Owing to a strong current, the survivors quickly drifted into several groups. Seven who were unable to swim to the shore they could plainly see when dawn broke were spotted by a group of Filipino natives. One of these was Teniente Bolo, a senior member of the local guerrilla organization, who led a rescue party that brought the survivors to safety.

At about the same time, the two other survivors managed to swim to the Onoda Cement plant, where they reported what had happened to their plane and the existence of other survivors, including Admiral Fukudome. The Japanese naval command on Cebu, alerted to the potential loss of two of the navy's most senior officers, launched immediate search and rescue operations throughout the central and southern Philippines. The area where the two survivors had last seen the admiral was searched, but no trace could be found. The incident was so embarrassing that the suspected disappearance of Admiral Fukudome was initially kept secret even from the Japanese army.

Surmising that the captives included high-ranking officers, Bolo, together with other Filipinos, decided to bring the Japanese, under guard, to their guerrilla headquarters at Tabunan in the central mountains. At that time, Cebu was the site of the most important Japanese base in the Philippines south of Manila. It also supported one of the most active guerrilla organizations operating in the Philippines. With an estimated complement of five thousand lightly armed men, the guerrillas gave the Japanese considerable trouble. The guerrilla units had come into being after organized resistance ceased following the surrender of all U.S. armed forces in the Philippines under the command of Lt. Gen. Jonathan Wainwright.

Already by ten o'clock on the morning of April 1, the guerrillas spotted a Japanese plane overhead looking for them. In the next few days, while on the march to their headquarters, they saw many more such planes but avoided being sighted. En route the prisoners were turned over to a crack guerrilla unit whose leader persuaded the admiral to exchange clothes with him in order to foil any sudden Japanese attempts at a heroic rescue. On the following day, Japanese headquarters on Cebu received word that members of Admiral Fukudome's party had probably been captured, and promptly set out to find them, arresting any Filipinos thought to have information on the whereabouts of the prisoners and torturing a number of them.

Meanwhile, the guerrillas embarked on a tortuous journey through the jungle. The exhausted admiral had to be carried on a stretcher after a short while, and two other Japanese who had been injured in the crash were carried on the backs of the guerrillas. Finally, on April 9 the Japanese prisoners were brought before the leader of Cebu's guerrillas, Lt. Col. James Cushing. A tall mining engineer in his late thirties from the American Southwest, Cushing had drifted to Cebu, picked up some of the Cebuano dialects, married a Filipina, and developed good relations with the local population. Although he had been preparing to flee to Mindanao as the Japanese closed in on Cebu, Filipino friends persuaded him to stay on. He then developed the concept of a regional guerrilla headquarters with fairly independent geographical subunits. Cushing interrogated Admiral Fukudome, employing the services of one of the Japanese captives who spoke some English. The admiral gave his name as Vice Admiral Furumi, and downgraded his position to that of naval commander of the Makassar Straits Command with responsibility for the seas between Borneo and Celebes (now called Sulawesi) Island. The prisoners were well treated.

Hot on the trail of the guerrilla headquarters staff, Japanese planes dropped leaflets on suspected guerrilla areas demanding the return of the prisoners and documents. They also ordered the father of a Filipino girl held prisoner in Cebu to proceed to guerrilla headquarters with the same demand. Cushing desperately sought instructions by radio from MacArthur's headquarters in Brisbane on how to proceed. At last, with pressure from a reinforced Japanese regiment growing by the minute and lacking any response from Brisbane, Cushing decided he could wait no longer. Early on the morning of April 10, his small band of guerrillas almost completely surrounded by the Japanese, Cushing called a conference of headquarters staff and leaders of subordinate commands. Virtually certain that they could not escape death or capture, he was also aware that the Japanese had rounded up hundreds of Filipino civilians as hostages for use in bargaining for the safe return of the Japanese prisoners. A decision was reached to propose a deal: the guerrillas would release the Japanese captives in exchange for safe passage out of the Japanese ring.

Cushing dictated the message addressed to Lt. Col. Onishi Seiichi, commander of the Japanese regiment that surrounded his guerrillas. Major Manuel Segura, Cushing's deputy, wrote it down. Commander Yamamoto Yuji, a planning officer on Admiral Fukudome's staff who had been on the Admiral's plane, then translated Cushing's offer into Japanese. The two documents were fastened together and entrusted to two Filipinos who, together with navy lieutenant Okumura Shotaro, pilot of the ill-fated seaplane, delivered them to Colonel Onishi under cover of a white flag. Colonel Onishi agreed to the deal without hesitation, apparently on his own responsibility. The messengers returned late in the afternoon with gifts of Japanese cigarettes and a demand that the prisoners be released immediately.

Cushing stalled, still hoping to receive further word from Australia. He offered to release four of the prisoners immediately and deliver the rest to Cebu City in four days to a week. Onishi replied, "All or none." After obtaining assurances from Admiral Fukudome that the Japanese would not harm any of their Filipino civilian hostages, Cushing agreed to release all the prisoners in return for allowing the guerrillas to escape the Japanese ring.

Thus, at 11 A.M. on April 10, 1944, the only POW exchange of the war took place. Cushing warmly shook Fukudome's hand as the Japanese officer was placed on a litter. Led by Lieutenant Pedro Villareal, one of the guerrillas, the captives and their Filipino escorts proceeded behind a white flag down to a ravine where the transfer was to take place under a mango tree. Fifty Japanese soldiers, armed only with swords and bayonets as had been mutually agreed, moved forward. Admiral Fukudome sat unsteadily on a chair supported by two bamboo poles. When the admiral reached his own lines, the

Japanese bowed deeply, providing ample evidence of Fukudome's high rank. The Japanese followed the return route to Cebu City prescribed for them by the guerrillas, and Colonel Onishi abided fully by the agreement he had made. Cushing and his men thus escaped to fight another day.

Meanwhile, a related drama was playing out on the southeastern coast of Cebu, where parts of the seaplane's wreckage had washed ashore. One of the locals, Pedro Gantuangko, picked up an important-looking leather portfolio that had been specially packaged to stay dry. He turned the portfolio over to Lieutenant Varga of the guerrillas. Fearing for his life, Gantuangko fled to the neighboring island of Bohol to avoid possible questioning and torture by the Japanese. Varga brought the two volumes of documents to Cushing, who assumed from their packaging that they might be of great importance, although none on his staff could decipher them. Their presence in the admiral's aircraft also suggested their great sensitivity. Cushing could not have known that the portfolio was actually in Admiral Fukudome's hands when his plane crashed into the sea. All of this information was relayed by radio to MacArthur's headquarters.

The long-awaited message from General MacArthur's headquarters came through that evening. It read: "Enemy prisoners must be held at all costs." The next message specified that the admiral was to be taken to Tolong on Negros Island and that a submarine was already on its way for the pickup. Cushing was crestfallen but convinced he had done his best. He prepared a report on what had transpired, emphasizing that his guerrillas still held the precious documents. These would now be hand carried to the designated rendezvous with the submarine, along with a German, Hans Ritter, who had somehow fallen into the guerrillas' hands. MacArthur's headquarters was so incensed by what it regarded as Cushing's disregard of orders that he was stripped of his command and demoted to private.

Upon their arrival in Australia, the Japanese documents were quickly brought to ATIS, G-2 (Intelligence Division) for translation by a team of three Caucasians and two Nisei. The documents included Plan Z, the Japanese plan for the defense of the Marianas and Philippines. Its capture represented one of the most significant intelligence successes of the war in the Pacific, providing the Allies with the report on Admiral Koga's just concluded personal inspection of Japanese defenses that had revealed significant weaknesses on Leyte, where the initial American landings subsequently occurred.[1]

Following the American landing on Leyte, the disgraced Colonel Cushing was summoned to MacArthur's headquarters. Since he had heard nothing more about the deal he had made to effect the guerrillas' escape from encirclement and whether those precious documents had been of value, Cushing probably still had considerable foreboding about the meeting. His fears were groundless, however, because the headquarters now fully understood the significance of his contribution for the return of American forces to the Philippines. "Private" Cushing was reinstated and after the war given a substantial cash award.

For the Japanese, the capture of Admiral Fukudome represented an unprecedented embarrassment. Never in Japanese history had a flag-rank officer allowed himself to be captured by enemy forces. Navy lieutenant Okumura Shotaro, the pilot of the ill-fated seaplane, told his surviving crew that they were never to talk about the incident to anyone, not even amongst themselves. It was to be regarded a "top secret" matter. Okumura said he would inform them when the time came to commit suicide. The crew expected they would all be executed, but a few days later a plane returned them to Saipan. The unfortunate occurrence, it appeared, would be disregarded. It was clear to those who took part in the episode that the special consideration they were shown had everything to do with their association with Admiral Fukudome during the incident.

Surviving passengers from the seaplane were flown back to Tokyo and taken directly to the navy minister's residence. Top officers in the navy ministry investigated the incident. After obtaining input from the army ministry as well, the navy informed Admiral Fukudome that, while not prepared to drop de facto *Senjinkun* policy, there was no rule that could not have exceptions. In this case grounds for an exception were found when the navy determined that the delicately termed "other side" (that is, the guerrillas who had taken the admiral captive) could not be considered enemy soldiers. Moreover, it was unclear whether Colonel Cushing had or had not acted under orders of the U.S. government. The Japanese navy ministry ruling determined that Admiral Fukudome's party was blameless in virtually all respects. Other than the pilot, nobody was responsible for the plane crash; the group had not actually "fallen into enemy hands," they had not conducted themselves in a manner that redounded to the enemy's benefit, and since the admiral maintained that the Plan Z documents had been destroyed in the flames that engulfed their plane, they had not violated the Military Secrets Protection Law.

In a memorandum neither signed nor marked with a personal seal—remarkable in itself—the ministry went on to reaffirm the navy's policy regarding personnel being taken prisoner. High-ranking officers in such an eventuality were urged in a "compassionate" way to commit suicide. The means for conveying to the officer the decision for him to commit suicide would be through a family member or fellow officer personally close to the officer concerned. The go-between's task would then be to determine the officer's "true intentions." If these were not in accord with the ministry's decision, the go-between was to convey the ministry's wishes indirectly, together with its "distress" and overall "benevolent affection."[2] With such convoluted phraseology, the ministry hoped to put the matter to rest.

The manner in which the Fukudome case was handled indicated clearly that the ministry was determined to retain the admiral's seasoned services for the difficult battles looming ahead, no matter what the facts of his capture demonstrated. This outcome flew in the face of considerable evidence the Japanese must have had from American-made matériel and documents captured from Philippine guerrillas demonstrating that the guerrillas were indeed operating under American command. Even had they been unable to decipher radio intercepts of communications between Colonel Cushing and Australia, they could not have been under the illusion that such channels did not exist. The navy ministry proceeding resulted largely in face-saving verbiage.

In any event, none of the survivors of the second seaplane ever had to face a court-martial. One of the "wise men" called on to rule on the Fukudome matter, Vice Admiral Nakazawa (the navy's personnel chief), wrote a memo on the navy ministry's deliberations that stated it was "not clear whether Adm. Fukudome in the bottom of his heart wants to commit suicide." If the admiral were "undecided about ending his life," the panel agreed that "we should permit him discretion in this matter in the light of doubts that had been raised." With such elliptical and hazy language, Fukudome's honor was preserved.

In his memoirs, Fukudome wrote that he had been determined to commit suicide, since he realized that he had indeed been taken prisoner by guerrillas. Accordingly, he had requested the navy minister, Admiral Shimada Shigetaro, to feel free to dispose of his case as he wished. The navy minister comforted him, stating that "because your resourcefulness resulted in your escape, you were really not a POW. You might as well lose this same life of yours in combat as in suicide." In his two-volume treatise on Japanese prisoners, the eminent historian Hata Ikuhiko noted that this "still amounted to no more than sophistry." It came down to an expression of sympathy for Fukudome's predicament. Since many other Japanese faced similar predicaments, however, the Fukudome episode ended up producing a blatant case of discriminatory treatment for a senior officer. The face-saving formula about saving his life to enable him to lose it later in combat was never applied to anyone else, notably not to the Japanese POWs released from captivity and returned to Japanese control on Bataan early in the war.

The at least equally embarrassing episode of the missing vital documents became a nonevent for the high command. Conveniently, nobody was officially informed about the loss up the chain of command, nobody was required to take responsibility, and nobody was ever punished for the loss. The Japanese command on Cebu must have at least suspected that the documents survived because as late as May 17 their unconditional return to Japanese hands was still being demanded in leaflets dropped over guerrilla areas. When interrogated about the documents, Fukudome gave his unqualified opinion that they had been consumed in the flames that engulfed the plane, despite the fact that they had been in his hands when the seaplane crashed and the impact forced him to release them.[3]

Saved from disgrace, Admiral Fukudome was subsequently entrusted with the command of the naval air defenses of Taiwan, a key ingredient in the Japanese defense of the Philippines and Okinawa. In October 1944, his Sixth Base Air Force gave a good account of itself but was no match for American airpower under Admiral Halsey that was clearing the skies in preparation for the invasion of the Philippines.

Aside from Fukudome, the other survivors of the seaplane crash all received promotions to seal their lips concerning their participation in a top secret event. Some perished in the latter stages of the war, but fate held still one more strange twist for the life of senior flight petty officer Imanishi Yoshihisa, copilot of the ill-fated seaplane. He was back on Saipan in June 1944 when the American assault began. When the Japanese garrison was eventually forced to retreat to the northern part of the island, Imanishi was severely wounded and thereby missed the *gyokusai*. A comrade carried him to a cave, where they both resolved to die, but the one remaining grenade in their possession malfunctioned, and Imanishi was again taken prisoner by the Americans. This gave him the dubious distinction of having twice become a prisoner of the Americans. In the postwar era he joined the Japan Air Self-Defense Force.

Admiral Fukudome survived the war unscathed. In August 1953, when Colonel Cushing died of a heart attack in the Philippines at the age of fifty-three, the admiral, by then executive director of the Japan Youth Aviation Federation, expressed "deep regret" over his death.

THE TALKATIVE INTELLIGENCE OFFICER

Aside from the unusual case of Vice Admiral Fukudome, navy captain Okino Matao was one of the three highest-ranking Japanese ever to fall into American hands, albeit in a circuitous manner.[4] Born in Tokyo to a well-to-do upper-middle-class family, Okino graduated from the Imperial Japanese Naval Academy in 1920. He became a Chinese language officer, which led to assignments in the intelligence field. He served in China for some time around 1927 and continuously from 1931 onward and was, at the time of his capture, resident naval officer in Hang-chou, a major city on China's central coast. In this position he headed naval intelligence operations in an important part of China, conducted liaison with the Chinese puppet government headed by Wang Ching-wei, and espionage and counterespionage operations. Yet he felt somewhat out of the mainstream.

A man with a restless, inquiring mind, he had gotten into the habit of flying once a month to Shanghai or Nanking just to catch up on what was going on elsewhere and to visit with colleagues. He was also angling for another command.

As Okino recalled in his memoir written shortly after the war, January 18, 1944, proved to be a fateful day. As usual, he had boarded the plane with an armful of diplomatic news reports on the Greater East Asia Co-Prosperity Sphere. His plane was the third of three that took off on that cloudy day. After a while he looked at his watch and realized that the plane should already have arrived in Nanking. It gradually became clear to him that the pilot was lost, flying through a mountainous region far from Nanking. Eventually the plane made a forced landing in a ravine. Nobody knew where they were. Villagers told them that Chinese Nationalist troops were over an hour away but that Japanese forces were close by along the Yangtze River. Most of the passengers, including Okino, had been injured in the landing, severely impeding their mobility. A small guerrilla unit took them into custody and several weeks later led them into a Nationalist-controlled area, where Okino's eyes were opened to Japan's poor reputation among the local population.[5] Okino was taken to a field hospital commanded by a Chinese graduate of Japan's military medical institute. The hospital, according to Okino, showed him every courtesy and treated him humanely.

At the time of his capture, Okino had already become disillusioned with Japan's China policies. A man who sincerely believed in a close relationship with China, he despaired over Japan's rejection of Chiang Kai-shek's peace overtures and its continuing efforts to undermine Chiang's attempts to unify his country. He believed that the rapid turnover of senior Japanese military commanders and diplomats served to shield Japan from Chinese realities, including the rising tide of nationalism. Okino was utterly convinced of the necessity for Japan to withdraw its troops and end the war with China, a concept that was anathema to the high command. Moreover, Okino had established close professional relations with Westerners over the years; when Japan attacked the Western powers, he believed that Japan had embarked on an "unjust, immoral" course of action that was doomed to fail in the end. From the start he had a realistic appreciation of the West's military potential and considered himself a "defeatist."

One day during his captivity the local Chinese commander came to his room to interrogate him about Japanese aircraft production, location of manufacturing plants for the latest fighters, and similar topics. He replied that he knew nothing about such matters but volunteered that he knew a great deal about China and proceeded to tell the Chinese officer about the position he held and his regret over the lost dream of Sino-Japanese ties based on a common humanity. Okino felt good about the encounter; his true feelings about China, he thought, were finally understood. Over the course of interrogations continuing over several months, Okino divulged considerable information about the organization and personalities of various security operations in China and the employment of agents. He also provided the Chinese with information on total Japanese tonnage lost to Allied attacks and on the number of aircraft losses Japan had sustained.

Okino was still recuperating from the amputation of a leg when he received a letter from the senior Japanese officer in An-ch'ing (now Anqing), a city on the Yangtze River and the site of the nearest major Japanese base. (It is unclear how such a letter could have reached Okino, but it was already known during the war that a good deal of information passed across the lines between Japanese and Nationalist authorities.) The letter informed him that the Japanese were aware of his situation but that efforts to effect his release had failed. It asked him to work for the future of good Sino-Japanese relations. Okino, though a captive, now saw a new role for himself. He described himself as "a man without a family, without a society, but as a naked individual standing alone."[6] As the senior Japanese officer then in captivity, he was assuredly very much alone, left to his own devices to carve out a personal mission. Despite ensuing bouts with depression and doubts, Okino continued to pursue his ideals even as a prisoner.

In due course Okino was brought to China's wartime capital of Chungking. He was amazed how modern a city it was. A Colonel Oh stopped by to explain that he would be in charge of Okino's interrogation. Oh had been enrolled in Japanese schools for eight years before attending a Japanese military college; to Okino he seemed to be "just like a Japanese." From young officers assigned as his "guards," Okino learned about Japanese atrocities—the brutality against Chinese POWs, rapes and murders of Chinese civilians. Meanwhile, the Chinese treated him well, seeing to his every need.

American officials in Chungking were apprised of China's prize prisoner but failed in efforts to interrogate Okino on their own. The Chinese provided American authorities with a translation of at least one interrogation, but the Americans questioned whether some material had not been included. After Nationalist authorities concluded that they had extracted all the intelligence they were going to get, they agreed to release Okino to American custody. Okino noted in his memoir that he had agreed to the move "on condition" he eventually be returned to Chinese custody. This never happened. Accompanied by an American army Japanese language officer, Okino left Chungking on October 27, 1944, and traveled across "the Hump," India, and North Africa to reach the United States.

In his memoirs, Okino noted that he was initially housed in a converted mansion in Mount Vernon, Virginia, a VIP facility reserved for cooperative prisoners. This strongly suggests he was actually at Fort Hunt, the highly secret interrogation facility. He was the only Japanese accorded this "distinction" until the end of the war in Europe. Most of the other "guests" at the facility were Germans along with a few Italians. He was provided with all kinds of reading material as well as great varieties of food and drink, all of which he consumed with gusto. All regulations, along with provisions of the Geneva Convention, were posted in his room, where he was greeted, not coincidentally, by navy captain E. S. Pearce, an acquaintance from prewar Peking and Shanghai.

Okino's initial interrogation was conducted by Captain Pearce and Marine Colonel Bales; a man Okino identified as Shappel interpreted. This first interrogation covered information on the Chinese Communists, relations between the Chinese Nationalists and Communists, special operations conducted by the Nationalists, and the possible reactions of the Communists to eventual American landings in China. On at least one occasion Okino was brought to the District of Columbia, in civilian clothes, for a party at the home of a senior American intelligence officer. Several other intelligence officers were in attendance on that occasion. The atmosphere was conducive to wide-ranging intellectual discussions about a variety of war-related and postwar issues. Okino clearly relished the easy camaraderie with professional colleagues.

In the ensuing months Okino was interrogated frequently, principally on Japanese intelligence operations. His interrogator was navy lieutenant Don Gorham (although Okino knew him as Lieutenant Smith), a superb bilingual choice. Gorham and his family had, moreover, lived in Shibuya, a borough of Tokyo where Okino also had his home. Gorham became completely convinced that the detailed information Okino provided was entirely truthful. At times he found it difficult to terminate the pleasant sessions because Okino was so garrulous.[7] Believing his mission to be a principal interpreter of Japan and its peculiar ways to the Americans, Okino was anxious to establish his credibility. For his part, Gorham was so impressed by Okino's sincerity that he proposed that this prisoner "be used with great profit in the consideration of broad policies . . . for the Allied government of Japan."

Hoping to play a role in postwar Japan, Okino took every opportunity to convey his views to American officials. Without being asked, he wrote a commentary on an article titled "To Break Japanese Morale" that had appeared in a journal called *Asia and the Americas*. His thesis was that Americans did not fully grasp the Japanese mentality and hence their countermeasures were often unsuitable. Also on his own initiative Okino commented on an article in the October 1944 issue of *Foreign Affairs* entitled "The Mikado Must Go." As that article was written by Sun Fo, a prominent Chinese Nationalist politician and son of Sun Yat-sen, it undoubtedly had considerable currency at the time. After accurately summarizing the arguments about the emperor, Okino not surprisingly advocated the emperor's retention by the Allies, arguing that the emperor's existence would not inhibit the growth of postwar Japanese democracy. He stressed the conventional wisdom of the time, to the effect that the emperor, a symbol of the "spirit of Japan," was kept in the dark about all the bad things that occurred in his name. In Okino's view, the emperor remained essential, if only to convince the Japanese people that surrender did not mean the final end of Japan as a sovereign entity.

Okino was excited by the thought that he was providing interpretive comments to senior American officials on events such as the political demise of Premier Tojo and the onset of the Koiso cabinet late in the war. He had long been convinced of Japan's ultimate defeat. When asked to comment on such weighty issues as Japan's governance under an occupation, Okino said he hoped that China would not have a role in the occupation. Despite his sympathy toward the Chinese, such a role, he thought, should be reserved for the United States.[8]

It is easy to see why for the Americans Okino was such an appealing conversation partner. He was unblinkingly candid about Japan's chances for victory in the war. While most POWs still believed that Japan would win, Okino was realistic enough to understand that since Japan had been unable to defeat a weak China, it could hardly be expected to best the Allies. Similarly, while Japan had claimed a "great naval victory off Leyte," the Americans had by then defeated Japanese forces on the island. Intelligent Japanese surely realized what was happening on the war fronts. His regular reading of American newspapers, furthermore, had convinced Okino that the Allies "possess a spiritual power against which the determination of the Germans and Japanese is weak."[9]

Okino still had periods of dark moods. On one occasion he dreamed of his family's reproach because he had become a prisoner; on another, he dreamed that navy minister Shimada ordered him to commit suicide and that his family would be punished for his transgressions in providing military intelligence to the enemy. But with the passage of time, he became more optimistic about the future. Best of all he had the chance to meet people like navy captain Kenny, with whom he could reminisce about times they had shared in Shanghai and Peking. They talked about old friends, dislike of respective army colleagues, and "shared military estimates and political information." Okino's meeting with Kenny once was topped off by a drive around the Virginia countryside near the District of Columbia.

In April 1945, Okino received a roommate, Iwai Suekichi. Having craved company at Fort Hunt, he was delighted by this development, especially because he could talk to Iwai about China to his heart's content. A civilian, Iwai had worked in the fishery business in Taiwan, Canton, and Hong Kong. He had lost his way while on a small boat off the China coast. Taken captive, he was held for some time in Chungking before being brought to the Washington area. While Okino and Iwai did not question their good fortune, it was hardly an accident that two Japanese with China connections were brought together. Okino's placement in Fort Hunt probably was primarily to provide him the best possible "home" for a POW and to keep him close at hand to senior officials in Washington; an ancillary reason may well have been to overhear Okino's conversations with Iwai. Given Okino's military background and readiness to reveal intelligence, it seems fairly certain that he was the source of as much or more intelligence than that provided by any other Japanese POW.

In the summer of 1945, Okino was glad to be fitted for a prosthesis. His new leg promised at least a limited return to some of the sports activity he had always enjoyed. During this same time he also met frequently with Gorham to discuss functions and relationships among the various Japanese intelligence organizations.[10] On June 19, 1945, Captain Pearce drove him to an apartment on Wisconsin Avenue in Washington, where Okino again met a group of American intelligence officers for a relaxed evening of banter. Okino dressed in a civilian suit for which measurements had been taken earlier. Everyone drank quite a bit, ate Chinese food, sang Japanese folk songs, and talked the evening away in a mixture of English, Japanese, and Chinese. As Okino put it in his memoir, his "heart danced" because he was among friends. He was able to forget that he was a prisoner, even "while our troops in Okinawa were being exterminated."[11]

Okino was abruptly reminded that he was still a prisoner on the following day, when he was transferred from one POW camp to another, never knowing the name or location of either. His morale plunged as his treatment became significantly worse. He was again interrogated by army officers but now gave them "insincere" answers. His complaints resulted in yet another transfer to a familiar earlier facility (likely Fort Hunt), where he shared a room with a Sergeant Sakai, a graduate of Tokyo Imperial University, who had served in China, Saipan, and Iwo Jima before being taken prisoner. Sakai told him about the shocking mistrust of officers that had developed among Japanese enlisted men, which even extended to some mistrust of the emperor.

Shortly after the emperor's surrender message, Okino met Okano Hideo, a Japanese diplomat taken prisoner in the Philippines. They had a long talk on politics and foreign policy. Life improved for Okino in some respects. He was transferred to Fort Eustis in Norfolk, where he joined a large number of POWs; all guards were removed, they were free to move about, and he received access to a radio. A group of five, including Okano, were separated out. Okino believed they were considered pro-United States and would receive special treatment. He felt sorry for them on that account, but he also worried about the reception awaiting him in Japan.

During wartime interrogations, Okino indicated that he did not wish to be returned to Japan once the war ended. Assuming the Allies would win, he thought that he could probably return home on his own without facing punishment, but he could not stand the shame of being returned as a POW. He requested therefore to be sent to China, where he hoped to work for peaceful Sino-Japanese relations, but there was never any prospect that such a request would be honored.

Okino disembarked at Urawa on January 6, 1946, in one of the first groups of prisoners of war to be repatriated to Japan. He was overcome by the sights and sounds of his native land and worried about how meetings with Japanese officials would go in the light of his POW status. The Welfare Ministry, which by then had taken over the repatriation work, was ready for him. Greeted by a former rear admiral, Okino was informed that his family was safe and his daughter engaged to be married. After routinely reporting on his experience as a POW, he completed the formalities and returned home.

If Okino had seriously believed that the Americans might wish to use his services in the Occupation, he was bound to be disillusioned. Professional military officers were purged and barred from government service. Despite his enlightened views on the ultimate outcome of the war and on the Sino-Japanese relationship, he would still have been considered a representative of the old order. Japan was in a period of basic internal reforms, with little room for a man of Okino's talents.

Unlike their interest in the first returning POW, the Japanese news media showed no interest in one of the highest-ranking former prisoners when he returned to Japan. Okino's memoir, published in 1946 when the energies of most Japanese were concentrated on just surviving another day, received scant notice and was soon forgotten. Okino eventually played a leading role in the Japan Disabled Veterans Association and the Japan Wounded Veterans Association. He died in 1978.

THREE WHO PROVIDED A WINDOW ON PEACE PROSPECTS

After American forces retook control of the central Philippines in early 1945, large numbers of Japanese civilians fell into American hands. Among these were two who evidently impressed their captors with their superb command of English; they were also well educated, well connected, and appeared to have a sophisticated understanding of social, political, and economic trends in Japan, as well as a hard-headed view of its remaining military capabilities. A third was a non-career officer serving in civilian functions. All three were realistically convinced that Japan's hopes for victory were gone.

American intelligence officers decided on the idea, remarkably bold for its time, that the three civilians might provide the Allies with insights on Japanese psychology and such key issues as attitudes concerning the emperor and Japanese atrocities. These officers were interested in the Japanese perspective on how the war came about, the attitudes of various Japanese interest groups and key individuals able to affect the future course of war and peace, and how the war might end. Instead of specific questions, the three civilians were provided only a broad framework for an essay that would cover these points. They were asked to pool their efforts and come up with a single text in English.

The team-written Japanese essay was completed in a little over a month and published as a confidential document by the intelligence section of the U.S. Sixth Army on May 7, 1945.[12] The foreword stated that it had been extremely important "to avoid the exertion of any influence or constraint whatever, conscious or subconscious, on the free expression by the authors of their own thoughts and opinions." The report was deemed especially valuable because it was written by Japanese whose firsthand knowledge of their people's psychology allowed them to explain many elements of Japanese civilization that often appeared paradoxical to Westerners. Every three days the group had been brought up-to-date with briefings on the latest world news, including domestic Japanese political events as provided by Japanese broadcasts. The finished report was presented to the military readers for their "personal evaluation and assessment."

This surprisingly open-minded approach to a dissection of delicate issues by the three noncombatants unfortunately also resulted in an extensive "analysis" by ATIS in General MacArthur's headquarters. This "analysis" gave its readers, presumably senior officers at General MacArthur's headquarters and intelligence officers in other commands, a slew of negative comments that could only be designed to negate the impact of the report in its entirety. It called the report an unsubtle, opportunistic effort by Japanese propagandists who had taken "full advantage of the unexpected opportunity gratuitously afforded them of rendering their country a service."[13] Some of the points made in rebuttal were simply wrong, especially in light of what subsequently became known about Japanese behavior in defeat. Other comments taken out of context were contradicted by reference to generalizations that preceded them. These interpretations provide a window on the fairly stereotypical and often narrow-minded preconceptions America's wartime military had of the enemy during the "war without mercy."

The oldest member of the triumvirate of this essay's writers was Okano Hideo, the same individual who met Captain Okino near Washington at war's end. His family had been in international trade, and his early education took place in France. A graduate of Tokyo Imperial University's Law Department, Okano joined the diplomatic service in 1933. He was posted at the Japanese Consulate General in New York between 1937 and 1939. En route to Tokyo from service in Chile, he was interned in Panama when Japan attacked Pearl Harbor and subsequently brought to the United States, along with other Japanese diplomats. Following repatriation to Japan in the wartime exchange of diplomats, he was posted to the Philippines, first with the military government and later accredited to the Japanese-supported Laurel government of the Philippines. Okano was taken into custody during the fall of Manila to American forces.

In the course of his interrogation, Okano stated that Japan's prospects for victory had become zero following the loss of Luzon. The reason Japanese soldiers continued to fight, he said, was not that they wanted to die for the emperor but because they feared disobeying their officers' orders. He advised that appeals to Japanese troops to surrender should stress the Allies' humane treatment of prisoners, massive Allied material superiority, and Japan's string of military defeats. In his analysis of Japan's domestic political situation, he expressed the view that the "crazy military" would have to make way for another type of leadership before Japan would sue for peace.

Okano accurately predicted that the Japanese people would accept Japan's defeat stoically, provided the surrender was ordered by the emperor. He also foretold that assuming the Allies treated Japan magnanimously, the Japanese people would not harbor thoughts of revenge for the humiliation of defeat but would be motivated to cooperate by their strong sense of obligation for favors received. Okano believed that the prevailing view among many highly educated Japanese was the following: "Defeat would be welcomed because it would put an end to the fanatical barbarism of which the intelligentsia were ashamed. It would also destroy the paranoiac dreams of empire which they had opposed from the start."

The authors of the essay expressed the view that a "graceful capitulation" that provided a small measure of saved face for the emperor would eliminate the possibility that Japanese forces in such places as Indonesia and Malaysia, which had not even been tested in battle, would continue to fight. In the event, when the emperor did surrender, these forces, numbering about a million and half men, gave up their arms without a murmur of dissent.

The second contributor to the essay, Kano Hisamichi, was a member of a prominent Japanese family with personal connections to influential persons in the peerage and business circles. At the time of the outbreak of war, his father, a viscount, was manager of the Yokohama Specie Bank in London. In his youth, Kano had lived in the United States and England. Inducted into the army upon graduation from Kyoto Imperial University, Kano was subsequently commissioned a second lieutenant. He landed in the Philippines in December 1941 and assisted in setting up a radio station in Manila. He also did some front-line loudspeaker work on Bataan. In February 1942 he was placed in charge of station KZRH in Manila and played a minor role as interpreter during General Wainwright's surrender of American forces in the Philippines.[14] Kano served as liaison officer and interpreter with the Laurel government until shortly before he was captured in Manila.

The third member of the group was Iimura Hiromu, who had lived since birth in Manila, where his father was in the lumber business. He had attended college in Manila and was interned by the Americans when war broke out. Released by the invading Japanese army, Iimura spent two years as a reporter for a Japanese news agency. Shortly before the collapse of the Laurel government, he served as liaison officer and interpreter at the Malacanan Palace, the historic residence of the Philippine president. Owing to his relative youth and inexperience, it seems likely that he contributed less to the essay than his colleagues in the POW camp.

Considering that the three analysts had no academic texts at their disposal and lacked full access to developments in their homeland, they did a remarkably good job of providing a fairly accurate picture of how various elements of Japanese society perceived their own country and its actions. They were not afraid to indicate their knowledge was meager on some issues, such as, for example, stocks of critical war materials. They were especially accurate about describing the attitudes of their own class toward other classes in Japanese society and toward other nations and peoples. In their explanations about Japan's war aims, they were correct in placing emphasis on the army's failure to bring the conflict with China to a satisfactory conclusion and pointing out that Japan's leaders plunged the nation into war with "little confidence in victory."

Most impressive were the trio's insights and speculations on how the war might end. They believed that Japan would not fight to the bitter end. Since the collapse of the imperial house was unimaginable for the majority of Japanese, an opening for a "graceful capitulation" that upheld the "honor of the Throne" would allow the

Japanese to cease fighting. On the other hand, the three predicted that Allied landings on Japanese soil would unleash bitter and meaningless resistance that would continue even after any semblance of a central government disappeared.

In these circumstances, "a negotiated peace or a formal surrender will be necessary to end hostilities," claimed the essay writers. A phrase such as "formal surrender" would have been anathema to all but a few Japanese at the time and demonstrated the authors' ability to transcend straitjacketed thought processes. The writers expressed the view that influential groups in Japan were already "gradually maneuvering themselves" to bring about a surrender of the sort they advocated. The essay concluded: "Offhand, it would appear that a complete blockade of Japan, full preparations for an invasion, continued heavy bombings, and then, secret informal negotiations, should bring about a way to formal capitulation." This was a remarkably prescient scenario, months before the dropping of the atomic bombs, massive conventional bombings of urban areas, and the Soviet Union's entry into the war!

Aware that substantial elements of Japan's army remained undefeated, the three authors believed that a surrender message from the emperor would also ensure the peaceful capitulation of the extensive Japanese army forces in China, Southeast Asia, Manchuria, and Korea. The paper assumed that Japan would be stripped of all its overseas possessions and that, with the elimination of its military, Japan would turn into "the most peace-loving and orderly nation of all." In the spring of 1945 such a prediction would have come up against enormous skepticism among the Allies, but it was pretty much on the mark.

8

UPRISINGS IN THE STOCKADES

Once Japanese POWs had passed through the trauma of surrender and the uncertainties and disorientation of being interrogated and moved through a number of POW enclosures, they normally arrived at a more or less permanent camp in the continental United States, Australia, New Zealand, or India. Some POWs, however, were shifted from one camp to another for a variety of reasons. Prisoner No. 1, Ensign Sakamaki, for example, passed through seven camps in the United States during his four years of captivity, including two separate stays at the same camp.

The location of POW camps for Japanese captives was determined largely by space availability at the various facilities. Until Japan's surrender, camps on the West Coast were judged unsuitable, owing to the region's intense anti-Japanese feeling. Such hostility was much less in evidence in Hawaii, some two thousand miles closer to the combat zone. Hawaii's large Japanese-American population was not, with some exceptions, deported to relocation centers on the mainland.

The Japanese always made up just a tiny part of the overall POW population in the continental United States and, for that matter, within the individual camps. In camps within the contiguous forty-eight states, Germans and Italians accounted for as many as 422,000 POWs in the late spring and early summer of 1945, while the number of Japanese prisoners there exceeded 5,000 only in the early fall of that year.

Roughly half of the Japanese in the continental United States were held at Camp McCoy in central Wisconsin, with smaller contingents at Camps Huntsville, Hearne, and Kenedy in Texas, Camp Clarinda in southwestern Iowa, and Camp Livingston in Louisiana. Late in the war Camp Kenedy housed most of the POW officers. Not long after the war ended, most of these installations closed and some of their Japanese POWs were temporarily transferred to camps in California before being repatriated to Japan.

Australia, New Zealand, and British India also maintained permanent Allied POW camps. Many Japanese taken prisoner late in the war, including those on Okinawa and the Philippines, were simply held in place, where they came under Allied control until the war ended. Once Japan surrendered, the number of Japanese POWs increased sharply with the surrenders of all those Japanese forces on the many Pacific islands that had been bypassed in the Allied offensive, as well as many more Japanese still hiding out in the Philippines and other Pacific islands. Japanese forces surrendered at the same time to British, Australian, and Dutch forces throughout Southeast Asia, in former colonies such as Burma (Myanmar), Malaya (Malaysia), French Indochina (Vietnam, Cambodia, and Laos), Thailand, and the Dutch East Indies (Indonesia).

Under a wartime agreement with the Australian and New Zealand governments, Japanese taken prisoner in General MacArthur's southwest Pacific Ocean area of command were sent to permanent camps in those two countries. Most prisoners captured in Admiral Nimitz's Pacific Ocean area of command were funneled through Hawaii to permanent camps in the continental United States. However, several hundred remained in Hawaii throughout the war, and one hundred forty-two were left behind on Saipan as late as April 1945 in the vain hope of effecting a POW exchange for American prisoners in Japanese hands.[1] This group performed so well on reconstruction work that an additional two hundred POWs were subsequently sent to Saipan to work on surplus property and base closures.

The U.S. Army had to overcome initial resistance on the part of local commanders to using Japanese POW labor overseas. In time these officers were won over by the excellence of the POWs' work. They often labored a twelve-hour day, including transit time, with no rest periods other than a lunch break. Once the war ended, they were employed on virtually all designated tasks. Essential military

projects had top priority, but POWs also worked on civilian reconstruction projects. In the Philippines they were paid six cents a day,
nine cents for skilled labor, based on civilian practices in the area.
The army had determined that "since Japan did not ratify the Geneva
Convention . . . nonessential features of the Convention could be
modified."[2] The American authors of a report on POW utilization
during the war also noted that the labor performed by eighty thousand Japanese in the Pacific was "excellent in quality and greatly
assisted in the rapid repatriation of American troops and equipment."[3]

At one time, the U.S. military employed eighty thousand Japanese POWs in the Philippines alone. Certain POWs there were armed
with clubs and flashlights to "police civilian areas and to guard U.S.
government property, effectively preventing thefts." There was no
danger that they might try to escape because they "preferred the security of the U.S. installations to encounters with the Filipinos."[4]

By the time Japanese prisoners arrived at permanent POW camps,
many had recovered from their initial depression, realized that the
Americans were not going to kill them, and had begun to come to
terms with their imprisonment. POWs whose bodies had been wracked
by malnutrition, disease, and wounds were usually well on their way
to recovery. The shame of their status, however, continued to haunt
many. They also became increasingly concerned about the fate of
their families at home as news of successive Japanese defeats and
reports of the bombings of Japanese cities filtered into the camps.
They also had plenty of time to ponder the future that awaited them.

Probably for the first time in their lives, Japanese POWs found
themselves living in a far more unstructured social situation than they
had been used to. Enlisted men were separated from officers, who
under the Geneva Convention were allowed their own quarters. Army
prisoners, in particular, rarely encountered more than a few POWs
they had known previously, either in civilian life or in the military,
because prisoners tended to trickle into the POW camps singly or in
very small groups.

In some camps internal discipline broke down. Many prisoners
hid their true identity and rank, not only from their captors but from
fellow prisoners as well. Although the Allies selected some POW leaders, when the Japanese were allowed to decide the matter among

themselves, it was not always certain that the most senior would assume leadership. Those who arrived first in a particular camp often attempted, with some success, to impose their leadership on later arrivals, forcing the newcomers to accept the established pecking order. In some cases, the most violent among the POWs, including criminal types, would simply assume leadership. Not coincidentally, these were often the most militant prisoners.

Without any preexisting social bonds of the type that normally enveloped Japanese, the POWs had to create new ones. In this situation, numerous factional groupings sprang up. Probably the most significant were based on attitudes toward their captors. By far the smallest numbers were inclined to cooperate actively with their captors, to varying degrees and from a variety of motives. This group was likely to be found among the best educated—those who, by the same token, most likely had had at least some previous contact with Westerners. Virtually all were draftees rather than career servicemen. It did not follow, however, that this breakdown necessarily correlated with the POWs' willingness to answer truthfully during interrogations.

Next in size were the hard-liners who maintained a fervent belief in Japan's victory and found the idea of its defeat unthinkable. They might have played along with their captors on the surface, but in their hearts they retained an implacable hatred of the enemy, having learned nothing from their unexpected capture and good treatment at Western hands. At times these true believers cowed the rest by insisting that all continue publicly to avow the beliefs of the past. It was this group that sought at times to carry on their war by such acts as taking extra helpings of sugar for their coffee, taking more bread on their plate than they could eat, and stuffing toilets with toilet paper. All such tactics represented pitiful efforts to weaken America's economic strength and to demonstrate to themselves that their active resistance was continuing even behind the barbed wire.

Hard-liners also reveled in putting something over on the Americans so that they could continue to feel superior. It was this group that felt the shame of captivity most intensely and continued to believe that only death could expiate their deeply felt transgression. Only a very few succeeded in individual suicide attempts, but several hard-liners masterminded so-called "breakout" attempts that were little more than thinly disguised mass suicides. These camp leaders were apt to have had a variety of backgrounds but were most likely career army and navy noncommissioned officers.

By far the largest number of Japanese POWs adopted a stance between the two extremes. Members of this group remained neutral, unwilling to commit themselves to either violence and petty annoyances against the Allies on the one hand or active cooperation with the Allies on the other. They carefully watched what was going on, seldom voicing their opinions. Members of this group mainly wanted to stay out of trouble, to remain alive to see what would develop, and to avoid anything that might be criticized as traitorous conduct. Most officers were in this category.

Attitudes toward their captors provided the chief, but not the only, criterion for the development of factions. Traditional frictions between the Japanese army and navy tended to intensify behind barbed wire. The navy's petty officers, who, unlike army noncommissioned officers, were all professionals, tended to identify with the hard-liners. Both services prided themselves on having undergone more severe privations than the other. Some of the army POWs were certain that, having survived numerous battles, illness, malnutrition, and exhaustion over extended periods of time, they had had the worst of it. The navy survivors, on the other hand, had known only a relatively brief period of acute discomfort from the time of their ship's sinking until they were rescued.

Tensions also arose between those who surrendered before the emperor's order to lay down arms and those who surrendered in compliance with that edict. A minority of those who surrendered in compliance with the emperor's message felt they were morally superior to those who had become prisoners before August 15, 1945. There was also hostility between prisoners who continued to respect the old rank order and those who ignored it in the belief that POW status made everyone equal. Since most prisoners found themselves in more than one category, it would be wrong to view the camps as being divided by clear-cut factional lines at all times.

So long as Japanese soldiers and sailors remained in organized military units, the writ of the *Senjinkun* was bound to be obeyed without much thought. It was understood by Japanese soldiers and sailors, with rare exceptions, as the natural order of things. It was even largely adhered to in situations where, their unit cohesion destroyed, on the run, and in retreat, Japanese had to deal with uncommon hardships just to survive. But, the real test for the *Senjinkun*'s power over Japanese minds arose when these men became captives. It was then that they had the time and opportunity to think for themselves, and influences from outside their culture began to make themselves felt. At the same time, the conflict between what was still considered the glory of living up to the *Senjinkun*'s stern message remained pitted against the innate urge to survive. Still, one soldier who ended up in a New Zealand prison camp reflected the thoughts of many in writing that the price for not choosing death over surrender was "a thousand deaths."

CAMP FEATHERSTON, NEW ZEALAND

By and large, Japanese POWs were fairly docile, resigned to their fate, and anxious to perform their assigned work tasks to the best of their abilities. In a few instances, however, a critical mass of hardline POWs succeeded in organizing a group suicide in the guise of an attempted outbreak. The first such uprising took place at Camp Featherston, located northeast of New Zealand's capital of Wellington, established in 1942 to receive POWs from the southwest Pacific area, including Guadalcanal.

The largest contingent of prisoners at Featherston came from the heavy cruiser *Furutaka* that had been sunk in the area known as the Slot, between Rabaul and Guadalcanal. Survivors clung to driftwood and a raft for thirty-six hours before being rescued by the Americans. The two highest-ranking officers were eventually sent to the United States for additional interrogations.

Trouble at Featherston began with the arrival of the *Furutaka* survivors. Hard-liners among the petty officers demanded action to terminate their lives in order to restore their honor. The higher-ranking Japanese officers became so concerned about these threats that they asked the camp commandant to physically separate the bitter-enders from the lower ranks.[5]

Although Ensign Ando Toshio was not the highest-ranking Japanese officer in the camp, he was the most senior officer of the combat arms, which led him to assume leadership of the POWs. The more senior officer in the camp had not only used a fake name but also lost his seniority when he told the interrogator that he was merely a noncommissioned officer. When the uprising took place, it was too late for him to step forward to assume command.

Unrest at Featherston boiled over on February 25, 1943, when hard-liners masterminded a sit-down strike by creating an issue over the interpretation of the Geneva Convention on a labor issue. At the time, POWs worked only sporadically, resulting in an excess of leisure and a resultant increase in gambling and fighting. The highly respected camp commander, Lieutenant Colonel Donaldson of the New Zealand forces, hoping to improve morale, ordered the prisoners to construct an athletic area for the guards. This was the kind of issue that the hard-liners wanted to exploit. They argued that work of this nature would benefit the enemy and as such was disallowed by the Geneva Convention.

The text of the convention in English was posted at the camp, but few POWs could read it. The camp interpreter, a Captain Aston, warned the prisoners that the refusal to work constituted a serious breach of camp discipline. When several Japanese junior officers insisted on speaking to the camp commander, thirty armed New Zealand soldiers appeared, surrounded the Japanese, and pointed their rifles at the prisoners. But Lieutenants Ando and Nishimura refused to back down. They appealed to the prisoners, over half of whom had served on the *Furutaka* with them, to stand fast and to be prepared to accept a "major sacrifice." With this act of bravery they won over the hard-liners, who had criticized their officers for being weak-kneed.

The New Zealanders promptly seized both officers, but Lieutenant Nishimura escaped to a nearby barracks, where the NCOs sought to protect him with their bodies. A melee ensued, with stones thrown and blood shed. POWs grabbed the New Zealanders' bayonets with their bare hands. Ando challenged the guards to shoot him, and the deputy camp commander, Lieutenant Malcolm, did so, killing him instantly. With that, the prisoners exploded with rage. The guards responded with a concentrated firing that lasted no more than fifteen to twenty seconds. In that time, forty-eight of the two hundred forty participants in what the New Zealanders considered a mutiny were killed and seventy-four wounded. Most of the casualties were not extremists but moderates who had played no part in creating the incident. Bad blood continued in the hospital, where one wounded POW struck a New Zealand nurse, provoking such resentment among the other POWs that the assailant eventually apologized.

After the open conflict, a more reasoned judgment took hold among the POWs. Moreover, the New Zealanders replaced the hard-line camp commander with a more conciliatory one. Tensions then eased and the situation returned to normal. New Zealanders even accepted the POWs' invitation to their semiannual plays, usually familiar period pieces. Toward the end of their imprisonment, social interaction between Japanese and New Zealanders increased.[6]

Not all of the Japanese participated in the uprising; even some hard-liners fled to a nearby barracks in the evident hope of saving their lives. A group of five hundred naval construction workers also watched the action but avoided involvement. After the mutiny was crushed, the camp received additional survivors from several Japanese naval vessels that had been sunk. Support for carrying on the resistance diminished, however, along with the earlier sense of solidarity and military discipline. In part this occurred because the POWs did not want to jeopardize their good treatment by the New Zealanders. This version of the events at Featherston was confirmed by the reports submitted to the Japanese government by the Swiss consul and representative of the International Committee of the Red Cross.[7]

CAMP PAITA, NEW CALEDONIA

The second incident took place at Paita, an American transit camp for Japanese POWs on the island of New Caledonia, a French possession in the South Pacific located roughly halfway between Guadalcanal and the northern tip of New Zealand. Early in 1944 the Paita camp was divided into five separate enclosures, each of which consisted of six tents of five to six beds. Prisoners were allowed to move freely within their own enclosure but prohibited from entering others. Surveillance was lax, however, and there were opportunities for the entire group to meet at mealtimes. The approximately one hundred sixty prisoners were almost equally divided between soldiers captured on Guadalcanal and sailors and fliers captured in the waters off Guadalcanal. Bad blood soon developed between the two groups with their vastly different combat experiences. The soldiers were dispirited and in terrible physical shape, while the sailors and naval airmen were relatively fresh in body and still full of the fighting spirit.

The "incident" at Paita was hatched following a series of episodes that had soured the atmosphere in the camp. A prisoner had approached one of the guards with shovel in hand, in a manner that appeared threatening to the young military policeman, who shot and killed the POW on the spot. Japanese prisoners responded with a hunger strike and protest to the camp commander, but the regulations clearly supported the conduct of the Americans.

The frustrations of dealing with the Japanese comes through in the memoir left behind by the American camp commander at Paita, a Captain Alter. Plaintively he asked: "What do you do when sixty or seventy prisoners being taken out to work in the garden and upon a signal which we never saw or heard they all just sat down and refused to move? When guns were leveled at them, many would pull back their fatigue jackets, bare their chests, and say 'shoot, me want to die'?"[8] Several American officers advised him to bayonet or machine gun the prisoners, but Alter could never bring himself to do that. Besides, it would have made him subject to a court-martial.

Innumerable small incidents followed that served slowly to build tensions. After each one, a leader of the prisoners would make "inconsequential demands" on the American authorities, such as asking to be allowed to cook their own rice or wanting a slight change in the time of the daily sick call. After lengthy negotiations, a "sort of tenuous compromise" would be struck, and life would return to normal. As Alter clearly saw, the Japanese saved face by winning a concession, while the Americans succeeded in avoiding bloodshed. Alter was also motivated by the desire to avoid, as far as possible, interference from higher commands. It was not unusual for the big brass to visit Camp Paita on a Sunday afternoon, "maybe to write home that [they] had been face to face with the Japanese." In the course of such experiences, the more senior officers were then prone to lecture him on Japanese psychology. This was seldom helpful, but if Alter did not succeed in keeping peace with his prisoners, he risked even more unwelcome interference from topside.

Alter freely admitted that it was not only the American officers and Japanese prisoners who caused problems. His own inexperienced military guards would occasionally insult prisoners or use their weapons in unauthorized ways that inflamed the atmosphere of fear and hatred. Even those POWs who felt indebted to the Americans for their good treatment complained about some of the guards who had, they believed, insulted their honor.

One of the soldiers at Paita who had been captured on Guadalcanal, Ouchi Shoshin, indicated that initially he had little desire to live. Later, however, he felt a need to repay an American medical orderly's selfless and wholly unexpected devotion to his recovery. Other POWs had been impressed by what army captain John Burden had told them on Guadalcanal about Western views on POWs. He had pointed out to the POWs that it was only the Japanese who believed it was shameful to become a prisoner of war and asked the POWs how their country could possibly benefit if they died. It would be criminal, not honorable, Burden told them, if they took their own lives in contravention to God's teachings. There was some indication that the solid support for the *Senjinkun* began to crack when confronted with arguments of this nature.

The situation at Paita might have remained uneasily peaceful for a long time. The overall treatment of POWs was good, and they knew it. However, the arrival of a new group of navy petty officers, and especially the appearance of a single strong hard-line leader, significantly altered the situation. One of his fellow prisoners described Senior Petty Officer Sato Mitsue as a dyed-in-the-wool Imperial Japanese Navy warrior type—"self-confident, dignified, exuding authority."[9] A tall judo master who sported an impressive beard, Sato had been a searchlight operator on the destroyer *Akatsuki* that was sunk in the Slot. Although Sato was not even the leader of one of the five sections, nobody disputed his rapid rise to de facto leadership of all prisoners. Sato's right-hand man was Senior Petty Officer Ogino Kyoichiro, a fighter pilot whom the Americans called "Zero." Sato was convinced that once he "united the will to die" of the prisoners, the rest would all fall into place.

Sato astutely used existing tensions and minor incidents to plot an uprising that envisioned the destruction of the Paita camp and the deaths of all Americans along with all POWs. Under Sato's guidance the Japanese prepared what Alter later termed an "almost foolproof plan" to seize the guard towers, murder the officers, gain access to American weapons, and kill their American guards. Until they could secure American weapons, the prisoners planned to use knives fashioned from pieces of metal inserted between the soles of the heavy New Zealand shoes they had been issued. Information eventually made available to the Americans suggested that the prisoners would then kill themselves since there was no way they could escape New Caledonia.

Ouchi, who lived to write about the incident, reported an even more grandiose and fanciful plot concocted by Japanese navy prisoners. After killing all the Americans and seizing the guard towers with their machine guns, the POWs were confident they could break out into the surrounding countryside. Plans were afoot to attack the American airfield in order to capture airplanes, while another scenario had them capturing Noumea harbor to steal a submarine and make their escape. The Japanese army contingent at Paita, however, was so skeptical about plans for an uprising that Ouchi believed they might well have decided to sit it out when the time came. Unable to voice their dismay over such a plan, the army faction docilely prepared for the worst.[10]

The Americans were well aware that something unusual was afoot but had no idea exactly what was going on. Guards reported that prisoners used sticks to draw maps on the ground, hastily erasing them when detected. Whispered conferences were observed. A sense of foreboding enveloped the camp.

The Japanese had devised a particularly clever way to overcome the major obstacle to their ability to exchange information about the planned uprising among the divided compounds. They asked for permission to put on a play for their own amusement. Permission was granted on the grounds that it might lighten camp atmosphere. The prisoners then requested that certain prisoners be transferred from one enclosure to another to rehearse and perfect their roles. The Americans were unaware that the play in question was Japan's most famous and beloved drama *Chushingura,* which dealt with forty-seven *ronin* (masterless samurai). In the play the *ronin* are determined to avenge the death of their former lord, who at court had been shamed by a rival and forced to commit suicide. For years they hide their identity while plotting together until able to carry out their revenge by storming the enemy's castle, beheading the evil lord and placing his head on the grave of their beloved master. Then, to demonstrate the "purity" of their act, all forty-seven *ronin* commit suicide. The play went off as scheduled on Saturday evening, January 8, 1944. That night the plotters were able to complete their final preparations.

The uprising was to take place the following evening, to coincide with "chow call." Alter had no doubt that it would have succeeded if it had taken place. The Americans had rifles and pistols and the prisoners had only crude, homemade weapons; the latter had the element of surprise, a three-to-one edge in numbers, and the determination to die whatever the outcome. That the intended bloodbath did not occur was termed a "miracle" by those who were spared.

In the tents that night, most of the prisoners brooded about what lay ahead. Survivors subsequently agreed that most kept their thoughts to themselves but were by no means in agreement with the course their leader had determined. The army contingent was especially skeptical about the planned revolt but felt paralyzed in the face of Sato's iron-willed determination to carry it out. One of the prisoners later admitted that he realized he only wanted to live but lacked the courage to buck the tide.

In another compound, a medical orderly named Zenpo Shukichi was endlessly mulling over what, if anything, to do when he was approached by Machinist Mate First Class Konosu Mitsuo, a gentle soul who had given the matter a great deal of thought. Konosu hated Sato, who had beaten him so badly that he was barely recognizable. Konosu whispered that Zenpo should approach the Americans and ask them "to do something." Konosu had chosen Zenpo for his good English, but Zenpo turned him down. Konosu then decided that he would have to act on his own since it was clear that, without decisive action, disaster would befall the entire prison population, not only the American guards.

On Sunday afternoon Konosu handed a note written in Japanese to an American medic informing Captain Alter of the uprising planned for that night. The medic, busy passing out Atabrine tablets to malaria fever-stricken prisoners, at first did not bother to pass it on for translation. Since it was not uncommon for POWs to send out notes with requests of one kind or another, the medic attached little importance to it. Fortunately, another prisoner, who apparently shared Konosu's views about the uprising, happened to read the note while it was lying around. He left the note where he found it and promptly informed the POW leaders that their plan had been leaked to the Americans and would therefore have to be aborted.

Knowing what fate was in store for him at the hands of the hard-liners, Konosu promptly feigned an appendicitis attack. He threw himself on the ground, gripping his stomach in apparent pain. An ambulance was summoned, and he was taken outside the POW camp to the section of the American hospital reserved for POWs. This ruse undoubtedly saved Konosu's life. An uneasy quiet settled over the camp, closely guarded by the Americans, but Alter noted that the prisoners did not sing their military songs that night, as had been their custom.

Early the next morning, on January 10, 1944, Alter was awakened by a subordinate's report that POWs had informed the guards that many Japanese prisoners lay dead in their tents. Accompanied by an MP sergeant carrying a pistol, Alter entered the compound and found a total of twenty prisoners suspended from tent poles, their feet barely a foot above the ground and their nostrils stuffed with pilfered cotton to hasten strangulation. Their hands were not tied. During their final moments any one of them could still have chosen to live. Only two were successfully revived. Entering a fourth tent, Alter was met by an even more startling sight. Sato and Ogino both lay dead beside an improvised Shinto shrine, their throats slashed. They had tied themselves together with a ceremonial sash fashioned from toilet paper, and apparently at a signal from a third prisoner had simultaneously attacked one another.

Two weeks later, another two prisoners hanged themselves, and on February 4 two more died after emulating their leaders by slashing each other's throats. A total of nineteen sailors and five soldiers had taken part in the suicide pacts. All had died to atone for their shame in having become prisoners in the first place, to apologize for their embarrassing failure to bring off the uprising, and to provide a standard for the comportment of all prisoners left behind. This series of events more than sufficed to convince the authorities that the camp should be shut down. All remaining prisoners were shipped off to the much larger Camp McCoy in the United States, where the Paita group could be widely scattered and brought under control.

Just before being shipped out of New Caledonia, Sergeant Major Nishino paid a farewell call on Captain Alter. In such situations, Alter routinely had his first sergeant stationed behind the prisoner with a blackjack concealed within arm's reach, just in case the prisoner tried some funny business. Nishino politely thanked Alter for the "fair treatment" he and others had received at Paita and said he merely wanted to say good bye. But before making his exit, Nishino let drop that he wanted Alter to know that, given the opportunity, he and any other prisoner would have had to try to kill Alter before departing. Nishino's farewell neatly encompassed the requirements of both his *tatemae* (that which was dictated by societal conventions) and his *honne* (the real feelings and opinions of the individual), leaving Alter to ponder "the inscrutability of the Japanese mind."[11]

There is no complete record of what happened to Konosu, but it is clear that the Americans took care to continue to separate him from his erstwhile comrades. He was first placed in a hospital for Americans only, but since Konosu was still fearful, he was then moved to a solitary cell in MP custody. One can assume that he was eventually returned to Japan, but probably under yet another assumed name. Before shipping out from Paita, Konosu left behind a detailed record of the planned assault on the Americans, adding, for good measure, some comments on how the camp should be run to avoid a repetition of the deadly incidents. He also named the individual POWs who in his view should be isolated from the rest in the interest of maintaining order and which ones could be trusted. Konosu urged that Americans, especially the military police guards, take greater care to avoid any remarks that could be interpreted by the prisoners as insulting or denigrating.

Konosu remained convinced that he had acted honorably and,

at least to some extent, had fulfilled his duty to his country. He realized that he owed his "very life" to the United States. While recognizing that many Japanese left behind in New Caledonia would think ill of him, "the joy of saving a multitude far outweighs [the pain of] seeing a few men killed."[12]

The most thoughtful Japanese account of the Paita incident was provided many years later by Ouchi, the eyewitness with an Imperial Japanese Army perspective. "For better or worse," he wrote, a "traitor" leaked the plan to the Americans, who easily aborted it.[13] The "traitor," Konosu, who had already fallen under suspicion by the POWs, was spirited away to another camp. But in the end, this "saving angel" was the reason he remained alive to tell the tale. Looking back on the planned event, he said that the uprising would have had a "gruesome result," with massive casualties and no benefits whatsoever. With the advantage of hindsight, he believed that all of his fellow prisoners thought in the bottom of their hearts that it had "turned out alright." Those who followed the *Senjinkun*'s strictures had their "splendid last moment." Immediately thereafter, everyone else (about one hundred thirty-five POWs) parried similar thoughts as "we groped seriously for a way to comport ourselves [thereafter]." For those who survived the aftermath of the failed "revolt," it was like a bad dream—they felt detached, looking on in blank amazement as events unfolded.

While the POWs from Paita were soon transferred to camps in the United States, they did not forget the events that had transpired on New Caledonia. How could those who remained alive apologize to those who had died? And what would they apologize for? For not having followed the example of those who killed themselves? For not trying to save them from death? Moreover, having experienced the hope of glory followed by the despair and relief at finding themselves alive, how were they to comport themselves now? They were left only with questions, no answers.

Torn from his lifelong moorings, Konosu was even more unsure where he stood now. In a poignant letter to Nisei sergeant Sasaki, an interpreter at the Paita stockade, he bared his heartfelt convictions and doubts. (Since American intelligence personnel often did not give POWs their true names, there is no certainty the sergeant's name really was Sasaki.) In the letter, which passed into Captain Alter's hands, Konosu was certain that he had found complete understanding with Sasaki; in a time of peace they would have been the best of friends, but fate decreed that it would be otherwise. He could not help but pray for Japan's victory; at the same time he urged Sasaki to do his best in the service of his country. Those who have Japanese blood in their veins are destined to do their best, no matter what country they fight for, wrote Konosu, certain that he himself "could never be happy again." It was just bad fortune that he was destined to be a soldier in a war over which he had no control. He felt extremely bad for causing his family such grief by his actions. Konosu explained that he could only deal with these realities by thinking of himself as having been reborn and by avoiding thoughts about Japan.

Turning to the motivation for the act that was seen by his countrymen as a betrayal, Konosu wrote that if the plan had been one of suicide alone, he would have gone along with his group. He opposed it because it would have involved the spilling of innocent American blood. The planned uprising's moral failure, as he saw it, lay in not considering the debt POWs owed the Americans for their very lives.[14]

COWRA, AUSTRALIA

If the failed uprising at Paita was the most bizarre, the revolt at Cowra, one hundred fifty miles west of Sydney, Australia, was by far the war's most serious incident involving Japanese prisoners. Cowra was initially used to house German and Italian POWs from the Australians' campaigns in the Middle East and Africa. Beginning in early 1943, Japanese prisoners were added to the mix. After eighteen months, about eleven hundred Japanese occupied one of the four subdivisions at Cowra, stretching the facility to its limits.

The Australian policy was to leave prisoners pretty much alone. They were required to perform only a few tasks, and leadership within the camps was left to the POWs. The first leaders were English-speaking navy pilots, normally senior NCOs, who had crash-landed in New Guinea. Later, a growing Japanese army faction in the camp, arising from the increased scale of ground combat in the southwest Pacific, seized control from the navy element and, in this instance, took a considerably harder line than its predecessors. Throughout this period, all the prisoners at Cowra believed that the Australians were dealing fairly with them and meeting their material needs.

The proximate cause of the Cowra uprising was the Australian decision to deal with an overflow of POWs by sending about seven hundred lower-ranked men to another camp while keeping the four hundred NCOs at Cowra. For the Australians, this was simply a rational answer to the problem of overcrowding. The Japanese equivalents of privates and privates first class, however, were led by their superiors to see the issue in terms of the imminent "destruction of our nation's family system." By threatening to send off their NCO father figures, the Australians were depriving them of their chief support in dealing with their shameful, alien existence in a foreign land. The NCOs were equally fearful of abandoning their "children." Both groups characterized the threatened separation of ordinary soldiers from their noncommissioned officers as the destruction of a "beautiful old custom." In their common view, therefore, the Australians were planning an inhumane course of action.

Either the POW spokesman lacked the ability to explain the subtleties of the situation or the Australians were simply unprepared to let Japanese dictate camp policy on a matter the Geneva Convention reserved to the government that held the prisoners. In any event, radical elements in this overheated emotional atmosphere quickly gained adherents from among the normally more passive "centrists." The hard-liners argued that Japan was still going to invade Australia and that, when the invasion came, the POWs would want to be in a position to assist such an effort. Moreover, news of a POW uprising would raise the spirits of frontline Japanese troops. The Allies would also be forced to withdraw troops from combat to deal with the uprising, and in that way it would provide concrete support to the Japanese war effort. The basis for such reasoning was flawed, but the spirited appeal was more than sufficient to win the day for the radical elements.

Moderates attempted to argue that the spirit of Bushido required a positive response to the goodwill demonstrated by the Allies in their treatment of POWs. Such favors should not be repaid by an attack on Australian barracks. After agonizing over whether to vote for life or death, however, most moderates reluctantly voted to go along because they felt powerless to oppose the hard-liners' pressure and feared being labeled cowards.

The POW leadership called a meeting of the forty section leaders to decide their course of action. Although a few section leaders voiced an opinion, most remained silent. Section leaders were polled on the proposition that all should participate in a mass attack, based on the premise that all would die in the process. Hard-liners monopolized the "discussion," virtually accusing any opponents of failing to live up to the high standards set for members of the Japanese military. Each section leader was asked to determine the sentiment within his section, but in the prevailing atmosphere it had become exceedingly difficult to withhold support for the preordained course. While there is no record of the vote taken within sections, an estimated 80 percent backed the hard-liners' plan, all others abstaining. Every section leader then voted to support the proposed course of action. The extremists among the POWs had successfully exploited a minor incident to carry out their cherished objective.[15]

And yet considerable doubt existed then and still remains that this resolution really reflected the majority will. As on many other occasions, there was a vast gulf between the *tatemae* and the *honne,* but when this tragedy played out, there was no contest. The *tatemae,* seen as the more honorable, unselfish, proper course of conduct, was bound to win out.

The prisoners prepared themselves for the uprising with the few weapons at their disposal. They used knives, forks, spoons, and razor blades, as well as baseball bats and whatever poles they could find. Almost as important, they had a bugle that would serve to rouse the troops for a charge, allowing them a brief, final moment of glory. On what was to be their last night on earth, the POWs quietly bade farewell to one another with talk of "meeting again at Yasukuni" (the shrine for fallen veterans). They spoke of fate and the "inevitability" of the action on which they were about to embark, but it was hardly a joyous occasion. One POW wrote that he "closed his eyes and thought of the mountains and rivers of his village, his parents, grandparents, and siblings." He heard that in another compound, three POWs had already hanged themselves, the first victim voicing the typical Japanese apology for "going first."[16] Some, undoubtedly including the author of this information, hoped that the enemy would discover the plot and stop the madness. He knew as well as others that with their pitiful arsenal, they had not the slightest chance of overcoming their well-armed guards and had sealed their own death warrants.

The uprising began with the POWs setting their barracks on fire. Then they sought to cross the first strands of barbed wire, using their bedding and baseball gloves to reduce the chances of injuring themselves. Some made it across, but most were killed or wounded. Lights went out and incendiaries lit the scene. The few who managed to get outside the enclosure roamed around aimlessly, survived awhile by eating grass, then hanged themselves. Some of the wounded asked to be killed by the survivors. One of the leaders of the uprising was gravely wounded but still managed to end his own life by cutting his jugular vein with a knife. Nobody knew anything about him—not his real name, rank, or even the prefecture he came from. One of the subordinate leaders who did not want to kill Australians or be killed by them committed suicide, telling his comrades shortly before his death, "[people] do some stupid things," hardly a resounding tone of conviction on embarking on the most important action of his twenty-six years.

Some of the Cowra prisoners preferred to commit suicide right at the start rather than participate in the uprising. They believed that suicide was the more honorable way out. Others may have feared facing a hail of enemy bullets without weapons more than they feared taking their own lives.

Saddest of all, as Moriki Masaru noted, when it was all over, more than half of the dead were from the moderate faction, while the radicals managed to survive quite well, their blood lust apparently sated by the deaths of others. One of the hard-liners who had urged suicide on those unable to join the uprising because they were too sick was a survivor himself. In the sulfurous atmosphere that hung over the camp in the morning, the resentments of the previous night concentrated on him, and he, too, hanged himself, taking responsibility for the fiasco. Many other hard-liners got off scot-free. In spite of the "unanimous vote" to carry out the uprising, more than a few had opted out at the last instant.

Although Moriki sided with the moderates, he wrote sympathetically of the hard-liners who succeeded in their quest to die. "Whatever the outcome [of the uprising], I respect them for their purity in living up to the ideal of death in battle according to the precepts of the *Senjinkun*. Equally, those who in the bottom of their hearts opposed the uprising, at the moment of their deaths splendidly reflected the resolve of the Japanese military."[17] To the Western mind, Moriki's sentiment lamenting the deaths of fallen comrades, irrespective of their diametrically opposite positions on the uprising, is clearer than his logic in assuming that the moderates would have embraced a glorious, if useless, death had they retained the will to carry it out. A Westerner would shed more tears for those who had to die in an action that was hardly a "battle," and one they considered neither meaningful nor necessary.

In this most violent of the uprisings of Japanese prisoners of war, there were 234 deaths (mostly by Australian bullets), and 23 men subsequently died of their wounds. Over a dozen killed themselves during and after the uprising. The Australians lost one officer and three enlisted men when the Japanese managed to seize one of the guard towers.

Unlike American prisoners plotting an escape in Europe, the Japanese had no real hope that a breakout from Cowra could lead to freedom and a return to Japanese-controlled areas. There was never a chance that the Japanese could meld into the surrounding native population, and they had absolutely no hope of leaving the huge island continent. The few prisoners who managed to escape were all recaptured within a few days.

Interviewed by an Australian in 1993, one of the main ringleaders of the uprising, Kanazawa Akira, expressed a "great bond" with the people of Cowra and with the Australians. Another survivor of Cowra characterized it as a deep philosophical experience, and others simply wanted to forget all about it. While some former POWs at Cowra were satisfied they had followed the appropriate Japanese custom in voting for a course of action they did not really believe in, many others who had approved the uprising wanted subsequently to distance themselves from it.[18] Cowra represents a clear example of the difficulty even today's Japanese confront in dealing with mass suicidal actions as in a *gyokusai* or its closely related breakout. In the abstract they can embrace such actions, but the reality strikes many as something of which they do not want to be a part.

BIKANER, BRITISH INDIA

The last Japanese POW challenge to Allied prison authorities took place in the spring of 1945 at the British-run facility in Bikaner, located on the edge of the Indian desert some two hundred forty miles west of Delhi. In this camp, originally constructed to house German prisoners of the First World War, the first prisoner was Senior Sergeant Aoki Akira, whose plane was shot down over Rangoon and crash-landed. He eventually became one of the POW section leaders. Although a Japanese citizen, as were all Koreans at the time, Aoki was a member of the royal house of Korea. Mizui Hajime, a Japanese fellow prisoner deeply imbued with the justice of Japan's cause, paid Aoki the ultimate tribute of noting that he possessed "a high degree of military spirit as well as strong leadership qualities," even though he spoke Japanese with a heavy accent.[19]

In a curious historical footnote, Aoki, reverting to his family name Rhee, achieved a measure of renown in 1949 when he became the first commandant of the Republic of Korea's nascent air force academy. In the following year, shortly after the outbreak of the Korean War, it was Colonel Rhee who took possession of a shipment of ten American P-51 Mustang fighters at Itazuke Airfield on Kyushu. After only three days of training on the new planes, Colonel Rhee, still full of the old fighting spirit, led a formation of three P-51s in a low-altitude raid on a North Korean concentration of T-34 tanks south of Seoul. Hit in the exchange of fire, Rhee crashed his plane into the enemy formation on a suicidal dive and was posthumously promoted to the rank of brigadier general.[20]

Back in 1945, the atmosphere at the Bikaner camp was tranquil. According to all accounts, including those of the International Committee of the Red Cross, treatment of the POWs was excellent. The food was good and adequate, there was plenty of recreation, and virtually no work was assigned because Indians performed all the menial tasks such as cleaning out the latrines. This peaceful scene was then disturbed by a hard-line faction that plotted to create disturbances. In contravention of the Geneva Convention, some of these hard-line

Japanese prisoners refused to salute Allied officers, believing it was improper for them to display any such respect for the enemy. The British were unhappy about this but declined to press the issue. Then, an inspection of the camp conducted by Admiral Lord Louis Mountbatten, the senior British officer in India, led to a sharp deterioration of the atmosphere. When the field marshal asked the assembled prisoners whether there were any complaints about their treatment, one of the prisoners, an army lieutenant who went by the name of Yamada although his real name was Iijima Kazuyoshi, brazenly asked Lord Mountbatten his name. Mountbatten genially responded, but the British camp commander, Lieutenant Colonel Hutchinson, understandably thought the question was a provocation meant to humiliate him and his command publicly.

Unable to ignore the provocation, Colonel Hutchinson resorted to a test of wills. He challenged the POWs to salute him, and when none did, this time the recalcitrants were sent to solitary confinement. This punishment backfired when one of the Japanese officers died of heat prostration in his hut, a victim of the Indian sun, handing further ammunition to the hard-liners. The British attempted to reach an amicable solution and released all Japanese from confinement. The POWs, however, remained obdurately opposed to saluting.

A few days later, Colonel Hutchinson ordered his armed military police to surround the enclosure. Addressing the assembled POWs, he demanded that the prisoners attend twice-daily roll call, that they salute all British officers, and that enlisted personnel perform light work assignments in the camp. If there was no compliance within a week, his guards would storm the facility. The hard-liners seized upon these not unreasonable demands to mobilize sentiment against their captors, countering with a hunger strike. The prisoners armed themselves with homemade weapons such as bamboo spears and welcomed the opportunity to die in the anticipated assault. Three days later the British tossed bread over the barbed wire. The Japanese threw it back. One POW caught eating the bread was summarily strung up and killed by fellow Japanese. The POWs also piled up their bedding and threatened to set it afire.

At the end of six days, the POWs were weak with hunger. Just as tensions were becoming intolerable, and with the deadline for compliance fast approaching, the British agreed to a truce on the basis of reverting to the situation that had existed before Lord Mountbatten's visit. The Japanese were jubilant, believing they had won a big victory. To show their goodwill, the British provided the camp with ample food and drink, even some sake. That night, while the POWs had their first good sleep in a week, Indian troops entered the camp. All prisoners were thrown out of their barracks and led to the exercise area. Called up by name one by one, they were asked whether they would now salute. Depending on the response, the POWs were divided into two roughly equal groups, which effectively isolated the troublemakers.

But the hard-liners were not yet done. They set a few buildings on fire, in which three POWs chose to perish, and even more talked about the idea of killing themselves. The Japanese did everything in their power to annoy the British. They sang the Japanese national anthem and occasionally tied written appeals to large stones that were then thrown toward the British barracks. They also engaged in petty acts of what they wanted to believe was "sabotage."

Eventually, the British lost all patience. Their Indian troops began to beat up the worst offenders among the POWs. In the end, most of the hard-liners at Bikaner were sent further west to a more primitive POW camp at Quetta on what is now close to Pakistan's border with Afghanistan. Even this drastic move failed to eliminate open expressions of anti-British enmity, and the test of wills did not end even with Japan's surrender. Unresolved, but less lethal than the other conflicts, this one ended only when the Japanese were repatriated.

The only time the Japanese government took cognizance of Japanese prisoners in Allied hands was when it seized on the Cowra and Featherston uprisings as opportunities to score propaganda points. Characterizing the mass killings as "massacres" on the basis of wire-service reports, Japan sent protests through diplomatic channels to the countries concerned. Following the Featherston incident, the Japanese government complained that the New Zealand guards made no effort to avoid a showdown and wantonly opened fire over a trifling pretext, characterizing the incident as an "unpardonable violation of humanity." This protest, dated March 13 1943, referred to "Japanese" and "Japanese nationals" but never used the unmentionable POW word.[21] In response, the New Zealand government noted that the Japanese prisoners had been defiant and failed to follow legitimate orders. When a New Zealand officer had fired a warning shot, he was met with a hail of stones, and the prisoners had then rushed the guards. At the ensuing official inquiry, most Japanese refused to testify. Those who agreed to testify blamed their leaders for the incident and their lack of understanding of the provisions of the Geneva Convention concerning the employment of POWs by the detaining power.

The Japanese government fired the last shot in this exchange. It sent a diplomatic note through Swiss channels reserving the right to take retaliatory action if New Zealand persisted in dealing with unarmed Japanese by force of arms.[22]

With the two exceptions of Cowra and Featherston, the Japanese government never recognized the existence of any Japanese prisoners, and even in these two instances, the reference was indirect. It follows that Japan did not permit relatives at home to communicate in any way with POWs.

CAMP MCCOY, WISCONSIN, UNITED STATES

Compared to the serious challenges to Allied authority in Australia, New Zealand, and India, the disturbance at Camp McCoy in May 1944 was minor. It resulted from a new policy on the use of POW labor. Initially, camp commander Lt. Col. Horace Rogers issued orders for a forty-hour work week. Work was restricted to nonmilitary projects and would take place inside McCoy but not within sight of civilians, to spare the prisoners the odium of having to endure the stares of curious Americans. Any food grown and harvested by the prisoners would be for their exclusive use.

When camp authorities required POWs to dry and clean tents and to clean barracks vacated by Europe-bound American GIs, the Japanese balked. Although clearly outside the meaning of prohibited labor,[23] the Japanese POWs insisted that the order was illegal. The Americans finally lost patience and went over to tough measures, including short rations and heavy labor, as permitted by the Geneva Convention in the case of recalcitrance. The officer POWs were physically separated from the enlisted personnel, and, more importantly, the nine NCO troublemakers were also separated from the rest.

When the remaining enlisted men refused to show up for roll call, Colonel Rogers called in a hundred armed soldiers to restore order and to get the POWs to work. The Japanese countered with a slowdown. The Americans then prodded the recalcitrants with their bayonets, which sent a few to the dispensary and the rest to work. This ended all defiance of legitimate orders.

The relatively restrained measures taken to deal with a potentially explosive situation earned added respect for the widely praised, fair, and courteous Colonel Rogers. Order was rapidly restored. The POW leaders, including Lieutenant Sakamaki, called for unity and moving forward to a meaningful future. Colonel Rogers's adept handling of the situation underlined the importance of the camp commander's personality in dealing with enemy POWs.

Although the suicidal uprisings in the POW camps have been a special interest of Japanese authors, they were the exception rather than the rule. They represented the final outward manifestation of some of the POW hard-liners' smoldering determination to end what little was left of what they firmly believed were their irretrievably misspent lives. It seems clear, however, that a substantial majority of prisoners wanted no further confrontations. Despite continued feelings of shame, they preferred to let events take their course. As many phrased it, if life became intolerable later, they could always kill themselves then.

9

EVERYDAY LIFE
IN THE STOCKADES

While uprisings were noteworthy, and tensions rose and abated from time to time in the prison camps, these were not what defined normal life for Japanese POWs. The great majority learned to adjust to the prescribed routines of work, self-generated sports and entertainment, meals, and plenty of boredom.

Since Japanese were never told what to do if captured, it is not surprising that only a few tried to escape from their POW camps. They were well guarded, and POWs who came up with the idea of gaining freedom could not, in their wildest dreams, believe that even if escape was possible they might remain free indefinitely. Given their circumstances, which included clothing painted with large "POW" letters, a lack of English skills, and the fact that few Oriental faces were seen in Middle America during the war years, it is not surprising that a successful escape was hardly possible.

While a total of fourteen Japanese prisoners did attempt to escape from Camp McCoy over a two-and-a-half-year period, the efforts were almost comical. One escapee headed for Mexico, in the mistaken belief that it was located somewhere three hundred miles to the south. Another wandered around aimlessly for a few days before he frightened a farmer's wife half to death, indicating through sign language that he was hungry. A third POW was spotted poling down the Mississippi on a homemade raft.

Allied forces also captured roughly ten thousand ethnic Koreans and Taiwanese working for the Japanese. Although some Koreans were integral members of the Japanese armed forces, most had either

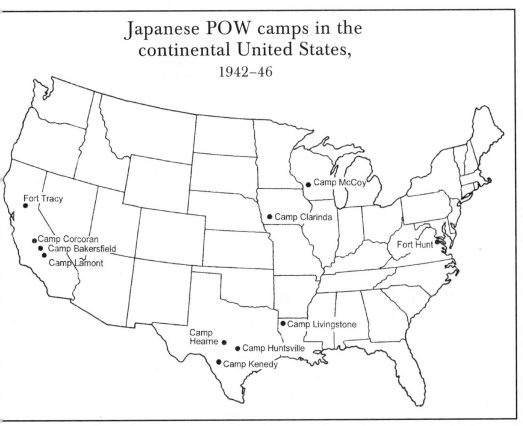

Japanese POW camps in the continental United States, 1942–46

Map 2. Japanese POW camps in the continental United States, 1942–46. California camps came into use only after the end of the war.

volunteered for or been drafted into labor battalions ordered into combat only when the tactical situation became desperate. Then they became little more than cannon fodder, along with the Japanese soldiers. The Koreans and Taiwanese in the labor battalions, however, did not share the Japanese preference for death over capture and surrendered to Allied forces in droves whenever it became feasible to do so. It was Allied policy to separate out captured Koreans and Taiwanese, assigning each group to its own enclosure. Cowra, in Australia, was the exception, in that it kept Japanese and the few ethnic Korean officers in the same enclosure. Koreans and Taiwanese were not imprisoned any further east than Hawaii, and many remained in the general area of their capture. Once the war ended, they were among the earliest to be repatriated.

There was never much love lost between Japanese and Koreans, and imprisonment did nothing to change that fact. Japanese POWs felt genuinely appalled, almost betrayed, to discover that the Koreans thought of themselves as victors once the war ended and looked down on the Japanese. Some Japanese POWs, including Takahashi Shigeru, realized that Japanese had discriminated against Koreans and Taiwanese and that the Koreans' gleeful attitude when Japan lost therefore "could not be helped."[1] In the few instances when Japanese were erroneously placed into an enclosure with Koreans, they were beaten up in revenge for earlier treatment at the hands of their colonial masters.

Most ethnic Koreans who had served as integral members of the Japanese military chose to maintain their Japanese identity in the prison camps. They may well have feared the wrath of fellow Koreans who had been pressed into the labor battalions and believed they would be more secure in the Japanese section. One of the reports from Cowra noted that Koreans caused no trouble for the Australians, except for a small minority who were "very pro-Japanese." This element compelled the rest to face east and bow reverentially after every roll call. When fellow Koreans disregarded this courtesy to the emperor, they were manhandled.

Taiwanese hostility toward the Japanese POWs was substantially less than that of the Koreans. American comments about Taiwanese prisoners, who never created problems, were entirely positive. When interrogated about possible American landing sites on Taiwan, they were uniformly eager to provide all the information they had.

On Okinawa the American army split up Japanese POWs in yet another way, separating not only Japanese and Koreans but Okinawans as well. Initially somewhat resistant to the idea of being distinguished from Japanese, Yamada Yuko soon became rather pleased to be called Okinawan rather than the pejorative "Jap" that was in common usage by Americans during the war. Given the Okinawans' widespread disillusionment with the Japanese military, especially its ruthless treatment of tens of thousands of civilians needlessly exposed to the hazards of war, it is hardly surprising that Okinawans relished this separate treatment, a difference manifested in a number of ways. Noting that Americans were eager to obtain Japanese swords as souvenirs, Okinawan POWs volunteered to help them find some. On several occasions they were even allowed to leave the prison camp without guards to search for souvenirs. Such complete trust was so greatly appreciated that the Okinawans could not think of betraying it. Nevertheless, when news of Japan's defeat filtered into the Yaka stockade, Yamada felt the humiliation, and when the Koreans held their victory celebration, he thought that his own feelings were no different from the feelings of those who came from other Japanese prefectures.[2]

Illustrative of POWs' widely differing objectives in the midst of a fluid situation that allowed for considerable private initiative, some Japanese POWs on Okinawa falsely gave themselves off as Okinawans and were shipped off to a POW camp in Hawaii. At the same time, there were Okinawans who identified themselves as Japanese in expectation of being sent, after the war, to one of Japan's main islands, where they hoped for a better economic future than had been available in their home prefecture.

Camp McCoy was unusual in that it initially held not only all ranks of the military up to field grade officers but also a sizeable contingent of Japanese civilians. Except for the relatively minor incident recounted in the previous chapter, Camp McCoy tended to enjoy trouble-free relations with its POWs. According to a former civilian employee of the Japanese navy's transportation division on Saipan, the civilian POWs constituted a solid bloc that was understandably opposed to the hotheads, whose suicidal intentions struck fear into the hearts of merchant seamen, businessmen, and journalists, among others. The civilians told the extremists that they would still have plenty of opportunities to kill themselves without involving the civilian element. When the hard-liners ultimately backed away from more confrontational tactics with the American guards and vented their frustration by beating up on the civilians, a larger group of civilians returned the favor a few days later.

Two of the Cowra stockade's four sections housed Italian soldiers. The Japanese found the Italians totally different from themselves. Italian POWs did not appear to feel any boredom or mental anguish.

On the contrary, they acted relaxed and happy, often singing joyously. All appeared to be writing home and receiving letters and even money from their families. These differences clearly bothered some Japanese, who felt unable to emulate Italian POW behavior. Many had assumed a false name and rank during interrogation. They had burned their bridges, and there was no going back.

Yamamoto Tomio recalled seeing German and Italian prisoners in an adjacent enclosure at a camp in Virginia, most likely Fort Hunt. In the evening, the Italians would sing. The Germans would congregate near the barbed wire fence to "show us the swastikas they had drawn on the inside of their prison garb. While standing erect and rigid they would salute us and boisterously told us that in ten years they would definitely join us in bringing down the United States."[3] Other Japanese POWs recalled that German prisoners were not at all ashamed of their status, and that some were unabashedly glad they no longer had to fight. By mutual consent, German POWs traded their rice rations for the potato rations destined for the Japanese, making both groups more content.

Japanese prisoners in Australia had almost no direct contact with German or Italian POWs from Rommel's Afrika Korps taken prisoner in North Africa, and those at Camp McCoy displayed only limited interest in their Axis allies. A *Collier's* magazine story, based on what one reporter saw and heard at Camp McCoy, concluded that the Japanese and Germans hated each other, at best an exaggeration because Japanese traditionally held Germans in high regard. Nevertheless, American guards told the reporter that the Japanese liked nothing better than to erect barbed wire fences for incoming German prisoners; the Germans reciprocated by leaving flower beds untended when they knew their compounds were going to be taken over by the Japanese.[4]

Such mutual disregard could be attributed to the physical distance between their enclosures and the linguistic barrier. It was, however, also a demonstration of a pronounced lack of affinity, even on an ideological basis, between the Japanese and their so-called Axis allies. Wartime cooperation between Germany and Japan was minimal, with little trust between them. The biggest impact on Japanese POWs came when Germany capitulated. German POWs could go home, and the Japanese realized that their homeland now had to face Western might alone.

In late 1944, the army Provost Marshal's Office became quite concerned about rumors of so-called "hara-kiri clubs" in POW camps and even queried the Canadian government about the existence of such "clubs" in Canada. At first, it was assumed that the name must refer to Japanese POWs. The Canadian response indicated, however, that it was not Japanese but fanatical German POWs, largely members of the SS and Gestapo, who were planning violence against anti-Nazi German prisoners. The "clubs" never went much beyond the rumor stage. Lending such a feared Japanese name to a German POW initiative may have been about the only "collaboration" between the two groups of prisoners of war.[5]

Japanese POWs incarcerated in the Midwest and South of the United States were effectively isolated from the surrounding civilian populations. Given the widespread American hostility toward Japan, this served to prevent any untoward incidents. Hawaii, however, presented a friendlier environment. There the Japanese POWs even enjoyed limited contact with Japanese-American civilians. Since Japanese immigrants constituted close to a third of Hawaii's total prewar population, there was really no way, and no need, to insulate Japanese prisoners from the civilian population. Japanese Americans occasionally had opportunities to supplement the prisoners' diet with Japanese specialties that were greatly appreciated.

Along these lines, Ouchi Shoshin cited his prison camp experience of establishing contact with Japanese-American laundry workers across the fence. In this way he even met a Japanese-American family, the Kuboyamas, who had emigrated to Hawaii from his home village. On one occasion Ouchi was permitted to leave camp in the company of a military policeman who drove him in an ambulance to visit this family. In their home he saw a picture of the family's son, an army volunteer who had fought and died with the all-Nisei 442nd Regimental Combat Team in Europe. Ouchi was sad for the fate they had had to endure but felt that, like so much else, "it could not be helped." As Ouchi left, the Kuboyamas gave him a fountain pen and a wristwatch.[6]

While POW camps under American control followed broad

guidelines set down by the Provost Marshal, individual camp commanders largely determined the extent to which prisoners were allowed to conduct their own internal administration. At Camp McCoy, the largest and perhaps best-run prison camp in the continental United States, Colonel Rogers left this to the Japanese POWs. Several camp inmates commented that Japanese noncommissioned officers ran the enlisted men's enclosure. These NCO "bosses" made sure that nobody ever talked openly about Japan's military reverses in the field, saying such talk was just American propaganda. The "bosses" retained some measure of credibility by claiming to possess a secret shortwave radio on which they received broadcasts from Japan. Many fellow prisoners believed them, although it would have been nearly impossible to keep a radio hidden through countless inspections. Holding fast to the Japanese version of events, however, allowed these POWs to avoid the emotional turmoil of facing reality. Even when Japan surrendered on August 15, 1945, several "bosses" remained unconvinced, and months later were still inflicting corporal punishment on those who dared to express openly the belief that Japan had lost the war. Only when Ouchi's group was transferred from Camp McCoy to Hawaii did the "bosses" get their comeuppance. There the newcomers were the ones to be beaten up by the already well-established "bosses" there.

While the war was still in progress, Ouchi believed that he could talk frankly only with two or three of his best friends about the adverse trend of the war. As more and more POWs arrived at Camp McCoy with accounts of successive Japanese defeats, POWs were able to update their knowledge on what was really happening on the battlefronts with firsthand accounts that validated the American version they were also getting from newspapers and the guards.

The situation was similar at Iroquois Point in Hawaii, where POWs asked a Japanese medical officer recently arrived from Peleliu, a key American target on the road to the Philippines, how the war was going. The officer responded factually that the Americans had taken the island and opined that "the war is lost." This was interpreted as a sellout rather than a sober assessment of Japan's desperate situation, and for this the officer was slapped around by several petty officers. His precious glasses that had survived even the battle for

Peleliu went flying. The doctor ruefully commented that he could not afford to use the word "defeat" in that section of the camp. If the situation had deteriorated further, he would have been forced to flee to Pen 8, where POWs willing to cooperate actively with the Americans were housed.[7]

Since boredom was a major enemy in the camps, most Japanese POWs readily accepted the necessity of performing work in accordance with the Geneva Convention. Officers were excluded from this requirement, and NCOs were normally used only in supervisory positions, unless they expressly requested remunerative work. Japanese prisoners were employed on tasks similar to those performed by Germans and those Italians who had been classified "noncooperative." Many Japanese POWs had been farmers with few skills beyond those required for agriculture. They easily adapted to tasks such as grass cutting, cleaning barracks, road maintenance, building fire lanes, and cutting wood on the bases. Owing to public hostility toward Japanese, they were not assigned to contract work outside the camps. The POW work system functioned most effectively when Japanese prisoners worked under their own leaders, in groups, and had ample time to complete tasks. For the most part, they were anxious to make a good impression and worked well.

Many Japanese believed that in becoming prisoners they were destined to remain "slave laborers" for the rest of their lives. They were therefore pleasantly surprised to learn that, under the rules of the Geneva Convention, they were entitled to a modest wage. At Camp McCoy, for example, they were paid for their labor at the rate of eighty cents a day, mostly in chits that could only be spent at the PX. POWs could buy what they wanted there, including limited amounts of beer. Not all POW camps for Japanese had systems in place to pay prisoners at all times, and prisoner pay was never high, but it added to the satisfaction of remaining busy.

When POWs at Camp McCoy were not working, they could choose from a wide variety of sports, self-generated entertainment, and education to while away the time behind barbed wire. Judo and sumo matches provided an excellent outlet for their energies. Volleyball and baseball were also popular. Prisoners often played mah-jongg and shogi (a Japanese form of chess) after making the required pieces themselves. Some of the *hana-fuda* (flower cards) for another popular Japanese game were so well made that they seemed almost professional. Used playing cards were made available by the guards. Gambling was a widespread obsession. Razor blades were officially forbidden in camp because of concern over possible suicides; however, this regulation was never enforced after the authorities became convinced that the prisoners used razor blades extensively in making games and had no intention to kill themselves.

Artistically gifted prisoners also kept busy producing souvenirs for their guards and other Americans who passed through. Handkerchiefs depicting cherry blossoms, Mount Fuji, or a geisha standing on a red bridge were especially popular items. There were also brisk sales of *shunga* (erotic pictures) drawn by the prisoners. The POW cottage industries were supported by the guards, who paid for their products with paint, brushes, extra beer, and cigarettes. Tobacco was not just smoked but used as common currency and to settle gambling debts among the prisoners.

Entertainment provided by the prisoners themselves was extremely popular, the more so because the Japanese military had never seen fit to provide USO-type shows for its men. Left to their own devices, POWs became adept at putting on shows that featured minstrel songs, Japanese-style storytelling, popular songs, and comedy acts. "The POW Returns," an especially successful skit put on at Iroquois Point in Hawaii, had the POW finally being mustered out at Uraga, an hour's train ride south of Tokyo, after a lengthy imprisonment. It made fun of the POWs' reluctance to return home and face their families "with shame." Accordingly, instead of heading south to his home in Shizuoka, the mustered-out POW first heads for Sapporo on the northern island of Hokkaido. A year later he is on a train to Kagoshima, the southernmost city on Kyushu in the south. In the following years he keeps bracketing his hometown, by ever smaller distances, until finally he screws up enough courage to get off the train in Shizuoka in central Japan. He crisscrosses the city, taking ever-shorter routes bracketing his home, but never enters it. The audience's anticipation grows. The storyteller ends his tale abruptly without getting to the inevitable final encounter, saying, "Sorry to have bored you for so long," amid long applause. In a case of life imitating art, one prisoner on returning to Japan avoided going directly to his home for a long time and bypassed it repeatedly. However, his hair did not turn gray before he overcame his inhibitions, as happened in the skit.

Most of the POW skits were comedies that dealt with prison camp existence. Appropriate clothing was usually stitched together from material available within the camp or occasionally provided from the outside. When female parts were essential, some of the younger prisoners were "persuaded" to cooperate, and the older prisoners were duly appreciative.

Some homosexual relationships were established under the abnormal conditions of prolonged imprisonment. They were not kept hidden, since such behavior was not considered aberrant, and certainly no weirder than becoming a prisoner of war. Moreover, homosexual behavior was not punishable under Japan's military code. One prisoner who was captured on Attu estimated that up to 20 percent of the soldiers on that island had engaged in homosexual acts. But this was an unusual reference to a subject otherwise seldom noted. Although interrogations occasionally covered a very wide range of subject areas, they hardly ever touched on this one.

Prisoners at Camp McCoy were allowed to visit the movie theater once a week, under guard. In the dark, they could forget for a while that they were POWs. Since Japanese movies were not available and American films lacked subtitles, only a small percentage of POWs would have understood the dialogue. Nevertheless, they enjoyed the opportunity to escape the routine of camp life.

Occasional social get-togethers of POWs from the same prefecture, or of POWs who entered their respective services at the same time, were organized, with beer and even other refreshments. To liven up parties, musical instruments, records and phonographs, and sports equipment were provided by the War Prisoners Aid of the YMCA.

By all accounts, life was good at Camp McCoy, better than in any other camp in the continental United States. Japanese POWs even received occasional meals of Japanese food that they judged to be much better than the food their guards were given. Nisei interpreters were often happy to get invited to join them. As one former POW put it, "Life was agreeable, human rights were respected and the commander and his staff showed deep understanding [for the POWs' needs]."[8]

The other prison camps, while they did not measure up to Camp McCoy, were not at all bad, as most of the same facilities for entertainment, sports, and education were provided. Nevertheless, when the Japanese officer POWs were moved from Camp McCoy to Camp Kenedy in late spring of 1945, they noticed the difference. There they had to deal with a Captain Taylor, who viewed POWs in a much harsher light, no doubt because he had been at Pearl Harbor when Japan launched its attack.[9] Captain Taylor was a stickler for meting out harsh punishments for minor infractions. For example, possession of a penknife could earn the prisoner a turn in solitary confinement. Ensign Sakamaki, among others, once spent a week in solitary on bread and water.

The American public apparently believed that its government was treating prisoners of war with excessive consideration. The Japanese were reputed to "complain too much," the Germans were "too happy" with their lot, and the Italians, most of whom, unlike Japanese and Germans, were free to work in the civilian communities, were "too affectionate" (with the girls). The *Collier's* article set the record straight. It pointed out that the prisoners were all treated "sternly but fairly," in accordance with international law.[10]

For virtually all Japanese POWs, prison camp was their first exposure to Americans and their ways, and for many it was an eye-opening, often bewildering, sometimes incomprehensible experience. They commented approvingly on the great care American troops lavished on sanitation, even near the front lines, as a means of preventing unnecessary casualties. This was totally unlike what they had known in their own military service. They had been taught to believe that dealing with the rigors of life in the jungle was simply a hardship that had to be accepted. Since the Japanese took virtually no public health measures, POWs were amazed by the extensive American campaigns to eradicate mosquitoes with DDT. Writing their autobiographies many decades later, former POWs often remembered what it felt like to be deloused with DDT when they fell into American hands.

The POWs' first encounters with the ubiquitous K and C rations of the Second World War were described in loving detail, even noticing that K rations were protected from dampness by paraffin. Takahashi Shigeru, a prisoner in the Philippines, and several other former POWs were fascinated by the indented GI aluminum trays on which warm food was ladled out to soldiers at mealtimes. Equally intriguing to them was the way Americans cleansed their trays and utensils by brief immersion in soapy hot water. He marveled at the extensive use of machinery such as bulldozers, trucks, and jeeps. But he also made good-natured fun of the Americans, rather like the postwar American TV series set in a German POW camp that mocked their German captors. Most significantly, perhaps, Takahashi realized in prison camp how much Japanese military regulations and codes of behavior had penetrated his very being, and how much more inhibited he was compared with the Americans. Seeing the variety and abundance of modern weapons in harbors, airfields, and depots, most prisoners wondered silently, if not out loud, how Japan's rulers could have believed they would win a war against a country so amply endowed.

Takahashi's eyes opened even wider with amazement when he was assigned to the American senior officers mess after the war. Some eighty "diligent" Japanese POWs had replaced an equal number of "sly" and "lazy" Filipino workers (as Takahashi phrased it) and were occasionally allowed to dine with the American mess sergeant on generous-sized steaks. The Japanese turned the rice provided by the Japanese mess staff into sake, and occasionally slipped some of the better food to their comrades in the camp. For Takahashi at this time, life was really looking up.

With his day of repatriation approaching rapidly, Takahashi screwed up enough courage one day to approach the American commanding general in his tent. To the amazement of his fellow POWs, he asked the general, in his halting pidgin English, for a letter of recommendation that he wanted to use in looking for a job in Japan. Takahashi was immensely pleased to receive such a letter. He was also quite aware that while perhaps permissible in America, the land of the free, this encounter could never have happened in Japan even if he had not been a prisoner at the time.[11]

Over time some of the prisoners became quite friendly with their

MP guards. Both prisoners and guards were often lonely and needed to talk with a fellow human being. For the Japanese, these meetings were gratifying and quite unexpected. Moriki Masaru, for example, wrote that he really came to like one of his guards, with whom he had learned to communicate through sign language. Most significant to him was that he never thought of his conversation partner as "the enemy," attesting to the Japanese propensity to think of interpersonal relations in terms of roles appropriate to various stations in life. Given the (to him) unbridgeable gap between his status as a POW and that of his soldier/guard, Moriki was amazed that his guard could even make him laugh. Moriki recalled that he strongly disagreed with his friend's confidence that he would be able to return to Japan one day with honor. Nevertheless, the American's insistence that Japanese were unique in believing that only death could cleanse one of the shame of having become a POW planted some seeds of doubt about his own beliefs.[12]

Several POWs also remarked how strange they found it that American soldiers could so easily shed their military role when off duty. Shockingly, some could even be seen flirting with girls! Japanese soldiers could never forget their status as members of the military, even when off duty, and especially could not conceive of engaging in such frivolities as pursuing amorous fancies. Ouchi, in writing of his experiences, expressed surprise at the prevalence of female nurses and that they were given officer status, so unlike Japan's practice. Even medical treatment was unaffected by the patient's enemy status or by racial discrimination. Ouchi noted that the ENT clinic at Camp McCoy had a young receptionist with a ready smile, and best of all, it was for POWs and Americans alike.[13] Along the same lines, Yoshida Osamu, a prisoner taken on Saipan, reminisced that melancholy over his status as a POW was erased by the kind treatment he received from nurses and other women at Camp McCoy. Thereafter he no longer cared whether the person he was dealing with was black, white, yellow, or green; it was enough that they treated him with the dignity of a human being.[14]

The long periods of leisure in the camps led at least some prisoners to reflect on what they had been taught about Americans and to contrast this with the daily reality of dealing with them in the flesh. At school they had learned that Americans were individualists with little or no sense of patriotism. Yet when the war began, they were now told, many Americans volunteered for military service even before being called up. In Japan, it was extremely rare for noncareer men to volunteer and virtually unthinkable that students, especially those in the university, would voluntarily give up their studies to join the army or navy.

From time to time, ordinary American soldiers drifted into the stockade, either out of curiosity, or boredom, or just to obtain some service, like getting a watchband fixed, and often they would stay to show pictures of their families or girlfriends. An American doctor who liked classical music occasionally visited the POW camp and asked a Japanese POW to sing Schubert lieder for him.

One prisoner who spent months recuperating from wounds in a hospital in Hawaii established an especially close relationship with his doctors and nurses. In the summer of 1945 he realized that the war must be coming to an end and figured out that, as a patient in Hawaii, he was likely to be among the first POWs to be repatriated. Although most POWs would have welcomed an early reunion with their families, this prisoner realized that it would interfere with his hopes of seeing more of the United States. In a remarkable story of a prisoner manipulating the system, he persuaded his doctor to discharge him from the hospital and to arrange his early transfer to a camp in the continental United States. It all worked out well for him. He received the "free trip" that included substantial train travel through parts of the continental United States, which satisfied his curiosity about the country that had captured him during the war.[15]

Prison camp life did not always go so smoothly. Misunderstandings and tensions abounded in the relationships between guards and POWs, owing to lack of a common language and the very different cultures from which they came. In one case, a guard constantly told the Japanese to "hubba hubba" (wartime GI slang for hurry up). All the Japanese thought the guard was trying to harass them with cries of "Pearl Harbor, Pearl Harbor," since the Japanese pronunciation of *harbor* comes close to "hubba." There were numerous accusations that Americans relieved POWs of personal items such as watches. But at least half thought these regrettable actions "could not be helped" since such practices were common during wartime.

Downtrodden and dispirited as prisoners of war, POWs relished finding ways in which they could feel superior to the Americans, such as the amount of time it took to "count off" at military formations and in mastering multiplication tables. Retaining a bit of "face" when they had already lost so much of it was clearly a matter of considerable importance.

Even at McCoy, regarded by all Japanese who spent time there as a model POW camp, there were minor disputes. POWs quickly learned to exploit the provisions of the Geneva Convention, posted in Japanese translation within the camp. In taking advantage of what they assumed were their rights, the Japanese often struck Americans as being uncharacteristically legalistic. Significantly, in many such controversies Japanese officers preferred to stay on the sidelines, permitting their NCOs wide latitude in dealing with the authorities.

One postwar incident at Camp McCoy reflected the mentality, often so different from that of the Americans, that infused Japanese behavior. The camp laundry was run by prisoners and was subject to rules set by prison authorities. It became the custom that half the money found by POWs in the Americans' clothing was turned over to the guards, and the rest was given to the guards to purchase items for the prisoners that they themselves were unable to buy at the PX. This led to grumbling among other prisoners who were not similarly favored. The practice was ordered stopped, but it continued. The POWs' leader then took matters in his own hands and decided to settle the issue in Japanese fashion. He chose, perhaps at random, one of the POWs assigned to the laundry who had been seen in possession of American money. This unlucky fellow was told that he was by no means the only one still engaging in unfair dealings. The punishment he was about to endure was not, therefore, a reflection on his personal honor; it was, however, his duty to accept responsibility on behalf of his group's inclination to persist in a harmful practice. The "culprit" accepted his responsibility without a murmur of dissent. He was beaten so badly in front of all the laundry workers that several weeks later he was still unable to walk. There was no official record of the incident, but the regrettable practice that threatened POW unity ceased. The "culprit" was held in the highest esteem thereafter by his fellow workers.[16]

The most intense interaction of the war between prisoners and their captors took place at a navy POW camp near Pearl Harbor. A group of POWs who were gradually beginning to consider cooperating in America's war effort engaged Otis Cary, the deputy camp commander, in a wide-ranging dialogue on how Americans perceived prisoners of war. At first it was inconceivable, even to this relatively enlightened element of the Japanese prisoner population, that Americans could think of prisoners of war as having acted honorably, even deserving of medals. They were still dubious until one day Cary thought of having this group look at the Japanese rendition of a card provided to all Americans flying bombing missions over Japan. For possible use if they were shot down, the card asked that its holder be taken to the nearest police because he "has a right to live as a prisoner." The POWs were also shown the scarves provided B-29 crews with a chart of the Pacific Ocean and its currents to help them avoid capture. Such evidence of America's deep concern for its own potential prisoners of war served to convince the Japanese that the American view of POWs was without doubt radically different from the one they were used to. It made them envious and contributed to their understanding as to why Americans might fight even harder, knowing that their government was behind them, no matter what the adversity. Cary also promoted the concept that Japanese POWs had given their all and now needed to remain alive to work for the Japan that would emerge out of the ruins of war. These were indeed radically new and different ways of looking at their fate and what the future might bring. While always a distinct minority, some prisoners proved receptive to ideas that provided a glimpse into a far more optimistic future than they had dared to imagine.

Among the two hundred prisoners of the navy in Hawaii in the summer of 1944, only about ten were convinced that Japan would lose the war. This group earnestly began a course of study to aid them in moving Japan in the direction of democracy once the war ended. They read widely in the literature given them by Cary. Some of these books were translated into Japanese for the benefit of prisoners who did not know English, and the many copies of such books subsequently transcribed by hand attest to the popularity of the project. The books dealt with the rise of militarism in Japan and Japan's imperialist record abroad. They provided viewpoints that had been suppressed in Japan in the years leading up to the war and were therefore novel to the POWs. One of the prisoners, to make such radical information palatable to the others, quoted Emperor Meiji to the effect that "the best kind of criticism is always made by the enemy."

With Cary's active support, this extensive reading program led to the establishment of the so-called "Hawaii College," in which POW lecturers in English language, history, and politics provided information to their fellow prisoners. These lecturers fully realized that a postwar Japan would require a new and different slant on Japan's past. Lectures were followed by free discussions. As at least partial converts to a more democratic outlook, they inevitably had greater credibility than the American authors of books the POWs had read. When students mispronounced words in the English class, MP guards outside the mess hall where the classes took place would helpfully yell the correct pronunciation through the windows. Not surprisingly, the guards also taught the students some quite inappropriate words and expressions, but gave them totally wrong meanings.

The activist-reformer POWs in Hawaii also put out a periodical with contributions about wartime experiences from camp residents. This "Camp Circular" was seen as unbiased, with contributions from all factions within the camp, and was therefore very popular. One prisoner was so motivated that he wrote a long novel with a progressive theme that was serialized in the "Camp Circular." Cary's efforts also produced a musical evening at the camp. He managed to find records of prewar Japanese popular hits and found, to his surprise, great appreciation as well for classical Western music, including Beethoven's *Emperor* Piano Concerto.

The student prisoners were also supplied with Japanese-language books borrowed from the University of Hawaii, one of the few libraries where such material could be found. The two newspapers of Hawaii's Nisei community, printed in both Japanese and English, were made available to the POWs in the hope of correcting their inaccurate understanding of the cause and course of the war. Hard-liners within the camp predictably derided the papers as American propaganda. Unfortunately, the newspapers were not completely convincing because their poor Japanese translations provided the camp's implacable elements with openings for attacking their authenticity.

The hard-liners' efforts to promote inaccurate Japanese claims of continuing victories made it imperative to counteract them with more truthful American accounts from the battlefields. Cary promoted the concept of a posted newspaper to provide prisoners with accurate translations from the English-language press. Many POWs would comment loudly that these articles were nothing but lies and more lies but came back the following day to read the news again. A number of POWs who had obtained cushy jobs, such as medical orderlies, spread invented stories about Japanese victories and Allied defeats simply in order to avoid being labeled American toadies. Ultimately, the fact that "Japanese victories" were moving ever closer to the Japanese homeland proved persuasive to increasing numbers of POWs.

POW COOPERATION TO END THE WAR

Leaflets encouraging Japanese on the battlefield to surrender had little success at first, largely because Japan's strategic position was then still far from precarious or hopeless, and the leaflets tended to be poorly conceived and badly phrased. They improved after Nisei were brought into the drafting phase and got even better when cooperating POWs in Hawaii and the Philippines provided advice on what would appeal most to Japanese soldiers. POWs counseled that wording that implied ineffective leadership by officers would resonate only if it matched the personal experience of those reading the leaflets. Leaflets stressing that Japanese forces were in a desperate situation might work to induce more soldiers to surrender but could also cause more Japanese to commit suicide. An appeal to give up in order to help create a new Japan would not be effective, the POWs advised, since nobody thought he would ever return to Japan after becoming a POW. References to Germany's fate and its surrender would have no effect, because the Japanese believed they were fighting a quite separate war. On the other hand, promises of good treatment of POWs, especially if accompanied by pictures that gave evidence it was already being practiced, would be most effective in assuaging the soldiers' fears.

Cooperative prisoners of the American army in the Philippines, Marianas, and Okinawa were similarly used to devise appeals for the Japanese military and civilians to leave their caves and live, rather than be killed by flamethrowers or be sealed in and die. Such appeals were often most effective when made in the name of a respected Japanese leader, such as an officer or senior NCO, who had been taken prisoner and who was known to the persons in the cave. Appeals of this nature were even more persuasive if the leader confirmed he was being well treated in American captivity.

Prisoners were also helpful in assuring that the language in the leaflets adopted just the right tone—not too slangy but not too formal, either. Certain words, like "surrender," were to be strictly avoided, they advised. Messages should not be too long or complex, and leaflets should be small enough to be easily folded so that they could be hidden in a pocket. One prisoner suggested that the appeal should be addressed to target recipients along the lines of, "To the soldiers fighting bravely in the southwest Pacific area front lines." Different ethnic groups had to be addressed separately, however, as in "To all Formosans." Several prisoners, citing Chinese successes in inducing Japanese to surrender, proposed a sentimental theme, while others believed a comics format might work to attract attention where propaganda leaflets would not be picked up.

POWs assured the Allies that the best possible inducement to surrender would be a guarantee that those who did so would be allowed to emigrate to such countries as Australia or Brazil. This made good sense to POWs unable to conceive a possible return to their own country. Believing that such a way out of their perceived dilemma was even remotely possible is a clear indication how far removed from reality they were.

Two events in February–March 1945 resulted in a quickening and expansion of the special POWs' work to help bring the war to an early conclusion. The last Japanese prisoners to arrive in Hawaii were the survivors of the Battle of Iwo Jima. Their experiences provided supporting evidence for the American claim that the Allies were closing in on Japan's main islands, and also disproved, or at least weakened, the hard-liners' contentions that Japan was still sure to win. Unlike most of their predecessors, the Iwo Jima veterans held their heads high, confident in the knowledge that they had given their best. They also had a more realistic appreciation of Japan's perilous strategic situation.

The arrival of the Iwo Jima survivors coincided with the start of the heavy, sustained aerial bombardments of Japan's urban centers from bases on Guam and Saipan. These evoked new cries of outrage at the Americans from among the ranks of the die-hard nationalists. These developments also brought home to the prisoners for the first time how dangerous the war had become for their families. Feeling guilty about their own safety when their families faced great peril, a somewhat expanded group of prisoners, including a few who had fought on Iwo Jima, began thinking about what more they might do to end the war as soon as possible in order to spare their families. Discussions among the small group of activists led to the conclusion that they would step up their cooperation, even if it led to Japan's "colonization," which some, even in that relatively enlightened group, still feared. These discussions also centered on who among the prisoners could be trusted implicitly. Twenty additional POWs were eventually chosen, for a total of thirty. They were not necessarily the best educated, but they were the most realistic as to what their homeland was facing.

Cary was at pains to remain in close contact with the group but did not want to become an intrinsic part of it. He wisely insisted that the Japanese had to arrive at their own conclusions based on their discussions. He was certain that no matter how sincere their motives, cooperating POWs would need to be exceptionally steadfast to deal with the inevitable hostility of their countrymen.

Finally Cary believed that he had the right group of men who would work together harmoniously and with strong dedication. This was sufficient for Cary to obtain permission from his immediate superiors to proceed with a noble experiment. If successful it would engage Japanese directly in winning the war against their native land, and perhaps, as Cary hoped, provide a nucleus that would work for the future democratization of Japan. The group of liberals, socialists, communists, and Christians was brought to a new site at Iroquois Point, located on the beach across from Ford Island in Pearl Harbor. There they were able to set to work far from the prying eyes of fellow POWs.

One of the first tasks they set for themselves was to draft a constitution for their organization that defined why they were about to engage in a project that most of their compatriots would have thought treasonous. In its statement of purpose, the constitution boldly proclaimed, "We have decided to manifest our unceasing patriotism in a small way by helping the American military campaigns and propaganda wars. When the war ends and Japan resumes its path toward a bright future, we will be in our homeland, and we swear to do our utmost for its reconstruction."[17] This group of Japanese that was working to bring down a militarist Japan was determined to do it for themselves, because they felt it was right for Japan.

Activists were subject to daytime work details like all other prisoners. Their evening tasks were entirely voluntary. They had the satisfaction of taking positive steps to bring the war to an early end, their work had a clear purpose, and they had the thrill of getting out of the prison camp and feeling human again. Although ambition and the desire for physical comforts may have played a part in their willingness to hasten the end of the war on behalf of the Allies, it was clear that, overall, the activists chose the far more difficult course. Although they laid themselves open to charges from their government and comrades of collaboration with the enemy, the activists had concluded that the times required that they take a stand, regardless of consequences to themselves.

There is little question that the ideology of this group of activists was far removed from the thinking of the vast majority of Japanese POWs. Most of the group looked forward to a postwar radical restructuring of Japan's politics and economy that would have included the destruction of Japan's imperial dynasty. The other POWs, however, could not possibly imagine changes of that magnitude since they could not even contemplate Japan's defeat.

One of the group's first projects was to improve the effectiveness of a propaganda newspaper, *Mariana Jiho* (Mariana Bulletin), which aimed to undermine the morale of Japanese forces at the front. Earlier it had provided minimal results, in part because it featured only translations of English-language articles, and often inadequate translations at that. A similar newspaper put out by the army in the Philippines employed much better Japanese and read as if it was written by Japanese rather than translated. It was successfully adopted by the navy contingent in Hawaii as its model. To provide an element of nostalgia and gain credibility, the bulletin even carried made-up "advertisements" of well-known Tokyo department stores.

Several members of this group even had the heady experience of being allowed from time to time to ride to the typesetter shop in Honolulu in a jeep chauffeured by Cary. They were dressed in ordinary fatigues that lacked the hated "POW" letters. While waiting for the finished product, they would even drop in on the Office of War Information to discuss possible themes for leaflet drops in the following week. Nisei friends occasionally took them out for a good meal at Japanese restaurants in town.[18]

Shortly before the war entered its final phase, Cary's group began to crumble. Some of the group's idealism started to fade when it came up against psychological warfare policies decreed from higher headquarters. The Japanese POWs who had cast their lot with the Americans believed that their true voice was not being faithfully transmitted to the Japanese audience. Cary was caught in the middle. He had bonded emotionally with these exceptional Japanese who were now accusing him of having deceived them. At the same time, Cary realized that he was a part of a huge military machine that would simply not permit POWs to dictate how the U.S. government was going to address the Japanese public in the final push to effect a surrender.

The most significant project undertaken by Cary's group was the speedy translation of the Potsdam Declaration in July 1945 as the war neared its end. The Big Three Allied leaders at Potsdam laid out the terms under which Japan was invited to surrender. The Japanese government remained undecided on its response to the declaration and had not permitted Japan's press to publish it in full. The complete translation of the Potsdam demand on the Japanese government was telegraphed to Saipan, printed in leaflet form, and immediately loaded aboard B-29s for wide distribution throughout Japan. The leaflet campaign, by informing the war-weary Japanese public of the Allies' terms, considered lenient and fair compared to what they had feared, contributed to their government's decision, finally, to accept the declaration.

In the spring of 1945, ten British soldiers had visited Iroquois

Point where Cary was directing activities to help bring down Japan. These men had become prisoners following the fall of Singapore to the Japanese. En route from Singapore to Japan, their ship was torpedoed by an American submarine that also rescued them. Put back on land in Hawaii, the men were curious to see Japanese POWs. What they saw in the camp could not have been more different from what they themselves had experienced at the hands of the Japanese. They were shown where the Japanese-language "Camp Circular" was put together and other activities that promoted Allied objectives. The Japanese were greatly troubled to learn that the British had been prisoners in their homeland. They did not have to be told that British POWs had been badly abused, and they were so ashamed that they wanted to hide. Several British soldiers smiled when they saw the discomfort of the Japanese and extended their hands, a gesture that was gratefully accepted.

The navy's democratization program at Iroquois Point had been fairly small-scale. Otis Cary had seen an opportunity to inaugurate such a program and managed to get it started without having it approved all the way up the navy's chain of command. By contrast, the army spent months debating the merits of a similar program before it finally got started late in the war. A State Department officer assigned to the CBI (China-Burma-India theater) command in India, John Emmerson, was impressed that Japanese POWs captured in Burma provided the Allies with a good deal of information. Emmerson explained that, "There seems to be no feeling that he is a traitor to his country, but rather that he no longer belongs to his own country."[19] Emmerson became even more convinced that the United States should exploit this phenomenon after speaking with Japanese POWs in Yenan, the headquarters of the Chinese Communist Eighth Route Army. Its extraordinarily humane treatment given the POWs had already resulted in a significant number of Japanese converting to the Communist cause. Emmerson resolved that the United States should take a leaf out of the Chinese book and indoctrinate Japanese POWs in the merits of democracy. He hoped that POWs held in the United States, Burma, China, and elsewhere who were convinced of the need to bring down the Japanese government might be induced to issue a common manifesto to influence forces within Japan wanting to bring about its surrender.

Emmerson attempted to push the Washington bureaucracy in the direction of establishing special camps to create new Japanese leadership for the postwar era and meanwhile provide a laboratory for better understanding Japanese psychology. However, the army's Office of the Provost Marshal General, responsible for all but a few of the POWs, saw the establishment of such training institutions as a potential source of trouble and strife. It was satisfied that the camps were kept clean and orderly and caused no serious problems such as had afflicted those in Australia and New Zealand. The Provost Marshal therefore dragged its feet. It raised doubts whether the program might not flout provisions of the Geneva Convention that prohibited political indoctrination. Elements in the State Department worried that the proposed program would provide Communist POWs with an opportunity to proselytize.

By July 1945, all such reservations were overcome by the perception of a compelling need to train suitable Japanese POWs to assist in the governance of postwar Japan. Prisoners judged most inclined to cooperate with the United States were sent, with their consent, to "reorientation centers" established at three POW camps in the American South. Unlike the perhaps more enlightened navy operation in Hawaii, which used POW instructors, the army relied exclusively on American lecturers. Its program provided a heavy dose of interpreted lectures on such topics as American-style democracy, English language and literature, comparisons between Japanese and American literature, and American newspapers and books. Naively, prisoners were also encouraged to attend American-style religious services in order to wean them from "traditional emperor-worship."[20] There is no evidence that any of the two hundred fifty participants in the program played their intended role in the occupation of Japan. Most likely, if they ever had the chance to assume a significant part, the moment had already passed by the time they were repatriated to Japan in December 1945. The new conservative Japanese government's cooperation with the Occupation's objectives laid down by General MacArthur saw to that.

SHINYA'S TRANSFORMING EXPERIENCE

With very few exceptions, once Japanese POWs returned home and reintegrated into society, their lives took the course they would have taken regardless of the POW interval. One such exception, Lieutenant Shinya Michiharu, a graduate of Japan's naval academy, found the experience of the POW camps life changing. He was on board the destroyer *Akatsuki* when it was sunk in a naval engagement that proved a key factor in the battle over control of Guadalcanal in the Solomon Islands in November 1942. Despite his attempts to die in the ocean, Shinya's elemental will to live resulted in his being taken prisoner. After passing through a number of temporary prisoner camps, he ended up at Camp Paita on New Caledonia. He was tormented by his desire to die and by what he considered the disgraceful striving to remain alive. Shinya was still grieving over having remained alive and trying to recover from the shame of becoming a prisoner when, on Christmas Eve 1942, he received a Red Cross parcel from Australia. The package contained cigarettes, candy, needle, and thread. That evening he heard, for the first time in his life, a choral group singing carols–his first contact with Christianity. Such a display of frivolity was unseemly in wartime, he thought. Not long after, Shinya was transferred to the Featherston stockade in New Zealand.

Shinya was one of a small group of officers among the roughly seven hundred fifty officers and enlisted POWs at Featherston. He sensed almost immediately the strained atmosphere between the officers and a relatively small group of NCOs bent on starting a fight with their guards. It troubled him greatly that, since any semblance of discipline and control had vanished in the unanticipated confines of a prison camp, the officers felt powerless to head off the impending disaster, even had they been able to present a united front. The uprising occurred at a separate enclosure from Shinya's, but when it was all over, he only reproached himself all the more for having remained a passive bystander.

Bereft of all the anchors on which he had built his life, Shinya's deep depression, demoralization, and dissatisfaction with his existence remained unresolved for many months. At the same time, his powerlessness as a POW led him to sympathize with those in similar circumstances. And as his desire to live began to assert itself, he wanted to make better use of the time on his hands. Shinya began studying English intensively and started to read books dealing with Christianity. Eventually this led to his joining the weekly classes on Christianity given by the prison chaplain.

Some of his barracks mates criticized Shinya: "Imagine listening to an enemy missionary talking about Christianity to POWs!"[21] The POWs viewed Christianity as something so fundamentally incompatible with the essence of being Japanese that it had to be shunned. Shinya's ultimate decision to accept Christianity led to weekly private meetings with the chaplain. Four months later he was baptized. Although this act was criticized as unpatriotic by fellow Japanese at the time, Shinya later recalled that his love for his homeland actually burned more brightly than before. He believed that he had transferred his loyalty from a narrowly based god-emperor to one God who existed for all mankind. Before the war ended, Shinya had enrolled in a correspondence course on the Bible offered by a Christian institution in Auckland, New Zealand. In postwar Japan, he became a Protestant minister.

REACTIONS TO HIROSHIMA AND SURRENDER

When the United States dropped atomic bombs on Hiroshima and Nagasaki on August 6 and 9, 1945, there was, according to one Japanese writer, a "high degree of anger" among the POWs at Pearl Harbor.[22] Nakajima Yoshio, who was there, wrote that he half believed and half doubted the reports of the atomic bombings. He also wondered why America would have paid such a heavy price in lives lost on Iwo Jima and Okinawa if it had weapons like that.[23]

As a Marxist, Ooka Shohei at first welcomed this awesome scientific achievement with the exquisite and ultimately faulty argument that it was bound to lead to the final destruction of Japanese capitalism. He believed it represented the biggest advance in planned progress since mankind's discovery of fire. Only later did it occur to him that his countrymen were its victims. It was the first time, he insisted, that he was shocked by the calamity that had befallen his country.[24]

For at least a few of "Cary's boys," the atomic bombings were the last straw. They asked themselves whether the United States really needed to drop weapons of such awesome destruction on areas where civilians lived at a time when the war appeared close to ending. But a few days later they decided that it made little sense to oppose the atomic bombings when they had not protested the massive bombings of Japan's cities, which had similarly killed tens of thousands of civilians in one raid. They were also deeply impressed that several American religious organizations spoke out on this matter; moreover, such protests had been covered by the press.

As much as the two atomic bombings had shocked the prisoners, the entry of the Soviet Union into the war on the Allied side may have jolted them into realizing that it had become imperative for Japan to surrender. Fear of the Soviet Union and its communist ideology was paramount among most Japanese, who had deep concerns about whether the imperial institution would survive an Allied occupation of their country. Despite these two momentous, foreshadowing events, Japan's ultimate defeat was a major shock. Most POWs could recall for the rest of their lives what they were doing when they first heard the news.

Word that Japan had surrendered hit POWs hard, although by then many had begun to believe, despite all they had been taught, that Japan might actually be defeated. Breaking the news of the emperor's surrender to the POWs was handled in a variety of ways. Some of the camp commanders let them hear the emperor's broadcast, or, when the reception was too poor to comprehend, simply told them outright that Japan had capitulated. At other sites, camp commanders concerned about a possible violent reaction from the POWs spoke elliptically in transmitting the message they had received on the radio, or waited a day or two before making the announcement. As it turned out, they need not have worried. A number of POWs, mostly bitter-end hard-liners, professed doubt about the authenticity of the report, though in their heart of hearts they must have known the war was over. A few days later, the POW camps received copies of Japanese newspapers that confirmed the bitter truth—Japan had truly lost the war.

The VJ Day celebrations at Pearl Harbor—the fireworks, sirens, pistols shot into the air—were watched and heard vacantly by the Japanese POWs. A few even cried openly, an unusual display of emotion. Some still harbored doubts that staying alive had been the right decision. They would now be forced to give up a secure present for a future that many still envisioned as precarious. First their military world had disappeared, and now their POW world was about to collapse, and nothing had yet occurred to take its place. Many POWs seriously believed that with Japan occupied by the Allies, they would be condemned to work as slaves for the rest of their lives.

At Camp Murchison in Australia, Japanese POWs were assembled to hear the emperor's surrender broadcast, but the ancient receiver picked up only static. An hour later the Italian compound erupted with even greater joy than it had when Germany surrendered. An Australian officer soon confirmed the news they had all expected. All leisure activities ceased as the Japanese digested the unconditional surrender of the fatherland. They avidly consumed news from home. Pictures revealed the widespread destruction and mass poverty, as well as Allied domination. Japanese newspapers were made available to them with such shocking items as "Japanese women's price is cheaper than pork" and "Adults steal lunches from school kids." Worry about how the home folks were coping began to supersede concerns about their own fate.

Nakajima wrote that on August 15, POWs at Camp Kenedy were brought together for an unprecedented assembly. They had a premonition that the news would be bad; in their hearts they had known defeat was only a matter of time, but none dared to voice it. Their POW leader, Ensign Sakamaki, whose four and a half years of imprisonment was about to end, told them of Japan's surrender and asked that order be maintained. The POWs observed a minute of silence, then dispersed to mull over thoughts of home and the future.

Stories that filtered into Camp McCoy about the cruel treatment of Allied prisoners by the Japanese filled Yoshida Osamu with fear of retribution. "We could only hope that they would have been well treated," he recalled much later, but even then he knew that his hope was misplaced.[25] Some of Yoshida's compatriots were beginning to believe that they, well-treated Japanese prisoners of the Western Allies, were the more unfortunate. Allied POWs could look forward to a future with confidence, knowing they would be received warmly by their country, families, and friends. Moreover, this was a genuine feeling on the part of American POWs. Japanese POWs, on the other hand, still could not be sure how their families and nation would receive them.

Reliving the time of his capture, Yoshida eventually came to the realization that he had managed to avoid death because of fear. He had known that dying was the "proper course" but had succumbed to his instinct for self-preservation. It was also true that he was a "coward." This thought process led him to decide that more basic even than being Japanese was the fact that he was a human being, and that as such, he had a right to life. It was a life that belonged to him, not to his country or to the emperor.[26]

Yoshida was far from the typical Japanese prisoner of war. His university education alone had placed him in a relatively small elite group in prewar society and had exposed him to substantial Western thinking. He probably harbored serious doubts about aspects of the myths propagated during the war concerning the emperor and, for that matter, the "invincible Japanese race of the gods." Yoshida was also special in his ability to rationally analyze his feelings and thought processes.

On August 15, 1945, the Camp McCoy commander announced the end of the war and asked the POWs to remain calm. Yoshida still could not bring himself to say that Japan had lost the war, yet his feeling of relief was palpable. He could go home and did not have to disguise his relief. A few days later, the head of the internal POW organization came over to him and asked with a serious mien, "So what do you think you are going to do?" Quite naturally, the answer welled up inside Yoshida: "I am going to return home alive." Those words filled him with immense joy.[27]

Understandably, not all Japanese prisoners of war were jubilant when Japan's surrender finally came about. However, there seems little doubt that, when the truth sank in, they could look forward unreservedly to "going home alive" after all. They would not have been human if that elemental striving had been totally erased. Moreover, with considerable rapidity the concept spread through the POW community that once the emperor had surrendered, all Japanese had become prisoners. No longer in the despised category set apart from Japanese fellow soldiers and sailors, Japanese POWs could once again draw a deep breath. With that breath they took the first important step in rejoining their countrymen.

POST-SURRENDER EXPERIENCES

Most POW accounts agree that their treatment at the hands of the Americans deteriorated soon after the war ended. It appears likely that a combination of factors worked against the Japanese at that time. First of all, the widespread cruelties perpetrated by the Japanese against American prisoners became widely known with the return of Allied prisoners from Japanese captivity, resulting in a desire for revenge, or at least a determination that Japanese POWs not be treated with kid gloves. Moreover, whatever restraint may have been exercised in wartime in a forlorn hope of avoiding even greater harm to Japanese-held American prisoners had evaporated. Possibly most significant, many of the officers and guards who had dealt with Japanese prisoners of war were being mustered out of the military at war's end, and with them went much of their often painfully built-up expertise. Finally, some camp commanders may have acted on the assumption that the requirements of the Geneva Convention no longer applied once hostilities had ceased, a moot point.

Ooka Shohei, the graduate of Kyoto University who became a prisoner in the Philippines, noted in his memoirs that after the war, guards with combat experience were replaced by callow youths of eighteen. The replacements had had no combat experience but were eager to show, in their treatment of POWs, that they were just as tough as their older brothers.

Camp McCoy was closed in October 1945, and all of its NCO and lower-rank prisoners were transferred to three facilities in the San Joaquin Valley of Southern California, taking the place of already repatriated German POWs. Their task was to harvest cotton, manpower in America being still extremely tight immediately following the war. The Japanese American Citizens League, which spoke for most of the Nisei community, protested the move of Japanese POWs to California on the grounds that prison labor would constitute unfair competition for civilian labor. In reality, it harbored unwarranted fears that the presence of the POWs might aggravate residual anti-

Japanese feeling at a time when the Nisei were drifting back to California from the relocation camps. California's governor Earl Warren issued a statement vowing to do all within his power to keep out the Japanese POWs, but to no avail. As it turned out, migrant workers from Oklahoma and Arkansas already on the scene in the cotton fields were not at all antagonistic toward the POWs, and local officials were cooperative with the federal government as well.

A civilian Nisei, Yoshiteru Kawano, who served as a Japanese interpreter first at Camp McCoy and subsequently in the POW camp at Lamont, California, provided a riveting account of his postwar service in an unpublished memoir. On the troop train from Wisconsin to Southern California, the American officer in charge informed the POWs on the first day that food on board was only enough to provide one K ration per person per day. The prisoners called this "insulting" and countered with a determination to fast for the entire five-day trip unless the food ration was increased. Finally recognizing the futility of using threats or force against such tactics, the lieutenant attempted, without success, to reason with the POWs. Miraculously, a search of the train then "found" sufficient food to provide prisoners with three meals daily, and tensions temporarily eased. To save face, however, the prisoners were told that the "additional" K rations had been ordered and taken on board along the way.

Once the large group of prisoners reached Lamont, new frictions arose. Cotton picking was conducted on the basis of quotas assigned by an agricultural agent. He had estimated that the daily quota should be no more than 250 pounds but recognized that it would take the inexperienced Japanese field hands some time to reach that degree of proficiency. In the first week, the POWs could barely pick 70 to 80 pounds, considerably less than the civilian labor force achieved. Another significant difference was that the POWs were being paid 80¢ a day while the civilians received $2.25 for every 100 pounds of cotton picked.

Prisoners trying to avoid the hard labor in the fields soon began to overwhelm the facilities of the medical clinic, claiming all sorts of ailments. Ouchi Shoshin, who was serving as interpreter at the clinic, recalled that this placed him in the "difficult situation" of having to break bad news to his fellow prisoners: POWs thought to be malingering were usually given castor oil for their "malady" and sent back into the fields. The tests of will continued until finally the POWs were required to get up as early as five o'clock to work thirteen hours a day without a lunch break as the camp commander tried unsuccessfully to get them to meet the quotas.

One day, a prisoner succeeded in remaining outside in the fields when the rest of the crew headed for camp. He managed to set fire to several bales of cotton and was found the next morning hanging from the tripod used to hang the scales for weighing the cotton. A spokesman for the prisoners came to Kawano with what he claimed was the POW's last testament. In his letter, the POW apologized for the "cowardly act" he planned to commit. He explained that he "felt unable to meet the quota and did not want to be responsible for lowering the average for his group" and thus denying his buddies the meals to which he felt they should be entitled. He predicted that others would follow his lead.

The camp commander, an inexperienced lieutenant, was so shaken by this incident that he never went out to inspect the cotton fields again. Every evening he got drunk instead. He knew that he had lost face but felt he had no means to rectify the situation. After several weeks this officer was relieved of his command. Not for the first time, Americans learned how difficult it was to overcome determined, solidly united opposition by Japanese willing to suffer and even die in order to win.

The suicide led to greatly improved medical treatment and ample food supplies when the new camp commander took over. The cotton quota was lowered to a more realistic 180 pounds, and an eight-hour workday was instituted. Occasionally POWs even met their quotas in just seven hours, which allowed them to return to camp early to play baseball.[28]

The work performed by the Japanese POWs in the cotton fields of California was probably the hardest of the war. Although the Japanese often complained of performing "slave labor," even in California they typically rejoiced in the spirit of accomplishment, mutual assistance, and camaraderie. In their minds, probably their greatest achievement was that, despite internal divisions, they retained their strong sense of group solidarity and thus were able to score some "victories" over their captors. For the American commander, "defeated" in these small ways, it was probably enough that with the return of tranquillity he had avoided triggering investigations of his conduct and other impediments to a successful military career.

With the big victory celebration at Pearl Harbor, Otis Cary worried what might happen to "his boys" when they were repatriated to Japan. He realized that the activities they had participated in under his direction had created huge fissures in the Japanese POW community. Hard-liners were generally aware of the work this special group had been doing. Muttered threats of revenge were heard, and rumors sprang up that "traitors" had already been thrown overboard from repatriation ships, although such scuttlebutt was proven false. Cary was also concerned how his collaborators would be accepted back home, whether they would now feel guilty about their activities, and whether they would be able to find work in the war-wasted cities of Japan. Although his genuine concern was appreciated, as it turned out he need not have worried.

The "pro-American element" faded into the mass of Japanese who all had to make their way in the new postwar environment. Cary's "boys" neither benefited nor suffered from their wartime association and went on to live pretty much the lives they would have had if war and collaboration had not occurred. Thirty years after the end of the war, the Japanese author of a complete account of the "pro-American" phenomenon concluded that "they had neither been heroes nor traitors; they had just been participants in a historic moment."[29] That statement may not have been much of an encomium, but it was a great deal more than any Japanese POW in the early 1940s had reason to hope for from his fellow countrymen.

When Cary was ordered to return to Japan to help assess bomb damage, his "boys" asked him to notify their families that they were alive and would be returning home. In late September 1945, Cary drove into Tokyo to visit the offices of the Domei (predecessor of Kyodo) News Agency and told management that one of their men was alive and well. Until then, Cary had not been certain how the Japanese would react to news that relatives and colleagues were alive, but he now discovered that they were delighted. Another contact thanked Cary for the letter he brought from his brother but uncomprehendingly said, "My brother is dead." The announcement of his death had just been received from the government, and the funeral was scheduled for the following day.

THE IMPACT OF WARTIME IMPRISONMENT

In accounts of experiences in American POW camps, mostly written many decades later, recollections varied widely. Some recorded contradictory impressions that appeared to reflect different periods of their imprisonment. For example, it was common for prisoners to have feelings of great despair at first but become considerably more accepting of their temporary status with the passage of time. Sakamaki wrote how imprisonment grated and strained the nerves. POWs tortured themselves with thoughts of having failed comrades who had died on the battlefields. They hated themselves for having failed to perform their duties, commenting: "We loathed our fate that caused us to live."[30] Yet, at other times, while imprisonment remained thoroughly distasteful, Sakamaki also considered it an experience during which he learned a great deal not only about himself but about America and its people as well.

Prolonged contact with Americans in the prison camps clearly had an impact on many prisoners, and for none more than those influenced by Otis Cary. One of the members of this group later recalled that his readings in the literature Cary provided changed his basic beliefs. Kobayashi Shigeyoshi, the graduate from Kyoto University's law department (see chapter 4), who never disguised his admiration for the Americans and was beaten by hard-liners for his views, had been made head librarian at Iroquois Point in Honolulu. In that position he had ample leisure to read widely on politics and society. Above all, participation in the life of Pen 8 allowed him to read in relative security, away from POWs still imbued with the ultranationalist thinking of the past. His discovery of "American-style democracy" and his readings in the history of democratic political theory provided him with an ideological basis for making sharp contrasts with the wartime Japan he had known. Writing with the genuine enthusiasm of a discoverer of new treasures, Kobayashi insisted that he had not planned to convert—"it just happened." He conceded that the Americans may have tried to brainwash him, but at least they never used force.[31] Despite Kobayashi's unstinting commitment to democratic principles, it bothered him greatly that he was twice accused of betrayal for cooperating with the Allied cause. Time and again he felt that he needed to refute the charge, arguing that his loyalty was not to ancient ways but to the future of Japan.

Accounts of Japanese POWs imprisoned in Australia and New Zealand largely tracked with the experiences of Japanese in American captivity. Differences depended more on the personalities of individual Allied camp commanders and the mix of Japanese prisoners than on anything else. Basic policy appeared to have been either the same or very similar regarding housing and feeding of prisoners and the type of work and leisure activities supported by the authorities.

Given the "White Australia" policy of the time, it was noteworthy that a number of Japanese POWs specifically mentioned the easy approachability of Australian guards who found opportunities to establish human contact with them. One of the guards even proposed that his POW "friend" join him in running his farm after the war. Aside from the totally unexpected good food, housing, and medical treatment received at Australian and New Zealander hands, it was such human gestures as these that meant so much to the Japanese.

Among the Western Allies only the British appeared to have done things somewhat differently. Unlike the other Allies, they apparently made a distinction between prisoners captured during the war, called POWs, and those who became prisoners once the war ended, whom they called surrendered soldiers. They kept the two groups separated after the war and treated them somewhat differently. The British also used their Indian troops extensively for POW guard duty and, according to one source, dealt with the prisoners largely through the Indians.

Two Japanese prisoners of the British returned from Burma with opposing viewpoints about their captors. Aida Yuji tended to be rather contemptuous of the British and believed they had exploited Japanese prison labor. He was harshly critical despite his observation that at the time of Japan's surrender he feared much worse retribution, having seen emaciated British POWs with his own eyes. When he first came into contact with British troops, with Burmese looking on, he felt so embarrassed being stared at as if he were a "devil" that he wanted to disappear into a hole. The first year of captivity in Burma was the roughest for Aida. All the food came from America, but rations were meager, especially in light of the heavy labor POWs were expected to perform. Worst of all, Aida hated having to clean toilets in the British barracks. When he complained about the degrading work, however, the British replied, "The Japanese military in Singapore had the British POWs ladle out the urinals—an eye for an eye."[32] Aida was most offended by female British soldiers, who were especially demanding and, he commented, dirty to boot. He felt utterly degraded when these women acted as if he did not exist, ordering him to work in their living quarters even when they were in various stages of undress. It was, no doubt, also the first time in his life that Aida had been ordered around by women.

In his memoirs Aida was still seething with contempt for the "uneducated" British and angry that they denied Japanese forces in Burma the opportunity for a ceremonial surrender, but he viewed the Indians in a much more favorable light. Indians saw the Japanese as their "saviors" and were friendly and impressed by Japanese work ethics. Aida recalled spending time with the Indian guards fantasizing about future Japanese military exploits in Southeast Asia to liberate the region from British rule, using Japanese military stocks that remained hidden away.

Unlike most POWs, who failed to use postwar opportunities to contact their families, Aida began exchanging letters in 1946; however, the long-term habits of worry concerning Japanese military censorship were not easily discarded, and only perfunctory messages were sent. Aida's letters and those of his comrades were confined to generalities and covered only good news. Likewise, news from home was kept vague so as to avoid raising anxieties. Some prisoners received no replies from their families and feared the worst.

According to Aida, the British kept the lid on Japanese hostility by threatening to delay the repatriation of anyone who stepped out of line. Rumors were rife that the British would keep POWs indefinitely for slave labor. Since the Soviet Union refused to return POWs promptly, it was widely believed that the British intended to do the same so as not to be disadvantaged. Prisoners mistrusted what little news they could glean about the outside world from discarded British newspapers. Despite their fears, however, repatriation from Burma began in 1946, and Aida was returned home a year later.

Morita Sukenao came away from imprisonment in Burma with very different impressions of the British. He, too, was forced to work hard, and some of it was unpleasant. Facilities at his camp in central Burma were minimal; his bed was a mound of grass, and a large sheet served as the roof for his makeshift tent. But he had some good chats with several "fine" Englishmen at the officers club where he worked. They gave him daily English lessons, and Morita got along well with both the British and Indian military.

Morita noted that tensions occasionally erupted over British demands for overtime work.[33] British military police had to be called in to subdue fights, but, remarkably, the issue was settled fairly. Unlike Aida, Morita came away from his POW experience praising the Englishmen's "correct attitude," for example toward the deceased, such as when the POWs' truck passed by Buddhist funeral processions or when Japanese POWs handed over the bones of deceased comrades.[34] Summing up his prison experience, Morita wrote that, while he spent a long time in captivity, it was by no means entirely bad. He learned about Western humanism and democracy. He came to understand that Japan lost the war not only owing to matériel shortages but also because its personal relations with other peoples were arrogant, despite claiming to have "liberated" them. While Morita indicated that the Burmese were relatively pro-Japanese, he made no claims to have had personal contact with them.

Few autobiographies of Japanese veterans, in fact, make reference to the local populations. In countries where the native peoples were largely hostile, as in the Philippines, this may have been inevitable, but such was not necessarily the case in other parts of East Asia, notably Indonesia, Thailand, and Burma. Nevertheless, accounts of the Japanese veterans' wartime experiences are written almost as if there had been no native inhabitants in the countries where they were stationed. Even as self-styled leaders of the Greater East Asia Co-Prosperity Sphere, Japanese soldiers hardly interacted in a personal sphere with those whom Japan wanted to enlist in its crusade to evict the colonialists from East Asia.

When the Japanese POWs embarked on Japanese-manned ships that returned them home, they were immensely relieved that their ordeal was almost over. Most were still unsure how they would be received. Only a few had availed themselves of the opportunity to reestablish communication with their families, preferring to wait and see with their own eyes what the atmosphere was like in Japan. They could hardly comprehend what a defeated Japan would be like, and quite a large number, especially among the less educated, still refused to believe that the emperor had capitulated, despite all the available evidence. To ease the transition, Americans provided these repatriates with newspaper pictures of GIs strolling along the Ginza, but they simply dismissed the photographs as "lying propaganda" that had been achieved by cropping. The shock of postwar reality would come more strongly to these doubters than to those who over the months and years of confinement had come to terms with the likelihood that Japan was going to lose.

10

RETURNING HOME ALIVE

No other prisoners of war have ever returned to their homeland with as much uncertainty about how they might be received as the Japanese. This became inevitable after they were taken prisoner and faced double jeopardy, a consequence of their own government's policy. First, that government had made it absolutely clear that they were to fight to their last breath, and when they could no longer fight, they were to commit suicide. Becoming a POW was simply unthinkable. Then, the government closed all avenues POWs might have used to notify Japanese authorities and their families that they were still alive. Indeed, it had inculcated in its people that becoming a POW was so shameful that it was equivalent to forfeiting one's citizenship and that families would no longer want to have anything to do with soldiers taken prisoner by the enemy. To spare their families, POWs believed with certainty that they had to refrain from ever informing them of their terrible fate.

Now, with Japan's surrender, everything had changed. Their Allied captors were not prepared to allow the POWs to remain in their countries. The Japanese government under Occupation control wanted them back and was making shipping and crews available to repatriate them. What made this transition so extraordinarily difficult was that the returning POWs knew what had meanwhile taken place at home: Their families would have received official death notifications, because the Japanese government routinely notified the next of kin of any soldier or sailor believed to be missing in action of their "glorious death" in battle. Many families would have received a box containing a hair or fingernail from the "deceased," or even his bones, although the government proved less than meticulous in making sure they had really belonged to the "deceased." The "departed" son or husband would then have been enshrined at Yasukuni Shrine, where, in the highest honor the state could bestow, he would have joined spirit warriors of the past in defending Japan from its enemies. The repatriates also knew that their families would have received a modest bereavement payment from the government, the amount dependent on the deceased's rank. They realized that their next of kin would have arranged for a private funeral and erected a gravestone. Finally, the repatriates surmised that their names would have been marked "deceased" in the family register, then and now Japan's vital document for any individual. Under these circumstances, wives believing themselves widows might even have remarried. It is widely believed that there were at least a few such cases, and probably many more instances where a man's fiancée had married or become betrothed to someone else. Few of the returning POWs, therefore, could be sure how their families would receive them.

POWs might have taken steps to assure themselves on some of these issues had they availed themselves of the ample opportunity to do so when the war ended. They could then have written their families via the U.S. military's mail service. Habits died hard, however, and the strong reluctance to inform families about their POW status was difficult to overcome. Meanwhile, the bureaucracy back in Tokyo continued to send out notices of "heroic deaths" for at least several weeks after Japan's surrender. Since Allied governments had sent the Japanese government lists of POWs they held, it would have been possible to assuage the fears of the POWs' relatives. But the Japanese government failed to take such action, perhaps owing to a respect for the perceived sensitivities of the recipients; it remained under the mistaken impression that notification that their next of kin was a prisoner would not be welcomed, despite the vastly changed circumstances after the war's end.

Repatriation of Japanese prisoners began in December 1945, with priority given to the sick and wounded, ethnic Koreans and Taiwanese, and POWs on the China mainland, where civil war was impending. By the end of 1947, virtually all POWs had been repatriated except those awaiting trial on war crimes charges or serving sentences.

The Japanese government, which continued to function under the Occupation, initially established two demobilization ministries (replacing the army and navy ministries). These evolved into a single Demobilization Bureau, subsequently subsumed under the newly created Welfare Ministry. These agencies were staffed by former military service personnel to process demobilized soldiers and sailors. Those repatriated from America, the central and southwest Pacific, and Southeast Asia landed at a number of ports where demobilization took place. Processing required two or three days, during which time former POWs were debriefed on their service histories and POW experiences. Mindful of the aura of shame that still enveloped POWs, this chapter of their lives was not pursued at length. Processing made no distinction between POWs taken prisoner before the emperor's surrender and those falling under Allied control after August 15, 1945.

Repatriates had to turn over all foreign currency, in return for which they received Japanese yen, then rapidly decreasing in value. Their greatest relief came when they could discard their distinctive red prison garb with its oversized "POW" letters painted on the back. The demobilized soldiers and sailors were provided with old Japanese military uniforms, minus the insignia. Most continued to wear these uniforms for some time, largely because no other clothing was available. They were housed in old-style Japanese military barracks and even bombed-out warehouses at the ports of debarkation. In winter they had no heat. There were beds but not always bedding, and at least one returnee noted that at this point he wished he could have stayed behind in the Philippines. The repatriates were given money to get home by rail, along with a small ration of food to see them through a few days of travel.

Some of the returning POWs attempted to contact their families immediately from the demobilization centers. This was difficult, especially in the year or so after the surrender, when Japan's telephone, telegraph, and postal services, as well as the railroad system, were still in a state of disrepair. Also, since all but a few of Japan's urban centers had been devastated by repeated air raids, repatriates could have little certainty that their relatives still lived in their prewar houses. Most contacts with urban dwellers had to be renewed through relatives with permanent domiciles on farms or in small towns. Returnees employed a variety of means to locate friends and relatives and to reestablish contacts, such as placing personal notices in newspapers and posting handbills on the ruins of houses. Already when descending the gangplank from their repatriation ships, returning soldiers were besieged by individuals trying to obtain information on the fate of relatives.

Until the family's likely reaction to the return of a "ghost," as some former POWs termed themselves, could be ascertained, returnees were often reluctant to appear unannounced at their former front doors. They felt intensely guilty for having failed to meet the expectations of their families and communities, and their hearts could not be at ease until they had tested the reaction of their kin and community to their returning home alive. It was therefore entirely predictable that the repatriates wanted to test the waters by resorting to intermediaries in approaching their families. They were hardly fearful about the reaction of their wives and children but deeply worried about what their parents and grandparents would think of them. The absence of any significant historical precedent to provide guidance in this situation added to their profound unease.

POW autobiographies abound with stories about how they approached their homes, along with tales of their families having received death notices. In one case the repatriate's mother had opened the box that supposedly contained her son's bones but found only a slip of paper with the son's name. All along, his mother relied on ESP to tell her that her son was safe. She was, therefore, not all that surprised when he appeared at her door while she was praying in front of the Buddhist altar in her home.

Ensign Aoki Takeshi had been a kamikaze pilot instructor and later volunteered to join the Special Attack Corps. It came as a "big shock," nonetheless, when he was selected on May 25, 1945, to take part in a night kamikaze attack on Allied naval vessels off the coast of Okinawa two days later. His pilot was seventeen-year-old Sergeant Yokoyama, whom he barely knew. Aoki was assigned the second seat as navigator, perhaps because on earlier suicide missions some young pilots failed to carry out their orders unless a more senior officer was present. This time, Aoki's plane missed its target, an American destroyer, and because of the pilot's inexperience, crashed into the sea. The crew were taken prisoner aboard the destroyer that had been their target, and Aoki wound up in Hawaii.[1] It was over a year and a half later before he was able to return home.

The personnel department of the Repatriation Bureau on February 10, 1946, officially informed Aoki's parents, then living on Taiwan, that their son had died a "glorious death." In extending condolences, the authorities further noted that Aoki had posthumously received a two-step increase in rank to lieutenant, as well as a decoration. The family held a private funeral in August, when nobody who had known Aoki was around. His father sent out notices of his death to friends and relatives, who sent condolence messages in return.

Meanwhile, a deeply conflicted Aoki awaited repatriation. As a kamikaze pilot, he knew exactly what his parents were going through. He did not know what his family would think about his safe return, so he proceeded cautiously. While Aoki was still in Hawaii, he had given a comrade his aunt's address in Hokkaido, the friend's destination. The friend duly called on the aunt, informing her that Aoki was alive and well in Hawaii and expecting to return home soon. The aunt was delighted to learn her nephew was alive. Convinced that a similar message must have been sent to her sister on Taiwan, Aoki's mother, she failed to pass on the message. When she received the death notice, however, she hastened to set Aoki's parents straight. But Aoki's father had greater faith in the government than in his sister-in-law and refused to believe his son was alive.

Aoki returned to Japan in October 1946. He was allowed to remain at the demobilization facility until he could determine the location of his parents, still uncertain because at the time all Japanese nationals were being repatriated from Taiwan. Aoki wanted to test the waters but did not have the courage to call his uncle, a retired army general, then living in Tokyo. Again, he prevailed on a friend to visit the appropriate borough office in Tokyo to find out whether the uncle still lived at the old address. The friend, however, exceeded his instructions. He proceeded to the uncle's house, and when the uncle appeared, momentarily "forgot" that he had promised to reveal nothing about Aoki. Asked to state his business, the friend blurted out that he was a friend of Aoki, who had asked him to find out about his family. Fearing that Aoki might be suicidal, the uncle urged the friend to convince Aoki to visit him soon. Aoki was greatly distressed that his plan had gone awry but overcame his concerns and called on the former general, who was very happy to see him, without a hint of reproach. He persuaded Aoki that times had really changed. Aoki would be able to return home without fear, the uncle assured him, but for the time being should live on the land with his aunt on Hokkaido. After getting settled there, Aoki finally found the courage to write his parents, spilling his entire story. When the parents returned home from Taiwan in January 1947, their reunion was joyous "beyond words." He felt fully accepted and reborn.

Before Aoki's life could assume normalcy, however, he had two more important missions to accomplish. Through his uncle's connections, young Aoki managed to obtain a temporary position with the Forestry Agency, where he was able to make use of his schooling. When the agency asked to see his family register, Aoki wrote the appropriate bureau in the city of Hiroshima, his last permanent address. That office replied that all records pertaining to family registers had been lost. Aoki then wrote the Repatriation Bureau, enclosing documentary proof of his having returned alive from service in the Special Attack Corps. The bureau was then able to reconstruct his family register, and Aoki could begin the long journey back to a normal life.

His second vexing problem was his given name, Takeshi, meaning "brave." Aoki thought that to start a new life in the dawning era of peace, a different name would be appropriate. Through a cousin well versed in fortune-telling, Aoki took his problem to a fortune-tellers association. The association pondered the matter and agreed with Aoki that his "was not such a good name." It was suggested that he change his name to Takayoshi (filial piety and righteousness) or Yasunori (protecting the law). He rejected Takayoshi because it sounded too much like the name he was giving up and chose Yasunori instead. The city office informed Aoki, however, that legally (at the time) he could not arbitrarily make such a change. Thereafter, he used Takeshi on official documents, but to his family and friends he became Yasunori.[2] Relieved of these bureaucratic tangles, Aoki was able to begin his "second life." A book published in 1988 on the "One Plane, One Ship Special Attack Corps" that dealt with Aoki's experience used his new first name, Yasunori. Aoki's transition to a new life was complete.

Two young naval officers during the Second World War, Mandai Hisao and Kojima Masayoshi, shared a common fate in that both became POWs and later resumed their careers in the Japan Maritime Self-Defense Force (JMSDF, Japan's postwar navy). Mandai was interrogated in Hawaii by Commander Huggins. Though as a young engineer he did not know much of intelligence interest, he did tell Huggins that the carrier *Hiryu* had eventually sunk as a result of aerial attacks during the Battle of Midway, a fact of utmost importance to American intelligence.

When Mandai was repatriated in January 1946, he was most reluctant to return home. He asked the demobilization staff what kind of work was most needed to reconstruct Japan. Because many Korean miners had been repatriated, he learned that the coal mines needed manpower and went straight to work in the mines, hired by an older friend. The friend understood Mandai's reluctance to visit his family but, after a lengthy discussion, persuaded him to go, if only to find out whether his parents were still alive. Mandai got as far as the railway station of his hometown when an old neighbor recognized him and told him that his funeral had already taken place. Though still hesitant, he went home to be reunited with his family. He apologized to his father, a veteran of the Russo-Japanese War, and was forgiven. At his mother's urging he stayed home for a week. During his stay he was given an X-ray examination that determined he had tuberculosis, disqualifying him from mining. Mandai then devoted himself to agricultural pursuits, another urgent national need in the immediate postwar world. Not long after the opportunity opened up, he joined the JMSDF. Mandai retired as a rear admiral.[3]

Kojima was piloting a plane assigned to antisubmarine duty in the Bungo Strait between Kyushu and Shikoku Islands in southwestern Japan in May 1945. Also in the area was the American submarine

USS *Atule,* on a "lifeguard" mission, prepared to pick up any American airman who was shot down. Overhead was a B-29 bomber that kept watch over the submarine and provided the means for its communications. Kojima's plane made for the submarine, then at periscope depth, but was shot down before he could launch an attack. The *Atule* picked up Kojima, tended to his burns, and only released him at Midway Island after completion of its one-month undersea tour. The crew called him Bungo.

Before arriving at the demobilization center, Kojima decided that he would cut all ties with his past life in Japan and live in quiet seclusion. Even more than his family's disapproval for returning home alive, Kojima feared the disdain of former Imperial Navy officers and especially the scorn of his classmates at the Naval Engineering Academy. In connection with administrative matters related to his demobilization, Kojima stayed a few days at a former navy facility and, to his surprise, encountered not even a hint of reproach when he later paid a courtesy call at the former navy ministry. On the contrary, he was treated sympathetically by his former associates. As a result, when briefly hospitalized for removal of a bomb fragment, Kojima wrote his parents. His siblings came to see him right away, surprised and overcome with joy over his safe return. They told him that the family had been notified of his death.

With such favorable reactions to his return, Kojima became convinced that Japan's value system had changed to its foundations and he no longer needed to feel ashamed. His anxiety had not evaporated completely, however, and thus he initially maintained the practice of never volunteering information about his capture, with one exception. On returning to Japan, Kojima had reaffiliated with a Buddhist sect and gained deep belief in its teachings. He told members of the sect about his experiences, attributing his safe return to the "grace of God."

The impetus for rejoining Japan's postwar navy came from one of Kojima's old professors at the naval academy, who knew about his wartime imprisonment and urged him to don his uniform again. Once in the Maritime Self-Defense Force at his old rank, Kojima did not volunteer information about his past. While many of the more senior officers were aware that he had been a prisoner, he never felt that he was being singled out or that his career was adversely affected. Like Mandai, he attained the rank of rear admiral.

Following his retirement, Kojima resumed contact with the officers of the USS *Atule* who had rescued him. He visited the United States twice to attend the crew's reunions. The second time was just to say "thanks" for his rescue forty-five years earlier. None of the participants at the reunions found it ironic or strange that former enemies who had sought to kill each other were now relaxing as friends at a resort in Florida.

Kojima even recounted his wartime experiences in the publication of former Imperial Navy personnel, *Suiko*. There was no significant reaction. For a period of time shortly after the war, Kojima and navy captain Okino, the China expert captured by the Chinese Nationalists (see chapter 7), organized get-togethers with all those who had shared their fate as former prisoners of war. But after a while, with everyone getting busy with their own affairs, the meetings ceased. Those still alive now live quietly in retirement, "having vanished from history." Kojima has remained active in his new faith and has written that without it, his existence in the present would "hardly have been possible."[4]

When Higashi Hatsuo returned home at long last, he did not have the courage to tell his family about having been captured in the Philippines in April 1945. Besides, just obtaining enough food to survive was far more important, as it was in all urban centers in the immediate postwar period. Still, his self-perceived stigma remained with him. It was not until six years after his repatriation that he screwed up the courage to confess to his family. They replied that they were just happy to have him back; they did not care where he had been. Higashi continued to feel a debt, however, to comrades whose bleached bones remained in the Philippines. Although he could never quite get over his personal shame, he was able to take pride in Japan's having become the world's second greatest economic power.[5]

While still in an American prison camp, Sugawara Yasuhiro received a letter from a comrade who had returned to Japan before him. This friend related that he was walking toward his home when he passed by a cemetery. He could not help but notice a beautiful fresh grave and, discovering it was his own, was pleased to learn that he had been advanced two grades to second lieutenant. The family was surprised and happy to have him home again. It was a great local media story for a while—"the military spirit who came home alive." A few months later Sugawara received word of his friend's sudden death. He speculated that it was probably a suicide, life in conservative, rural Ibaraki Prefecture having proved too difficult for a hero who had returned home from the dead.

Sugawara did not beat around the bush when he returned home. He told all his friends and relatives in Hokkaido exactly what had happened to him. His life had been returned to him in an American field hospital after he was badly burned. Unlike many others, he returned with his head high; he felt that he had done nothing to be ashamed of. Back home little had changed. Sugawara's parents surprised him somewhat by not appearing shocked by his sudden appearance, a friend having tipped them off that he was alive in Hawaii. A half year before his return, however, the Demobilization Bureau had informed his parents of his death. They had traveled to Sapporo to pick up his bones, even though his father felt rather foolish about the trip, knowing by then his son was safe. And as he had expected, the box was empty. Apparently all relatives of "deceased" servicemen received bones, even the kin of navy pilots who crashed at sea, where the retrieval of bones was, at best, unlikely. Shortly thereafter, Sugawara's parents were invited to attend a ceremony jointly honoring the community's fallen heroes. His father demurred. However, the family register had already received an entry for his death in battle, and for six months thereafter Sugawara remained "officially dead."

In beginning life anew, Sugawara was determined to live it based only on logical reasoning and what he himself believed to be right. He expected that this would probably entail clashing with superiors, no matter what employment turned up, but it all worked out perfectly. As a pilot flying privately owned planes, he was his own man in the postwar era. At age seventy he was still flying his Japanese-made YS-11 to Africa and the rest of the world.[6]

In a similar case, a Nisei soldier brought word to a Japanese family from their brother-in-law, who was thought to have died but had been taken prisoner. The news arrived just as his funeral was being planned, part of a community ceremony, as was then common. Since the family of the "deceased" thought it tactless to withdraw from the community funeral, the family decided it should see the charade through to its end, but they quietly canceled the family-only funeral. At the mass funeral, however, the "deceased's" wife balked at carrying the white box that allegedly held her husband's ashes. She asked a relative to carry it in her stead and was roundly criticized by the neighbors. The family then had to worry how the former POW would be received by the neighbors in their small village, fearing their "cold looks."[7] When the husband did return, however, he was able to reintegrate into the community as if nothing unusual had happened.

Yokota Shohei's wife received word from Otis Cary that her husband was alive on the very day her village was conducting a community funeral. She had already received official word of Yokota's death and was conflicted about attending under these circumstances, but the village chief advised her to take part. "Naturally, I did not feel at all sad on the occasion. Since I did not shed a single tear, I earned the reputation that I was an ogre of a wife," she later recalled.[8]

On his return home, Yokota did not much feel like talking, especially about his wartime experiences. He never did speak to his children about that era of his life. Mrs. Yokota's brother occasionally talked with his brother-in-law about the war and later remarked that it had changed Yokota's personality. Toward the end of her husband's life, Mrs. Yokota believed that he was trying to tell her something about wanting to return to Guam to find his identity papers and dog tags, but he died before he could make the trip.

The first stop for Ishii Shuji after the demobilization procedures was his former newspaper office in Tokyo. He shed tears of joy at seeing the office intact and functioning. The staff was most happy to see him back; nobody had imagined that he might still be alive. In traveling to his home in Niigata by train, however, he noted that not only had "things" burned to the ground but also the human spirit had burned and fractured in the harsh postwar climate. Order and decency had been impaired. The few things he brought back from imprisonment in America were stolen on the overcrowded train.

Ishii's reunion with his family was highly charged emotionally.

He was startled to see his name engraved as a spirit on the Buddhist household altar, together with incense and a candle. He fluctuated between dreams and reality and fell in love once again with his country.

Some of the villagers called him, teasingly, "a spirit with legs," with reference to his having returned alive, Japanese ghosts never having been known to have legs. Ishii determined to live the rest of his life to the fullest to justify his return from the dead. He would change his ways by living not just for Japan but for the world. He also proclaimed that those who had died on Iwo Jima had not died in vain and dedicated his life to the men who made the ultimate sacrifice and to their families.[9]

Sakurai Jinsaku began his wartime recollections with the observation that the price for his failure to choose death over the dishonor of surrender was "a thousand deaths." Captured on Tulagi Island off Guadalcanal, he ended up at Camp Featherston in New Zealand. On returning to Japan in early 1946, Sakurai hesitated over which name to give the demobilization interviewers. Eventually he decided to use his real name rather than the one he had used during his three years of captivity, so that he could again assume his place in the family register. Before heading for his parents' home, Sakurai first stopped off to see his elder sister to test the atmosphere. At first she did not recognize him; when she finally realized who he was, she burst out "Jin-chan [Sakurai's nickname] was killed in the war and we already held a funeral for him." At home, his mother examined him up and down; then, still half in doubt, she asked, "Since you were said to have died, where were you all along?"[10]

In an afterword to his memoir, Sakurai explained that writing down his personal experiences had helped him come to terms with his past. Nevertheless, fearing the wrath of villagers who had lost sons in the war, he refrained from telling his own son more than a fraction of what had really happened to him. His grandson is now convinced that Sakurai's experiences were as unbelievable as the samurai dramas he sees in the movies. At meetings with World War II veterans, Sakurai admits to having been a POW but adds, "Hey, that was only slightly different from those of you who served on the home front."

Yamajo Tomio had served in Manila with a communications unit. His military service taught him to be distrustful of all military organizations. He came to realize after listening to the Voice of America that much of the information turned out by the Japanese were "lies." When I interviewed him at his home, I recognized a free spirit. Yamajo told me that his wife had been dead twenty years and that he had little interest in his family, or they in him. He had run a good business, made plenty of money, invested wisely, and got out of the stock market before the bubble burst. Now he lived alone in his home of sixty-five years. Still, he was restless, and he fondly recalled his wartime contacts with Americans. Yamajo was playing with the idea of perhaps emigrating to the United States. Although he spoke no English, I thought he just might fit in.[11]

Moriki Masaru, a survivor of the bitter combat on the Owen Stanley Range in New Guinea as well as of the Cowra uprising, sent a telegram to his rural family when he was mustered out. Although he informed them of his arrival time, he was shocked when nobody was at the station to greet him. The family was certain that the message had been a mistake because Moriki had been given a big funeral two years earlier when news of his "glorious death" had been received. When the reality dawned that Moriki was really their son and not a "ghost," there were tears of unrestrained joy in his family and his community.

Moriki immediately reported to the village chief to restore his official status as a live human being. Seeing his tombstone, he reflected on the strange fate that willed he should live while so many comrades had died.

In 1983 Moriki headed a group of veterans of the New Guinea campaign for a reunion in Sydney with the Australians against whom they had fought. They exchanged gifts, recalled long-ago wartime events, and told each other about their families and postwar experiences.[12]

The Japanese government, in time, automatically removed from the list of deceased veterans submitted to Yasukuni Shrine the names of those who were known to have survived. This act voided their earlier memorialization at Yasukuni. Many individuals who had survived the war voluntarily returned to the government the monetary gift their families had received.

Irrespective of whether they were captured before or after Japan's surrender, most Japanese veterans did not talk with their family members to any great extent about their battlefield experiences. This clearly had much to do with ultimately losing the war. The deafening silence enveloping the war in the years after it ended also related to their need to address the daily problems of survival, a particularly urgent matter for urban dwellers. As the years passed, the opportunity for dialogue about the war, including POW experiences, was lost. As one former POW remarked, "My children and especially my grandchildren would never understand what I went through." Life had changed too radically to permit understanding.

Large numbers of Japanese have become members of veterans organizations of their wartime military units, including many former POWs. Some who were prisoners before the war ended decided not to join, for a variety of reasons. Those who have not identified themselves outside their families as wartime POWs are still fighting their own personal battles, not a forgiving society at large.

There is no distinction between pre– and post–August 15, 1945, prisoners in their continuing motivation to return to former combat sites where their comrades died. They return to gather recoverable bones of their deceased comrades to ensure proper burial, and they visit memorials to Japanese war dead scattered throughout the Pacific. Such occasions usually include Buddhist religious services. These memorials can be found on such places as Saipan, Guam, New Guinea, and Iwo Jima. Twenty years after the war, the citizens of Cowra, where the bloodiest POW uprising took place, transformed the Japanese cemetery into a beautiful park with a monument to the fallen POWs, cherry trees, and a traditional Japanese garden. This Australian effort to transcend the past has helped bring about today's amicable Japanese-Australian ties.

The most remarkable such war memorial is located on the south coast of Okinawa where the last major Japanese stand on the island occurred. There, the Okinawan prefectural government laid out an impressive park with row upon row of granite blocks with the names of all the Japanese military and Okinawan civilian dead, as well as the names of all the Americans and British who perished on and around Okinawa in 1945. Numbering almost three hundred thousand names, it is a remarkable expression of generosity on the part of the Okinawans, who lost around a quarter of the prefecture's entire population in the conflict.

11

REFLECTIONS ON JAPAN'S WARTIME NO-SURRENDER POLICY

The *Senjinkun* achieved its hold over the Japanese people because their leaders represented it not as a departure from old values but as their reaffirmation. Even if this representation was not entirely accurate, the concept's success was assured because it fitted into the fabric of a highly nationalistic society at the time. The *Senjinkun* demanded unlimited service to the state and a romanticized and moral notion of death.

The spirit of the *Senjinkun* prevailed during the war at an unknowably high cost, certainly in many tens of thousands, even hundreds of thousands, of lives, especially if civilians are included in the totals. The toll included not just the men who participated in the well-known kamikaze and *gyokusai* attacks that inflicted substantial casualties on the Allies. The *Senjinkun* also exacted a price in the deaths of the many Japanese who perished in the jungles from Burma through New Guinea and the Philippines to the caves of Iwo Jima, Saipan, and Okinawa and who followed its dictates rather than face the shame of surrender. To this list must also be added the countless thousands too ill, too badly wounded, or too malnourished to fight on who chose to end their own lives, often far from the battlefields. Their fate did not just happen; it was a consequence of the policies pursued by the Japanese government.

The Japanese author Mikuni Yudai wrote his book on the Special Attack Corps (or Tokkotai, popularly known in the West as the kamikaze) because he believed that the intrinsic beliefs of Japanese society had brought forth what he termed the "pitiless strategy" of the kamikaze. They fought bravely and well though their cause was wrong, and those who sent them into battle will have to accept the judgment of history. Theirs was a strategy that rested on a "fundamental contempt" for the value of human life. Mikuni also recognized that underlying Japanese societal values similarly created agonizing problems for prisoners of war that no human being should ever have to face. This applied especially to kamikaze pilots. Mikuni concluded that, while Japanese society has made substantial changes since the war, some undesirable elements from the past remain rooted in today's society.[1]

The Japanese government was clearly mistaken in its assumption that the Japanese spirit would suffice to overcome whatever material advantages the United States and its allies possessed. In the light of history, it is not even certain that the *Senjinkun* conferred any advantages to the Japanese cause. The ferocity of the Japanese attacks engendered not only fear but a desire among Japan's enemies to meet fire with fire. *Gyokusai* charges in such areas as Guam and Okinawa may have delayed the American advance at times, but they also allowed well-entrenched Americans to kill large numbers of the enemy whom they might otherwise have had to pursue into caves and well-protected defensive positions at a high cost to themselves. The final kamikaze attacks against Allied navies around Okinawa undoubtedly exacted a high toll in Allied lives and ships. At best, these suicidal tactics only put off the ultimate Japanese surrender by a few months at most, perhaps only weeks.

The *Senjinkun* had another, quite unintended, consequence. Simply because the Japanese government willed that there be no surrenders, it acted as though none occurred. Ignoring the information on POWs provided through the International Committee of the Red Cross, the Japanese government failed to take account of the existence of Japanese POWs because to do so would have contradicted the Japanese myth. Inevitably, when Japanese prisoners were taken, the policy of their own government placed them in an impossible position that played into the Allies' hands. Denied, as the POWs saw it, the possibility of returning to their own country with honor, and uninstructed on how to behave in such a contingency, they would often, perhaps unwittingly, prove to be a significant source of military intelligence. As a result, superior intelligence in Allied hands undoubtedly shortened the war, perhaps by as much as Japan's kamikaze tactics lengthened it.

The longer-term consequences of Japanese policy embedded in the principle of the *Senjinkun,* though even more difficult to assess, nonetheless deserve mention, in no small part because the *Senjinkun* as a concept, and even as a word, has simply dropped from sight. Many veterans have written about it, some even in a disparaging manner. Many more have remained silent. A large number of returning prisoners have come to terms with that phase of their lives so that they could talk about it with family, friends, and erstwhile comrades. For a minority, however, the experience of becoming POWs was so painful that they remain loath to talk about it. In a 2001 NHK (Japan's government-run television network) documentary on Japanese POWs, one veteran agreed to speak on camera only if his identity and face remained hidden, fifty-six long years after the war ended. It appears likely that he now represents a distinct minority point of view. Even Japanese convicted by the Chinese of astoundingly brutal war crimes have come forth in recent years to talk about their deeds before television cameras. Surely, if the Japanese public today can deal with behavior of that nature, it can sympathize with those who became prisoners of war in a merciless conflict.

Despite the publicity about wartime events, today's younger generation, either by accident or by design, has remained largely ignorant about government policies that resulted in immense suffering and death, policies compounded by the *Senjinkun.* An informal survey of this population segment showed that many professed complete ignorance of the *Senjinkun.* Of those who knew about the *Senjinkun,* some heard about it from parents or grandparents, while fewer still learned about it in school or from the media. Even elements of the population somewhat informed about the government's wartime policy tended to be quite vague as to the edict's bitter consequences. The most hopeful sign of change is that youths acquainted with what the *Senjinkun* stood for reject it almost unanimously.

The *Senjinkun's* role in the Japanese war effort appears to be part and parcel of an entire bundle of shameful war-related issues that many Japanese institutions and individuals still prefer to leave shrouded in silence, unfit for public discourse, although the past decade has witnessed a growing readiness to face such issues. It is a difficult matter to address since it involved routinely reckless expenditure of lives in an ultimately losing cause. In particular, veterans and their families are understandably loath to voice criticisms that could be interpreted to take away from the supreme sacrifice made by their fallen kin. Survivor's guilt, while not expressed in those words, still plays a role in the wartime generation. Very few veterans' autobiographies criticized the *Senjinkun* as such. More frequently they mentioned their wartime desire not to "die a dog's death" and complained that government policies placed a low value on human life.

Several factors may explain the amnesia toward significant issues arising from Japan's conduct of the war. Many Japanese today shy away from questioning the behavior of those who, in a very different time, subscribed to different values. Moreover, the concept of sacrifice, especially on behalf of the family, is one that still resonates strongly. Today's Japanese also understand the fatalism of that era—hardly extinct now—which made it appear that one had no choice but to conform to the prevailing mores of that long-ago time.

Significant elements of the population also would not like to abandon the belief that Japan waged war in the noble cause of ridding East Asia of colonialism, however little real basis exists for that contention. Wartime Japan voiced such a lofty goal, but its actions belied its words, even though the war clearly had the effect of speeding up the inevitable course of decolonization. Others still contend that the war was forced on Japan by the antagonistic policies of the Western powers. This is an untenable position. The United States, and especially Great Britain, were not looking for a fight with Japan when the conflict with the more dangerous Germany was already in progress. Moreover, the Western powers' major demand concerned Japan's military withdrawal from China, a clearly anticolonial position.

More than five and a half decades after a devastating war, Japan seems still in the grip of national pacifism, having learned well its lesson that war does not pay. It continues to believe that the postwar constitution, embodying the concept that Japan would never engage in a military conflict, provides it with a moral high ground.

This clearly marks a 180–degree turnaround from World War II beliefs, but it remains to be seen whether this position can withstand the stresses of the twenty-first century. At the same time, a certain nostalgia lingers on for a nobler, simpler time of long ago when people seemed less self-centered, less materialistic, and more willing to make sacrifices for high ideals than does the present generation.

Has Japanese society unalterably changed to such an extent that a gladly embraced phenomenon such as the *Senjinkun* is not even remotely likely to reappear again? And does the *Senjinkun* now seem so hopelessly old-fashioned as to be inconceivable as a part of today's Japanese military?

Most of the evidence suggests that the appropriate behavior prescribed by the *Senjinkun* is very far removed from today's Japanese society. This generation's youth has received an entirely different kind of education, one that, if anything, uncritically propounds the virtues of pacifism without examining the basis for Japan's ability to avoid international conflict since 1945. Japan's democratic political system, though it incorporates Japanese cultural traits, allows a wide expression of views, and its free press readily voices opinions that are not always mainstream. Japan is also far more attuned than ever before to what is going on in the rest of the world, especially in Europe and America. Japanese now know that the West has a different, more enlightened attitude toward becoming prisoners of war than Japan once did. Many probably read about an American POW of the Vietnam War, Senator John McCain, becoming a viable presidential candidate.

The growing influence of women, another major change in Japanese society, gives hope that they, perhaps more than the men, can be relied upon to avoid making the errors of the past. Even if some of today's Japanese males remain enamored of the "purity" of an aesthetic death, the women, who would become the ultimate victims of a revived *Senjinkun* as widows and orphans, surely hold more realistic views.

Japan's wartime propaganda expounded the view that, historically, their heaven-blessed nation had never experienced the ultimate shame of defeat at the hands of a foreign enemy. Until modern times, Japan was so remote geographically that it rarely became embroiled in international wars, and in Imperial Russia and China it picked foes that loomed large and powerful but were ultimately proven weak. The profound defeat experienced by Japan in the Second World War will never again allow it to proclaim that its heritage can protect it from defeat. Like all other nations, it has experienced both victory and defeat. The end of the war also brought home the truth that Japanese not only could but did surrender and return alive to their native land. While most returning POWs did not initially feel they were returning home with honor, many came to believe that they had done their duty. The veterans' restoration of honor, at least in part, also came about through their role in producing Japan's "economic miracle."

Do we then need no longer be concerned that patriotic frenzy could once again engulf Japan and lead to another disaster? Though chances remain remote, some Japanese today warn that it could yet happen. The media's highlighting of political developments that suggest a slight rightward shift in public opinion may contribute to this perception.

Many Japanese understand instinctively that underlying cultural values could conceivably make their country vulnerable to a recurrence of the past. Brought up in a society that values harmony above all, they tend to shrink from voicing frankly conflicting opinions. And once embroiled in conflict, with their personal honor at stake, they have had difficulty in constraining their conduct. It is hardly accidental that Japanese society still employs go-betweens to avoid angry confrontations much more frequently than Westerners do.

Another trait that Japanese themselves note is their difficulty in standing up for what they truly believe when an apparent majority takes a different position. Japan's society even today sees as a virtue the all too human tendency to want to go along and not make waves rather than honestly express contrary viewpoints.

I found it rather surprising that several of my Japanese correspondents used the word *bigaku,* to which the dictionary attaches the meaning "aesthetic," in commenting on the widespread wartime belief that committing suicide was the honorable, virtuous way to avoid being taken prisoner. This word, written with a combination of the Chinese characters for "beauty" and "learning" or "study," still evokes in the minds of many Japanese the thought that those who died were exemplary in their "purity" and models of "manliness."

Such feelings about the war contrast with the true horror that many Japanese veterans reflect in their writings on the war. Morimoto Shinji, who survived intense, prolonged combat on Guam, believes he was hardly a human when it was over. "Those few who survived the war know its craziness and the inhumanity and emptiness it leaves behind. And I feel we have only survived to be messengers and tell today's world about it."[2]

In writing me about conduct pursuant to the *Senjinkun,* some Japanese prefaced their well-considered comments with the observation that Westerners would not understand such a manner of thinking and acting. They may well be right. We certainly believe there is a place for manly behavior and sacrifice but refuse to believe these should be limitless. The United States, for example, rewards those who perform military service "above and beyond the call of duty" with the Congressional Medal of Honor, the nation's highest military decoration. In this manner, the nation applauds the individual who sacrifices his life for the common good but does so on his own initiative. Society as a whole rewards those who zealously work for a cause or project they believe in but shuns the fanatic zealot.

Like all societies, we fall short, but as a democratic society we have the correct instinct to avoid the extremes and praise "moderation in all things." It was no accident that Western attitudes toward POWs evolved together with a deepening and broadening of democratic practices and a heightened valuation of individual human rights, which by their nature are moderate positions. There is ample reason to believe that Japan's attitudes will evolve in a similar manner over time.

Considering all the available evidence, it appears quite unlikely that Japanese will ever again embark on the reckless course that led to abject defeat. Now that the wartime generation has all but completely passed from the scene, the time seems right for a thorough airing of all the issues that have lain dormant in the intervening years.

In response to my inquiry to the Japan Self-Defense Forces (JSDF) on how they address the issue of prisoners of war, the National Institute for Defense Studies wrote that the matter is dealt with briefly in the context of learning about international law. The JSDF has no special "doctrine" concerning prisoners of war, but they hope to expand studies in this field.[3]

When all the arguments are heard—from left, right, and center—I still trust the Japanese people to deal with the immense problems of the future in a moderate, sensible way. Sooner or later, the issue of how to treat its own and its enemy's POWs will have to be addressed even in a pacifist Japan.

NOTES

INTRODUCTION

1. Cantril, *Public Opinion, 1935–1946,* pp. 500–502.

1 PRISONER NUMBER ONE

1. Sakamaki, *I Attacked Pearl Harbor,* 28; published originally in Japanese as *Horyo seikatsu yon-ka-nen no kaiko* (Recollections of four years as a prisoner of war).
2. Fukiura, *Nihonjin horyo* (Japanese prisoners of war), 111.
3. Krammer, "Japanese Prisoners of War in America," 79.
4. Fukiura, *Horyo no bunmei-shi* (Prisoners of war in the history of civilization), 224.
5. Fukiura, *Nihonjin horyo* (Japanese prisoners of war), 117.

2 JAPAN'S POLICY ON PRISONERS OF WAR

1. Sansom, *History of Japan to 1334,* 369.
2. ATIS-SWPA Current Translations, no. 131, 10 March 1944, 4, National Archives, Entry 366A, RG 208, 330/73/30/5, box 205.
3. Ibid., 2.
4. Ibid., 7.
5. Ibid.

3 INDOCTRINATION INTO THE *SENJINKUN*

1. Suzuki, *Guntai no omoide* (A military memoir), n.d., n.p.
2. Sugawara Yasuhiro, interview by author, Zushi, Japan, 11 May 2000.
3. Hata, *Nihonjin horyo* (Japanese prisoners of war), 161.
4. Ibid., 18.
5. ATIS-SWPA Research Report no. 76, 4 April 1944, "Self Immolation as a Factor in Japanese Military Psychology," 11, 28–29, National Archives, Entry 366A, RG 208, 350/23/30/5, box 31.

4 HONORABLE DEATH OR SHAMEFUL LIFE

1. Gilmore, *You Can't Fight Tanks with Bayonets,* 151.
2. Ichinokuchi, *John Aiso and the M.I.S.,* 96.
3. Uemae, "Taiheiyo no seikansha" (Survivors of the Pacific War), 101.

4. Essay by marine captain John Burden on how to deal with Japanese POWs, National Archives, RG 165, 390/35/15/5, box 769.

5. This account of Ishii Shuji is based on Ishii, *Iwo-to ni ikiru* (Alive on Iwo Jima).

6. This account of Kobayashi Shigehiko is based on Kobayashi, *Saipan ryoshu no ki* (The story of the Saipan prison camp).

7. This account of Yamamoto Tomio is based on Yamamoto's articles "Waga furusemba Guam-to wo tazunete" (Visit to my old battlefield on Guam), *Koto Gakko Doyukai* 10, no. 8 (October 1972): 8–9; "Nihon-gun wa naze seimei wo karonjitanoka" (Why the Japanese military made light of life), in *Sekai-shi no naka no Nihon-gun* (The Japanese military in world history), ed. Eguchi Mikio (Tokyo: Sanju-ichi Shobo, 1995), 164–96; and "Seikanshita eirei no ki" (The story of a spirit of one who died in the war and returned alive), YMCA League of Japan, 15 September 1946; Yamamoto's letters to author dated 26 May 1999 and 15 September 1999; and his interview by the author, 30 May 2000.

8. This account of Konoye Makoto is based on Konoye, *Senjin* (Dustbin of war).

9. This account of Matsubara Shunji is based on Matsubara, *Gakuto, senso, horyo* (Student, war, prisoner).

10. This account of Aoki Takeshi is based on Mikuni Yudai (pen name of Ubukata Murao), *Tokko* (Special attack unit).

11. This account of Miyamoto Masao is based on Miyamoto, *Okinawa-sen ni ikinokoru* (Remaining alive in the Battle of Okinawa).

12. This account of Sato Kazumasa is based on Sato, *Guam-to gyokusai senki* (An account of the suicide charge on Guam).

13. This account of Takahashi Shigeru is based on Takahashi, *Luzon-to haiso nissho* (Diary of the rout on Luzon).

14. This account of Watanabe Norio is based on Watanabe, *Nigeru hei* (Escaping soldiers).

15. This account of Yokota Shohei is based on Yokota, *Gyokusai shinakatta heishi no shuki* (Recollections of a soldier who did not die in a suicide charge).

16. This account of Kojima Kiyofumi is based on Kojima, "Senso to nin-gen" (War and human beings), lecture delivered at the 177th Joint University Seminar, sponsored by the Association of Noncombatant Servicemen, in *Seminar House News*, no. 153 (Oct., Nov., Dec. 1998).

17. This account of Ooka Shohei is based on Ooka, *Furyoki* (Memoirs of a prisoner of war); available in English as *Taken Captive: A Japanese POW's Story* (New York: John Wiley & Sons, 1996).

18. This account of Nakajima Yoshio is based on Nakajima, *Iwojima*.

19. This account of Yoshida Osamu is based on Yoshida, *Gyokusai no shima Saipan kara ikite kaeru* (Returning alive from Saipan, the island that chose death over dishonor).

20. ATIS Analysis of Prisoner of War Reports, no. 1, National Archives, Entry 366A, RG 208, 380/73/30/5, box 208.

21. Headquarters Sixth Army, G-2 Weekly Report, 17 January 1945, "Imperial Headquarters Discusses 'Rotation,'" 24 October 1944, National Archives, Entry 366A, RG 208, 350/73/30/5, box 228.

22. Gilmore, *You Can't Fight Tanks with Bayonets,* 134.

23. Prof. Benjamin Hazard, letter to author, 20 June 1999.

5 AMERICA'S SECRET WEAPONS:
THE ARMY AND NAVY JAPANESE LANGUAGE SCHOOLS

1. Frank Tenny, "Experiences in War and Japan," unpublished memoir, n.d.

2. Oral History Project, Japanese-American Historical Society, San Francisco.

3. Japanese-American Schedule for Rating, Referral, or Rejection, P.S.D., rev. 24 March 1943, National Archives, Entry 480, RG 389, 290/90/18/7, box 1732. This document had fifty-six detailed questions about the individual's past, affiliations, and abilities. For example, a person employed as a Japanese language instructor was given three minus points, a Shintoist was rejected, a Buddhist got one minus point, but a Christian got two plus points.

4. *Deseret (Utah) Post,* n.d.

5. *Japanese-American Veterans Association (JAVA) Newsletter,* October–November 1995.

6. Oral History Project, Japanese-American Historical Society, San Francisco.

7. Report of the Roberts Commission, January 23, 1942, in *Hearings before the Joint Committee on the Investigation of the Pearl Harbor Attack,* 79th Cong., 1st sess., pt. 39 (Washington, D.C.: U.S. Government Printing Office, 1946).

8. Cantril, *Public Opinion, 1935–1946,* 380.

9. Cary, *Yokoito no nai Nippon* (The Japan that lacks the weft), 48.

10. Ibid., 94.

6 THE INTERROGATIONS

1. "Summary of Prisoner of War Interrogation/Translation Conducted on Guadalcanal" (the Burden Report), under cover of Headquarters Fourth Army, Foreword signed by Col. John Weckerling, published 10 November 1943, under cover of a memorandum issued by G-2, Headquarters, Fourth Army, National Archives, Entry 165, RG38, 390/35/15/5, box 769.

2. Ibid.

3. Cary, *Nihon no wakai mono* (Japan's youth), 55.

4. Cary, *Yokoito no nai Nippon* (The Japan that lacks the weft), 48.

5. Samuel Jacobs, former intelligence officer with the Fortieth Division, e-mail to author, 15 March 1999.

6. National Archives, Entry 366A, RG 208, 350/23/30/5, box 28.

7. Ooka, *Furyoki* (Memoirs of a prisoner of war), 148.

8. Moriki, "Goshu Cowra horyo shuyojo hoki" (The insurrection at the Cowra stockade in Australia), 156.

9. Toyota, *Senso to ryoshu no waga hanseiki* (My reflections on war and becoming a POW), 54.

10. Matsubara, *Gakuto senso horyo* (Student, war, prisoner), 203.

11. Ishii, *Iwo-to ni ikiru* (Alive on Iwo Jima), 101.

12. Nakajima, *Iwojima,* 195.

13. Maj. Sherwood F. Moran, "Suggestions for Japanese Interpreters Based on Work in the Field," 17 July 1943, National Archives, Entry 165, RG 38, 390/35/15/5, box 769; also available at the University of Colorado at Boulder library. Major Moran served as a missionary in Japan for forty years before and after World War II. On Moran's retirement in 1956, the emperor awarded him the Order of the Sacred Treasure, Fifth Class.

14. Cary, *Yokoito no nai Nippon* (The Japan that lacks the weft), 40.

15. National Archives, Entry 165, RG 38, 370/35/15/4, box 759.

16. Ibid., 390/35/15/5, box 768.

17. Ibid., 390/35/15/2, box 750.

18. Camp Tracy interrogation records, National Archives, Entry 179, RG 38, 370/15/10/6, box 2.

19. Moore, "Getting Fritz to Talk," 266.

20. Navy Department, OP-16-2, Office of Chief of Naval Operations, "Report on Crew Members from the Japanese Submarine I-24," 25 July 1945; National Archives, Entry 179, RG 38, 370/15/10/6, box 2, folder 22. (See page 142.)

21. Interrogation record of POW Shinoda Toshikazu in the China-Burma-India theater, 31 August 1944, National Archives, Entry 366A, RG 208, 350/23/30/5, box 228.

22. Report by Military Intelligence Service, Captured Personnel and Material Branch, Supplement to Report no. 1353, 16–19 February 1945; National Archives, Entry 165, RG 38, 370/35/15/4, box 750.

7 A FEW VERY SPECIAL POWS

1. Toland, *Rising Sun,* 481.

2. Hata, *Nihonjin horyo* (Japanese prisoners of war), 559–60.

3. Toland, *Rising Sun,* 40.

4. Another high-ranking Japanese prisoner was Col. Yahara Hiromichi, chief operations officer of the Japanese command on Okinawa. The English translation of his autobiography, *The Battle for Okinawa,* relates Yahara's strong reservations about the Japanese government's requiring "the sacrifice of an entire people." He thought it was "ridiculous" that Japanese pride stood

in the way of the rational course that should have dictated surrender before Okinawa was lost. His failure to commit suicide was severely criticized after the war. The third high-ranking POW was Capt. Yamaga Moriji, one of the Japanese navy's top meteorological experts, who, in this capacity, provided the Allies considerable information on Japanese and Russian capabilities. His interrogators also learned that, while some four hundred fifty Japanese crypt-analysts encountered great difficulty in attempts to break the codes of the Western Allies, they succeeded in breaking Soviet weather codes.

5. Okino, *Ikeru shikabane no ki* (Journal of a living corpse), 34.

6. Ibid., 39.

7. Lt. Don Gorham, interview by author, 6 January 2001.

8. Interrogation of Okino at Fort Hunt; National Archives, Entry 366A, RG 208, 330/73/30/5, box 229.

9. Morale Sidelights, A-178, National Archives, Entry 366A, RG 208, 330/73/30/5, box 229.

10. Okino, *Ikeru shikabane no ki* (Journal of a living corpse), 125.

11. Ibid., 178.

12. Published 7 May 1945 as Interrogation Report no. 0447, 162d Language Detachment, G-2, Sixth Army.

13. Published 2 July 1945 as Intelligence Report no. 751, ATIS, G-2, GHQ.

14. Toland, *Rising Sun,* 315.

8 UPRISINGS IN THE STOCKADES

1. Lewis and Mehwa, *History of Prisoner of War Utilization,* 248.

2. Ibid., 256.

3. Ibid., 261.

4. Ibid., 258.

5. Sakurai, *Jigoku kara no seikan* (Returning alive from hell), 134–35.

6. Hata, *Nihonjin horyo* (Japanese prisoners of war), 239.

7. Ibid., 249.

8. From an eleven-page fragment of an unpublished memoir by a Captain Alter, obtained secondhand by the author from Captain Alter's son Steve, who had passed it to a University of Michigan professor known to the author.

9. Ouchi, "Senjinkun 'ryoshu no hazukashime' wa omokatta" (The heavy burdens of the *Senjinkun's* shame in becoming a POW), 117.

10. Ibid., 121.

11. Alter, unpublished memoir; see n. 8.

12. Ibid.

13. Ouchi, "Senjinkun 'ryoshu no hazukashime' wa omokatta" (The heavy burdens of the *Senjinkun's* shame in becoming a POW), 121.

14. Alter, unpublished memoir; see n. 8.

15. Hata, *Nihonjin horyo* (Japanese prisoners of war), 256.

16. Moriki, "Goshu Cowra horyo shuyojo hoki" (The insurrection at the Cowra stockade in Australia), 189.

17. Ibid., 82.

18. Gordon, *Voyage from Shame,* 128.

19. Mizui, "Sannin no yakishin jutsusha wo dashita Bikaneru horyo shuyojo" (The Bikaner POW stockade and the three POWs who committed suicide by setting themselves on fire), 213.

20. Hata, *Nihonjin horyo* (Japanese prisoners of war), 357.

21. National Archives, Entry 452, RG 389, 290/34/11/2–3, box 1388.

22. Ibid.

23. General Policies Governing Use of POW Labor, issued by War Department on 18 January 1944; National Archives, Entry 480, RG 389, 290/90/18/7, box 173.

9 EVERYDAY LIFE IN THE STOCKADES

1. Takahashi, *Luzon-to haiso nissho* (Diary of the rout on Luzon), 115.

2. Yamada, "Yaka horyo shuyojo" (The Yaka POW stockade), 9.

3. Yamamoto Tomio, letter to author, 26 April 1999.

4. DeVore, "Our 'Pampered' War Prisoners," 57.

5. National Archives, Entry 452, RG 389, 290/35/13/5–6, box 1846.

6. Ouchi, *Senjinkun 'ryoshu no hazukashime' wa omokatta* (The heavy burdens of the *Senjinkun*'s shame in becoming a POW), 141.

7. Uemae, *Taiheiyo no seikansha* (Survivors of the Pacific [War]), 145.

8. Nagata, "Taiheiyo senso"(The Pacific War).

9. Hata, *Nihonjin horyo* (Japanese prisoners of war), 198.

10. DeVore, "Our 'Pampered' War Prisoners," 57.

11. Takahashi, *Luzon-to haisho nissho* (Diary of the rout on Luzon), 138.

12. Moriki, "Goshu Cowra horyo shuyojo hoki" (The insurrection at the Cowra stockade in Australia), 153.

13. Ouchi, "Senjinkun 'ryoshu no hazukashime' wa omokatta" (The heavy burdens of the *Senjinkun*'s shame in becoming a POW), 134.

14. Yoshida, *Gyokusai no shima Saipan kara ikite kaeru* (Returning alive from Saipan, the island that chose death over dishonor), 165.

15. Takahashi, *Luzon-to haiso nissho* (Diary of the rout on Luzon), 138.

16. Yoshiteru Kawano, "Experiences with Japanese Prisoners of War," unpublished memoir, n.p., n.d., given to the author by the sister of the writer, a postwar Nisei interpreter, and used by permission of his son.

17. Cary, *Yokoito no nai Nippon* (The Japan that lacks the weft), 101.

18. Uemae, "Taiheiyo no seikansha" (Survivors of the Pacific [War]), 399.

19. Emmerson, *Japanese Thread,* 216.

20. Krammer, "Japanese Prisoners of War," 87–89.

21. Shinya, *Shi no umi yori sekkyodai e* (From the sea of death to the pulpit), 113.

22. Uemae, "Taheiyo no seikansha" (Survivors of the Pacific [War]), 258.

23. Nakajima, *Iwojima,* 209.

24. Ooka, *Furyoki* (Memoirs of a prisoner of war), 333.

25. Yoshida, *Gyokusai no shima Saipan kara ikite kaeru* (Returning alive from Saipan, the island that chose death over dishonor), 185.

26. Ibid., 199.

27. Ibid., 218.

28. Kawano, "Experiences with Japanese Prisoners of War."

29. Uemae, *Taiheiyo no seikansha* (Survivors of the Pacific [War]), 310.

30. Sakamaki, *I Attacked Pearl Harbor,* 91.

31. Kobayashi, *Saipan ryoshu no ki* (The story of the Saipan prison camp), 150.

32. Aida, *Aron shuyojo* (Ahlon POW camp), 36.

33. Morita Sukenao, letter to author, 25 June 1999.

34. Morita Sukenao, interview by author, Osaka, 16 April 2000.

10 RETURNING HOME ALIVE

1. Toland, *Rising Sun,* 714–18.

2. Mikuni, *Tokko* (Special attack unit), 184.

3. Rear Adm. Mandai Hisao, interview by author, 11 May 2000.

4. Rear Adm. Kojima Masayoshi, letter to author, 15 June 1999, and interview by author, 10 May 2000.

5. Higashi Hatsuo, letter to author, 6 April 1999.

6. Sugawara, *Seikan* (Returning home alive), n.p., n.d.

7. Shikiba, *Furyo no shinri* (The psychology of prisoners of war), 41.

8. Yokota, *Gyokusai shinakatta heishi no shuki* (Recollections of a soldier who did not die in a suicide charge), 347.

9. Ishii, *Iwo-to ni ikiru* (Alive on Iwo Jima), 172.

10. Sakurai, *Jigoku kara no seikan* (Returning alive from hell), 182.

11. Yamajo Tomio, interview by author, 9 May 2000.

12. Moriki, *Cowra shutsugeki* (The Cowra uprising), 236.

11 REFLECTIONS ON JAPAN'S WARTIME NO-SURRENDER POLICY

1. Mikuni, *Tokko* (Special attack unit), 204, 211.

2. Morimoto also left behind the following poem, included in a letter to the author dated 2 September 2000: "Buried deep in the ground/Their names forgotten/My fellow soldiers of long ago./By the full moon I remember them/Our youths full of agony/And my heart aches with sorrow."

3. National Institute for Defense Studies, Self-Defense Research on Military History Section, letter to author, 21 February 2000.

BIBLIOGRAPHY

ENGLISH LANGUAGE BOOKS AND ARTICLES

Allen, Louis. *The End of the War in Asia.* New York: Beekman/Esanu Publishers, 1976.

Asada, Teruhiko. *The Night of a Thousand Suicides: The Japanese Outbreak at Cowra.* New York: St. Martin's Press, 1970.

Benedict, Ruth. *The Chrysanthemum and the Sword: Patterns of Japanese Culture.* Boston: Houghton Mifflin, 1946.

Bix, Herbert. *Hirohito and the Making of Modern Japan.* New York: Harper-Collins, 2000.

Boller, Paul F., Jr. *Memoirs of an Obscure Professor and Other Essays.* Fort Worth: Texas Christian University Press, 1992.

Buruma, Ian. *The Wages of Guilt: Memories of War in Germany and Japan.* New York: Farrar, Straus & Giroux, 1995.

Cantril, Hadley. *Public Opinion 1935–1946.* Westport, Conn.: Greenwood Press, 1951.

Carr-Gregg, Charlotte. *Japanese Prisoners of War in Revolt: The Outbreaks at Featherston and Cowra during World War Two.* New York: St. Michael's Press, 1978.

Cary, Otis, ed. *War-Wasted Asia: Letters 1945–46.* New York: Kodansha International, 1975.

Crost, Lynn. *Honor by Fire: Japanese Americans at War in Europe and the Pacific.* Novato, Calif.: Presidio Press, 1994.

Davis, Winston. *Japanese Religion and Society: Paradigms of Structure and Change.* Albany: State University of New York Press, 1992.

Daws, Gavan. *Prisoners of the Japanese: POWs of World War II in the Pacific.* New York: William Morrow, 1994.

de Bary, Wm. Theodore, et al., comp. *Sources of Japanese Tradition.* Vol. 1, *From Earliest Times to 1600.* New York: Columbia University Press, 2000.

DeVore, Robert. "Our 'Pampered' War Prisoners." *Collier's,* 14 October 1944, 14, 57–60.

Dower, John W. *Embracing Defeat: Japan in the Wake of World War II.* New York: W. W. Norton, 1999.

——. *War without Mercy: Race and Power in the Pacific War.* New York: Pantheon Books, 1986.

Drea, Edward J. *In the Service of the Emperor: Essays on the Japanese Imperial Army.* Lincoln: University of Nebraska Press, 1988.

Emmerson, John K. *The Japanese Thread: Thirty Years of Foreign Service.* New York: Holt, Rinehart and Winston, 1978.

——. *A View from Yenan.* Washington, D.C.: Institute for the Study of Diplomacy, Edmund A. Walsh School of Foreign Service, Georgetown University, 1979.

Gibney, Frank, ed. *Senso: The Japanese Remember the Pacific War.* Armonk, N.Y.: M. E. Sharpe, 1995.

Gillin, Donald, with Charles Etter. "Staying On: Japanese Soldiers and Civilians in China, 1945–1949." *The Journal of Asian Studies* 42, no. 3 (May 1983), 497–518.

Gilmore, Allison B. *You Can't Fight Tanks with Bayonets: Psychological Warfare against the Japanese Army in the Southwest Pacific.* Lincoln: University of Nebraska Press, 1998.

Gordon, Harry. *Die Like the Carp! The Story of the Greatest Prison Escape Ever.* North Melbourne, Australia: Cassell, 1978.

——. *Voyage from Shame: The Cowra Breakout and Afterward.* St. Lucia, Australia: University of Queensland Press, 1994.

Hall, John W., and Richard K. Beardsley. *Twelve Doors to Japan.* New York: McGraw-Hill, 1965.

Harrington, Joseph D. *Yankee Samurai: The Secret Role of Nisei in America's Pacific Victory.* Detroit: Pettigrew Enterprises, 1979.

Hasbrouck, Fr. John Baptist. "The Story of a Soul and Body, 1939–1946." N.p., 1997.

Hata, Ikuhiko. "From Consideration to Contempt: The Changing Nature of the Japanese Military and Popular Perceptions of Prisoners of War Through the Ages." In *Prisoners-of-War and Their Captors in World War II,* edited by Bob Moore and Kent Fedorowich. Oxford and New York: Berg Publishers, 1996.

Ichinokuchi, Tad. *John Aiso and the M.I.S.: Japanese-American Soldiers in the Military Intelligence Service, World War II.* Los Angeles: MIS Club of Southern California, 1988.

Iriye, Akira. *Power and Culture: The Japanese American War 1941–1945.* Boston: Harvard University Press, 1981.

Keene, Donald. *On Familiar Terms: A Journey across Cultures.* New York: Kodansha International, 1994.

Kluckhohn, Clyde. *Mirror for Man.* New York: McGraw-Hill, 1949.

Krammer, Arnold. "Japanese Prisoners of War in America." *Pacific Historical Review* 52, no. 1 (February 1983): 67–91.

Lamott, Kenneth. *The Stockade.* Boston: Little, Brown, 1952.

Leighton, Alexander H. *Human Relations in a Changing World: Observations on the Use of the Social Sciences.* New York: E. P. Dutton, 1949.

Lewis, George G., and John Mewha. *History of Prisoner of War Utilization by the United States Army, 1776–1945.* CMH Pub. 104–11. Fort McNair, D.C.: Center of Military History, U.S. Army, 1955.

Linebarger, Paul M. A. *Psychological Warfare.* Washington, D.C.: Combat Forces Press, 1948.

Moore, Bob, and Kent Fedorowich, eds. *Prisoners-of-War and Their Captors in World War II.* Oxford and New York: Berg Publishers, 1996.

Moore, John Hammond. "Getting Fritz to Talk." *Virginia Quarterly Review* 54 (1978), 263–80.

Nakasone, Edwin M. *The Nisei Soldier: Historical Essays on World War II and the Korean War.* White Bear Lake, Minn.: J-Press, 1999.

Reischauer, Edwin O., and John K. Fairbank. *East Asia: The Great Tradition.* Boston: Houghton Mifflin, 1958.

Sakamaki, Kazuo. *I Attacked Pearl Harbor.* New York: Associated Press, 1949. Also published in Japanese under the title *Horyo seikatsu yon-ka-nen no kaiko* (Recollections of four years as a prisoner of war). Tokyo: Koenkai, 1947.

Sansom, George B. *A History of Japan to 1334.* Palo Alto, Calif.: Stanford University Press, 1958.

Segura, Col. Manuel F. *Tabunan: The Untold Exploits of the Famed Cebu Guerillas in World War II.* Cebu: MFSegura Publications, 1975.

Stewart, Sidney. *Give Us This Day.* New York: W. W. Norton & Co, 1957.

Toland, John. *The Rising Sun: The Decline and Fall of the Japanese Empire, 1936–1945.* New York: Random House, 1970.

Warner, Denis, and Peggy Warner. *The Sacred Warriors: Japan's Suicide Legions.* New York: Van Nostrand Reinhold, 1982.

Yahara, Hiromichi. *The Battle for Okinawa.* New York: John Wiley & Sons, 1995.

Yoneda, Karl G. *Ganbatte: Sixty-Year Struggle of a Kibei Worker.* Los Angeles: Resource Development and Publications, Asian American Studies Center, University of California, Los Angeles, 1983.

JAPANESE LANGUAGE BOOKS AND ARTICLES

Aida Yuji. *Aron shuyojo: Seiyo hiumanizumu no genkai* (Ahlon POW camp: Limits of Western humanism). Tokyo: Chuo Koron Shinsha, 1962.

Cary, Otis. *Nihon no wakai mono* (Japan's youth). Tokyo: Hibiya Shuppansha, 1950.

——. *Yokoito no nai Nippon* (The Japan that lacks the weft). Tokyo: Simul Shuppankai, 1976.

Deguchi Hanju. *Buki-naki tatakai: Horyo taikenki* (Fighting without weapons: A record of POW experiences). Taiheiyo Senso Shogen Shirizu (Pacific War testimony series), edited by Deguchi Hanju, vol. 16. Tokyo: Cho-shobo, 1990.

Eguchi Ken. *Sekaishi no naka no Nihongun* (The Japanese military in world history). Tokyo: San Ichi Shobo, 1988.

Fujimoto Satoshi. "Shingaporu horyoki" (Diary of a prisoner of war in Singapore). *Koato* (Ship's wake), journal of Ichigyokai (One Torpedo Association), vol. 40 (10 November 1986), 8–13.

Fukiura Tadamasu. *Horyo no bunmei-shi* (Prisoners of war in the history of civilization). Tokyo: Shinchosha, 1990.

——. *Nihonjin horyo: Kikigaki* (Oral history of Japanese prisoners of war). Tokyo: Tosho Shuppansha, 1987.

——. *Taiheiyo senso horyo dai ichi-go to iu jinsei* (The life of the person called prisoner number one of the Pacific War). Tokyo: Shinchosha, 2000.

——. "Senjinkun to Nihonhei horyo" (*Senjinkun* and Japanese prisoners of war). *Rekishi to jinbutsu* (History and character), special issue on testimonies of the Pacific War. Tokyo: Chuo Koronsha, 1994.

Hata Ikuhiko. *Nihonjin horyo* (Japanese prisoners of war). 2 vols. Tokyo: Genshobokan, 1998.

Ishii Shuji. *Iwo-to ni ikiru* (Alive on Iwo Jima). Tokyo: Kokusho Kankokai, 1982.

Kamisaka Fuyuko. *Iwo-to imada gyokusai sezu* (In opposition to the suicide charge on Iwo Jima). Tokyo: Bungei Shunju, 1995.

Kobayashi Shigehiko. *Saipan ryoshu no ki: Hito heishi no mita senso to minshushugi* (The story of the Saipan prison camp: War and democracy as seen by one soldier). Nagoya: Shuppan Service Center, 1977.

Kojima Kiyofumi. "Senso to ningen" (War and human beings), lecture given at the 177th Joint University Seminar. *Seminar House News,* no. 153 (Oct., Nov., Dec. 1998).

Konoye Makoto. *Senjin: Tada hitori ikinokotta gun-i* (Dustbin of war: The only military doctor left alive). Tokyo: Kingo Shuppan, 1964.

Kuwabara Sueo. *Watakushi wa ikite ita* (I remained alive). Tokyo: Hyakuai Shobo, 1950.

Manaka Yoshio. *PW Doctoru.* N.p., 1962.

Matsubara Shunji. *Gakuto, senso, horyo: Watakushi no Leyte senki* (Student, war, prisoner: My account of the war on Leyte). Tokyo: Kaihatsusha, 1989.

Mikuni Yudai. *Tokko: Kono hijo na senpo* (Special attack unit: This pitiless strategy). Tokyo: Higashi Ginza Shuppansha, 1998.

Miyamoto Masao. *Okinawa-sen ni ikinokoru* (Remaining alive in the Battle of Okinawa). Tokyo: Ogawa-cho Kakaku Shuppanbu, 1984.

Mizui Hajime. "Sannin no yakishin jutsusha wo dashita Bikaneru horyo shuyojo" (The Bikaner POW stockade and the three POWs who committed suicide by setting themselves on fire). In *Rekishi dokuhon,* 15 (213) (History Reader): *Senso saiban: Shokeisha issennin* (Military tribunals: One thousand sentenced). Tokyo: Shinjinbutsu Otosha, 1993.

Moriki Masaru. *Cowra shutsugeki: Sei to shi no kiseki* (The Cowra uprising: Between life and death). Tokyo: Toko Insatsu, 1986.

——."Goshu Cowra horyo shuyojo hoki" (The insurrection at the Cowra stockade in Australia). In *Buki-naki tatakai: Horyo taikenki* (Fighting without weapons: A record of POW experiences). Taiheiyo Senso Shogen Shirizu (Pacific War testimony series), edited by Deguchi Hanju, vol. 16. Tokyo: Chobosho, 1990.

Nagata Teruo. *Taiheiyo senso* (The Pacific War). Tokyo: Confor, 1999.

Nakajima Yoshio. *Iwojima*. N.p., 1993.

Okino Matao. *Ikeru shikabane no ki* (Journal of a living corpse). Tokyo: Toho Shobo, 1946.

Ooka Shohei. *Furyoki* (Memoirs of a prisoner of war). Tokyo: Shinkosha, 1998. Available in English as *Taken Captive: A Japanese POW's Story*. New York: John Wiley & Sons, 1996.

Ouchi Shoshin. "Senjinkun 'ryoshu no hazukashime' wa omokatta" (The heavy burdens of the *Senjinkun*'s shame in becoming a POW). In *Buki-naki tatakai: Horyo taikenki* (Fighting without weapons: A record of POW experiences). Taiheiyo Senso Shogen Shirizu (Pacific War testimony series), edited by Deguchi Hanju, vol. 16. Tokyo: Chobosho, 1990. Expanded from a magazine article by the same title.

Sakurai Jinsaku. *Jigoku kara no seikan: Gadarukanaru-sen ikinuku* (Returning alive from hell: Surviving the Battle of Guadalcanal). Tokyo: Mamenoki Kobo, 1995.

Sato Kazumasa. *Guam-to gyokusai senki* (An account of the suicide charge on Guam). Tokyo: Kojinsha, 1999.

Senda, K. *Horyo ni natta dai-hon-ei sanbo* (General staff officers who became POWs). Tokyo: Mainichi Shimbunsha, 1977.

Shikiba Ryuzaburo, ed. *Furyo no shinri* (The psychology of prisoners of war). Tokyo: Sogo Shuppansha, 1946.

Shinya Michiharu. *Shi no umi yori sekkyodai e* (From the sea of death to the pulpit). Tokyo: Seibunsha,1988. Published in abbreviated English form as *Beyond Death and Dishonor: One Japanese at War in New Zealand*. Auckland: Castle Publishing, 2001.

——.*Tamashii no ikari* (Anchor of the spirit). Tokyo: Seibunsha, 1988.

Sugawara Yasuhiro. *Seikan* (Returning home alive). N.p., n.d.

Suzuki Michiya. *Guntai no omoide* (A military memoir). N.p., n.d.

Takahashi Shigeru. *Luzon-to haiso nissho* (Diary of the rout on Luzon). N.p., 1998.

Toyota Jo. *Senso to ryoshu no waga hanseiki* (My reflections on war and becoming a POW). Tokyo: Kodansha, 1953.

Uemae Junichiro. *Taiheiyo no seikansha* (Survivors of the Pacific [War]). Tokyo: Bungei Shunju, 1993.

———. "Taiheiyo no seikansha." *Bungei shunju,* August 1970.

Watanabe Norio. *Nigeru hei: Sangosho no hi* (Fleeing soldiers: The coral monument). Tokyo: Maruju, 1988.

Yamada Yuko. "Yaka horyo shuyojo" (The Yaka POW stockade). In *Naha-shi shiryohen, shimin no senji sengo taikenki* (Wartime and postwar experiences of the citizens of Naha), Naha Municipal Documents no. 3, vol. 8. Naha, Okinawa: City of Naha, 1981.

Yamamoto Taketoshi. *Nihonhei horyo wa nani wo shabetta ka* (What Japanese POWs told their captors). Tokyo: Bunshun Shinsho, 2001.

Yamanaka Akira. *Kanruban shuyojo monogatari: Saiaku no senjo zanchi butai* (Story of the Kanruban stockade: The unit that remained behind in the worst war zone). Tokyo: Kojinsha, 1987.

Yamanaka Takayoshi, ed. *Oo-ii, sora-yo umi-yo* (Hey there, sky and sea). Vol. 1. N.p., 2000.

Yokota Shohei. *Gyokusai shinakatta heishi no shuki* (Reflections of a soldier who did not die in a suicide charge). Tokyo: Soshisha, 1988.

Yoshida Osamu. *Gyokusai no shima Saipan kara ikite kaeru* (Returning alive from Saipan, the island that chose death over dishonor). Tokyo: Kyodo Publishing Company, 1973.

INDEX

Page numbers in *italics* refer to maps and sketches.
Boldface numbers preceded by **ph** refer to unnumbered photo insert pages.